T5-AVP-333

Credit Risk
From Transaction to Portfolio Management

Butterworth-Heinemann – The Securities Institute

A publishing partnership

About The Securities Institute

Formed in 1992 with the support of the Bank of England, the London Stock Exchange, the Financial Services Authority, LIFFE and other leading financial organizations, the Securities Institute is the professional body for practitioners working in securities, investment management, corporate finance, derivatives and related businesses. Their purpose is to set and maintain professional standards through membership, qualifications, training and continuing learning and publications. The Institute promotes excellence in matters of integrity, ethics and competence.

About the series

Butterworth-Heinemann is pleased to be the official **Publishing Partner** of the Securities Institute with the development of professional level books for: Brokers/Traders; Actuaries; Consultants; Asset Managers; Regulators; Central Bankers; Treasury Officials; Compliance Officers; Legal Departments; Corporate Treasurers; Operations Managers; Portfolio Managers; Investment Bankers; Hedge Fund Managers; Investment Managers; Analysts and Internal Auditors, in the areas of: Portfolio Management; Advanced Investment Management; Investment Management Models; Financial Analysis; Risk Analysis and Management; Capital Markets; Bonds; Gilts; Swaps; Repos; Futures; Options; Foreign Exchange; Treasury Operations.

Series titles

- **Professional Reference Series**
  - The Bond and Money Markets: *Strategy, Trading, Analysis*
- **Global Capital Markets Series**
  - The REPO Handbook
  - The Gilt-Edged Market
  - Foreign Exchange and Money Markets: *Theory, practice and risk management*
  - IPOs and Equity Offerings
  - European Securities Markets Infrastructure
  - Best Execution in the Integrated Securities Market
- **Operations Management Series**
  - Clearing, Settlement and Custody
  - Controls, Procedures and Risk
  - Relationship and Resource Management in Operations
  - Managing Technology in the Operations Function
  - Regulation and Compliance in Operations
  - Understanding the Markets

For more information

For more information on **The Securities Institute** please visit:
www.securities-institute.org.uk

and for details of all **Butterworth-Heinemann Finance** titles please visit:
www.bh.com

Credit Risk

From Transaction to Portfolio Management

Andrew Kimber

AMSTERDAM BOSTON HEIDELBERG LONDON NEW YORK OXFORD
PARIS SAN DIEGO SAN FRANCISCO SINGAPORE SYDNEY TOKYO

Elsevier Butterworth-Heinemann
Linacre House, Jordan Hill, Oxford OX2 8DP
200 Wheeler Road, Burlington, MA 01803

First published 2004

British Library Cataloguing in Publication Data
Kimber, Andrew
Credit risk: from transaction to portfolio management – (Securities Institute. Global capital markets series)
1. Credit control
I. Title II. Securities Institute
332.1

ISBN 0 7506 5667 0

Typeset by Charon Tec Pvt. Ltd, Chennai, India
Printed and bound in Great Britain

Contents

Preface

The last few years have seen enormous change within the credit markets posing considerable challenges to the author. Not least amongst these is to distinguish between long-term structures and short-term trends.

In particular, we have recently seen concerted efforts to develop a secondary market in tranched products, together with any number of portfolio models to assess their risk characteristics.

Rather the attempt has been to take a step back and to develop on themes common to all types of credit exposure. The convergence of the loan and traditional fixed income credit business, due in part to reasonable quantitative modelling, has made this a worthwhile exercise. Consequently, rather than elaborating upon disparate portfolio models the text focuses on underlying structural models and their application within the industry.

The central idea is a 'credit portfolio' and the core business areas are covered within the initial chapters. Subsequently, the idea of credit derivatives and securitization as a way of modifying portfolio exposure is treated within the remainder.

Andrew Kimber
Dublin 2003

Acknowledgements

In such a large marketplace it is impossible for any one individual to be an expert in all areas. Consequently my first acknowledgement goes to all the financial service professionals, too numerous to mention personally, who have assisted in my understanding. Particular thanks to Moorad Choudhry at JPM Chase, Dominic O'Kane at Lehman Brothers, Heinz Gunasekera at Citigroup and Tim Barker at Deutsche Bank.

Several parts of the text rely on core analysis. Thus, I am grateful to RiskMetrics for allowing me to reproduce a number of ideas behind their products, and in particular to Fabrice Rault for proofreading. I will also mention Duffie and Singleton for inspiring the section on jump models.

Thanks also Roger Noon, the staff at Elsevier, in particular Mike Cash, Jackie Holding and Jennifer Wilkinson.

Inevitably this book is a consequence of my exposure to the cutting edge of credit gained at Warburg. I acknowledge the expertise of my former colleagues and wish them continued success with their product.

Finally, my parents for putting up with me 'being in the middle of something' every time they call. Perhaps they appreciated the reason, maybe now even understand.

1

Fixed income credit

Managing credit within a fixed income portfolio

1.1 The credit product

Introduction

The debt capital markets are very, very large. A conservative estimate of global indebtedness is of the order of tens of trillion in dollar terms. They are very large for the simple reason that the prevalent economic system in the 21st century is based around Anglo-Saxon capitalism. Only the public marketplace can meet the financing needs of the entities comprising this edifice.

Although external financing had been important in some economies the spur for more general growth of the international debt markets was the rise in the price of oil in the 1970s. This had a secondary effect of creating large capital flows directed at the developing economies. The majority of this capital found its way into deposits, indeed the term eurodollar was coined to represent pooling of capital outside of the US.

The 1980s and 1990s saw further large growth. This was caused by the easing of capital controls and exchange rates together with the recognition that the international debt market was a viable source of financing. Simultaneous advances in technology contributed to capital becoming much more liquid. Consequently cross-border activity had become as important, or more important than domestic flows.

Perhaps the best way of understanding the debt capital markets is from the user's perspective. On one hand the borrower will wish to finance as cheaply as possible. The choice available was historically restricted to their domestic marketplace assuming that an efficient, liquid bond market existed. Nowadays corporations, supranationals

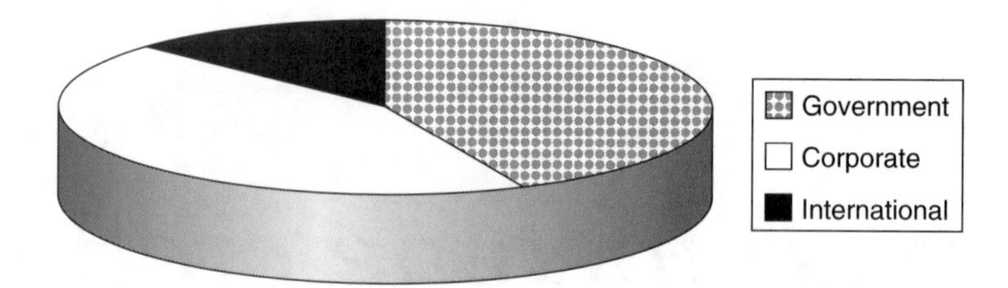

Figure 1.1 Debt outstanding by bond type (May 2003). *Source:* Deustche Bank.

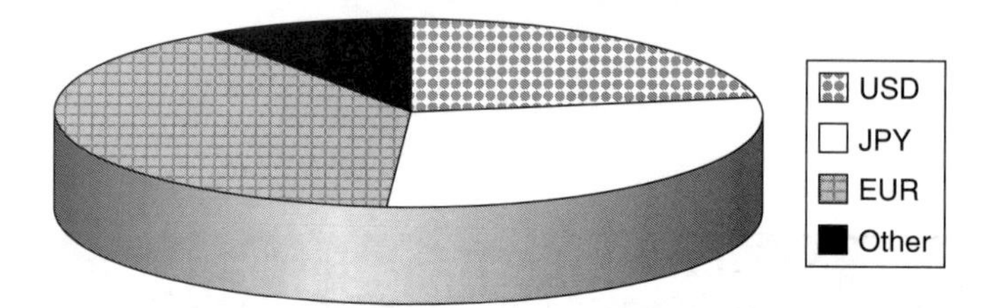

Figure 1.2 Government debt by country (March 2003). *Source:* CitiGroup.

and some governments look beyond the borders as the prime source of cheaper funds. Thus enters the supplier of capital driven by the requirement to secure the maximum return on investment. This decision is now one of international analysis. The major supplier of capital is the institutional investor. This category has become increasingly dominant at the expense of the private saver.

To give a brief example of the current financing environment it is now commonplace for a US corporate to borrow funds in the European marketplace denominated in euros and then thence swapped back into dollars. The purchaser of this debt could be an Italian pension fund manager.

Or to take a more recent example: a German insurance company may wish to have exposure to the US high-yield markets, but may be restricted through regulatory requirements to domestic paper. There is now a way (we explore the CDO markets in due course).

Figure 1.1 shows the components of the global debt markets. We can see that one of the main categories is the government issue. These are important in the context of setting the risk free rate of borrowing and consequently in the pricing of all categories of bonds. It is in a government's interest to ensure a liquid bond market because this will allow a cheap source of capital for public schemes but a further indirect effect is the possibility of cheaper financing to the economy as a whole because the rate of corporate borrowing will be determined in part by the government curve. Figure 1.2 shows the major government bond markets.

Most governments have a benchmark programme whereby bonds of different maturities provide the risk free rate of interest for borrowings of differing maturities. This can be ideal because general increased fiscal rectitude within the public domain has led to some head scratching over the role of the government security in providing a reference. A particular example was occasioned by the 30 year treasury throughout 2000 which became increasingly scarce due to a government buy back program. Consequently the yield for this maturity became dominated by liquidity considerations and not particularly representative of the risk free rate of interest.

This has touched on the controversy of whether government bonds should be a benchmark for corporate bond portfolios. We will explore this theme in more detail in due course.

The domestic corporate bond market constitutes all issues other than governments. This phrase is rather misleading as you could have a so-called corporate bond issued by a financial institution. This category also includes the so-called 'foreign' bonds comprising paper issued by a non-domiciled borrower. Examples include the 'Yankee' bonds. For example if a European borrower wanted to issue US domestic paper it would 'do a Yankee'. You will also encounter 'Bulldogs', 'Alpine', 'Samurai' and 'Matador' which are synonyms for sterling, Swiss franc, yen and Spanish denominated bonds issued by foreign borrowers.

The third category of bond is the international which latterly used to be called the Eurobond. These are both issued and traded cross border. This is now one of the largest fixed income markets.

The final major category of bond is the so-called global, now often included within the international classification. This is issued both domestically, so it would trade like a normal corporate but there will also be a simultaneous international issuance having the same characteristics (i.e. coupon and maturity). They are the province of institutions with large financing requirements and would be almost exclusively either supranationals such as the World Bank and the US government-backed agencies, or large corporates.

All non-government bonds and indeed many government issues are exposed to a source of risk which is the theme of the book, that is credit risk as distinct from the market risk to which they will also be exposed. This credit risk will be partially dependent upon the bond rating and sector.

1.2 Government bonds and credit

Why the need for an entry on government bonds when the target is credit?

The reason for the interim discussion on government bonds is because a large part of the behaviour of the fixed income credit instrument can be described in terms of the government security.

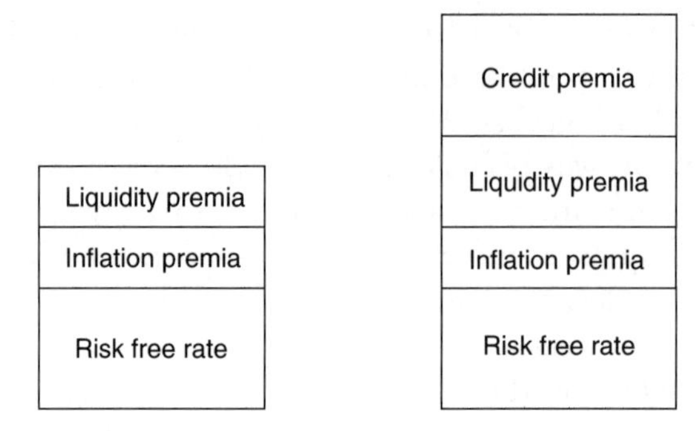

Figure 1.3 The components of return on government and corporate issues.

A picture of the components of return inherent in a corporate bond will hopefully make this statement transparent. These are displayed in Figure 1.3.

We can see from comparison in Figure 1.3 that both the government bond and the corporate bond share elements of their return, that is the risk free and inflation premia. This means that the return on the corporate bond will be correlated with the government marketplace. The credit bond also has an extra return component which is the compensation due to the holder bearing credit risk. The liquidity within the credit marketplace is also generally different. Ranging from almost non-existent, in the case of speculative grade credits, to highly liquid and comparable with the most actively traded government issues. Notice that the government bond in the diagram is considered to be credit or default risk free. This is because the perception of governments is that they are unable to go bankrupt because they have a monopoly on printing money, raising taxes and issuing into the domestic market.

In the opening period of the new millennium there are a number of strong qualifications that need to be attached to the above paragraph. First up, not all governments are free of credit risk. Strictly this would be limited to the debt of developed countries. There have been many occasions in the past decade where holders of emerging-market government bonds have visited the financial equivalent of Siberia.

It is also questionable now how much latitude governments of the developed countries have when it comes to fiscal policy and monetary policy. Certainly the rather more drastic measure of printing money is almost unknown in western economies. Given the role of the government now seems to be broadly one of maintaining stability, their debt is important in the context of acting as a benchmark for corporate borrowing and funding a certain amount of public expenditure.

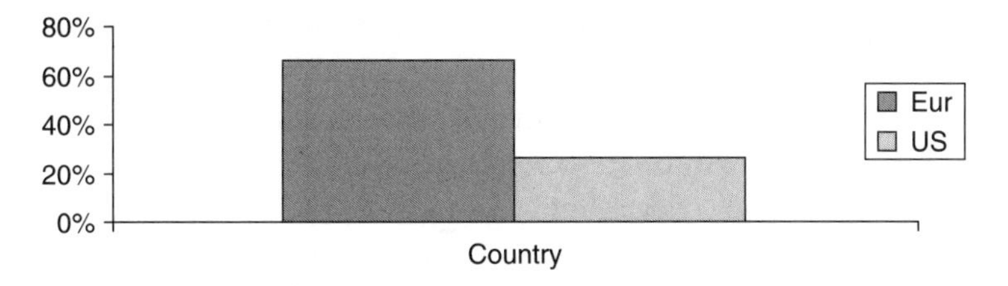

Figure 1.4 The importance of government securities (2002 supply). *Source:* Lehman Brothers.

We also hear the claim from some commentators that the dragon of inflation has on the whole been slain. So in the diagram above perhaps the government return should just be represented as a risk free rate and a liquidity spread. With these qualifications behind us we can still state that government bonds generally form the foundation for the entire domestic debt market and without exception are the largest in relation to the overall market as a whole. Figure 1.4 demonstrates that the government sector is still a major participant within the debt markets.

Government bonds represent the benchmark for all issuers in that denomination regardless of whether they are other governments or corporates. Every bond will be quoted at a spread to the government benchmark for that maturity.[1] Typically we also use the benchmark for pricing the issue through a combination of the risk free rate implied from the government par curve together with a credit spread dependent upon the credit worthiness of the borrower. This methodology will be particularly important for pricing new issues.

However there are often circumstances when the risk free rate cannot be determined in a straightforward manner. This can lead to erroneous conclusions on the pricing of credit. For example throughout the last year of the millennium within both the US and UK there has been a decline of government bond issuance leading to widening credit spreads. Obviously this is not a statement about the credit worthiness of the companies within the economy but rather the matter of supply and demand imbalances within the government bond market.

These types of scenario have led to the promotion of alternative benchmarks. Most prominent of the candidates is the swap market. This is perhaps the most transparent and liquid of all the fixed income markets, consequently it is easier to hedge both rate and credit exposure

[1] When there is not a comparable bond of the same coupon and maturity the benchmark curve is interpolated.

through the swap mechanism. Practitioners will use the swap rates to derive an underlying pricing curve which will be employed both as a reference point to measure the credit risk premia and an underlying benchmark for performance analysis.

Alternative benchmarks used to establish the risk free rate include the US agencies which have near guarantee status. Within Europe some of the large corporates and supranationals are vying for the market to confer benchmark status on their debt.

1.3 Benchmarks for credit

The term is used by corporate bond portfolio managers in the sense of providing a set of returns on a comparable asset class forming the basis of the fund performance. The assets should have the broad characteristics of the credit vehicle. Consequently we see from Figure 1.5 that a credit investor should not want to use the government bond market as a benchmark because the portfolio characteristics of this asset class are different from the credit product. This represents a plot of various spreads to the government rate.

By characteristic we partially mean the level of correlation. A good credit benchmark should have a high level of correlation with the credit spread. Figure 1.5 reveals that government bonds simply do not have this characteristic, swaps spreads however are quite well correlated with the credit product and this is manifest in the increasing

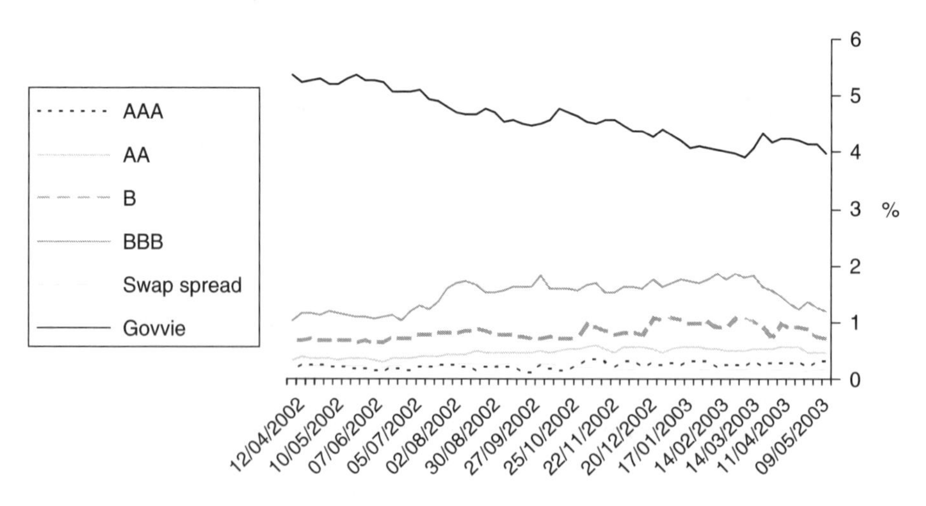

Figure 1.5 Evolution for various credit categories. Euro 10 years. Fair Market Curves. *Source:* Bloomberg LP.

use of the so-called TED spread[2] as a suitable benchmark for credit analysis. The graph was determined using weekly samples of spreads to the treasury.

Swap spreads

A lot of effort is expanded among the investment banking community in trying to explain the level of this spread. The reason for this is that it represents a generic proxy to the health of the credit market. In particular the measure that is commonly adopted is the difference between the fixed leg of the swap and the yield on an equivalent maturity government bond. The reason these two are not the same is because the fixed coupon is partially determined by the general banking communities' ability to service a commitment, this will be different to the government. In particular the interbank market is representative of an AA credit, while governments are perceived to have a higher-credit worthiness. While a driver of this spread is credit the reader should beware when interpreting Figure 1.6. An example is furnished from the events surrounding September 11. In particular the yield of a generic 10 year dollar denominated bond widened by 16 basis points over a 2 week period, while the 10 years swap spread narrowed by eight basis points. To understand this it is necessary to appreciate that the supply of government bonds also influences the spread. In this particular example, the market anticipated that the form of the government reaction would have to be funded through the debt markets placing downward pressure on spreads. Heavy corporate bond issuance also influences this spread; post-issuance the corporate will usually transact an interest rate swap which will change the profile from fixed to floating. This is desirable because fixed debt is less risky from a valuation perspective. This effect will cause the spread to narrow. In the chart below we have depicted the evolution of the 10 year dollar swap spread over a period of 5 years. The long-term historic average over 10 years is approximately 40 basis points. During President Clinton's tenure the budget

---

[2] We should say a word on the TED spread since it is one of the expressions where everybody nods in understanding but some surprising responses comeback when asking for definitions. The majority of the credit industry thinks of the TED spread as simply the difference between the yield on the swap market and the government bond at a comparable maturity. However this is quite a loose definition and a more rigorous statement would be the asset swap margin between the government bond and the swap market. We will go into greater depth in this area in due course. In the meantime we can discuss a little bit of a perennial favourite, beloved of market practitioners and that is speculation regarding the direction of 'swap spreads'.

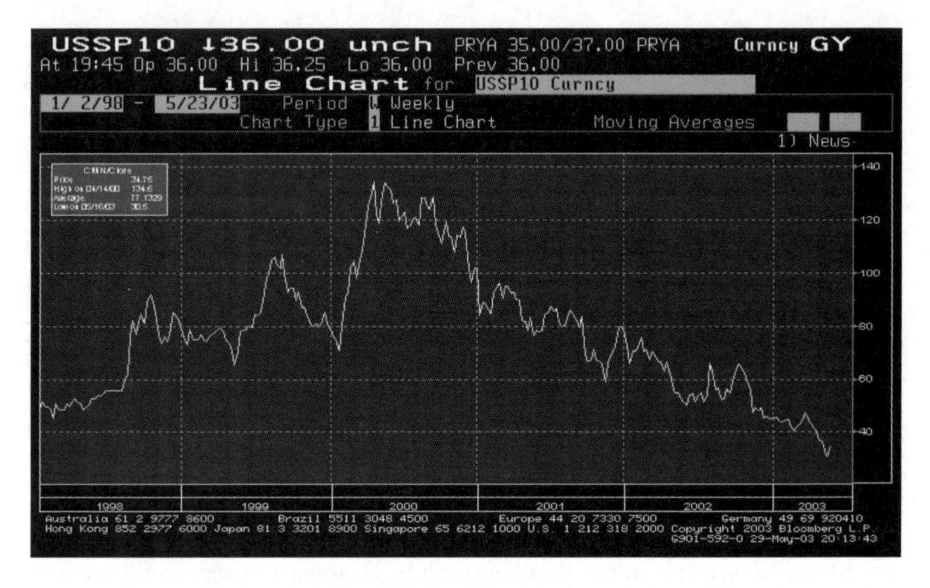

Figure 1.6 US$ swap spreads. *Source:* Bloomberg LP.

surplus grew rapidly, indeed at one stage it was anticipated that the 30 year 'Bellwether' treasury would be fully redeemed. This had the effect of pushing spreads out to a historical high of around 140 basis points. More recently in a somewhat typical government funding environment swap spreads have contracted to something like their long-term historical average.

1.4 Corporate bonds

The term corporate bond covers all domestic bonds issued by non-governments. This term can be somewhat ambiguous because the international class can sometimes be included. We use corporate in the domestic sense and consider internationals later. The market is very large approaching $10 trillion outstanding in 2002. The major denominations are in dollars, euros and yen. Figure 1.7 shows the breakdown by currency.

Corporate bonds are on the whole plain vanilla instruments. Meaning they have a fixed time to maturity and pay a fixed coupon. The corporate bond can either be secured on the general assets of the company, or certain specific assets, or unsecured. These assets are used to pay off the debt in the event of the company defaulting.

The proceeds of the corporate bond issue are used to finance medium to long-term projects and acquisitions. The yield on the bond is set within the secondary market and represents the credit quality of

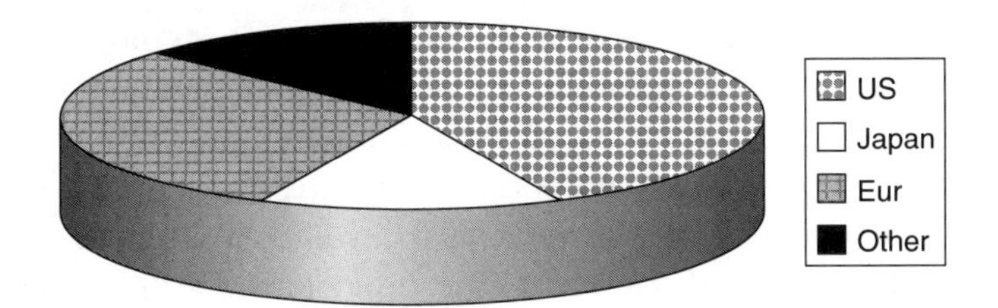

Figure 1.7 Corporate debt by currency (May 2003). *Source:* Deutsche Bank.

the borrower as well as the underlying interest rate environment together with other factors such as liquidity. The relevant weighting accorded to these components is dependent upon both the issuer and the details of the issue. The credit worthiness of the borrower drives the spread over a similar maturity government. If this is high-investment grade then the bond will tend to trade at a small spread over the comparable government bond. Similarly if it is speculative grade the credit will trade at a wide margin to the governments.

It is not just the rating accorded to the borrower that drives credit spreads but also the sector and maturity of the bond. The behaviour of the credit bond is explained largely by the anticipation of *default*. This is defined as the borrower failing to pay either interest or to redeem the principal on the issue at maturity.

The majority of bonds are issued at maturities of less than 10 years. Beyond this date it is normally costly in terms of the level of coupon that would have to compensate investors. Indeed the window of 10 years or more is normally only available to borrowers of high-credit quality. Even then there will be a number of provisions advantageous to the lender. We now issue a warning to the reader that the forthcoming text will discuss the major types of 'frills' packaged into the corporate bonds. Unfortunately not all corporate bonds are plain vanilla for the simple reason that they would never be launched because of credit concerns about the issuer.

The most common 'frill' is the level of security. There is a clear food chain in the event of company defaulting; this is shown in Figure 1.11.

If the debt is secured then it will be redeemed in the event of a foreclosure. This can take the form of either a specific fixed asset tied to the issue or a float which is tied to the general assets of the company. There is also a type of bond known as a debenture which confers the right over pledged general assets, usually physical in nature, called a lien.

In some cases the advantage lies with the borrower. For example, a provision may exist to pay back some or all the issue before maturity. A sinking fund is just such a contractual pre-payment and enables the issuer to redeem at a predetermined amount at regular intervals. The repayment may be designed to retire the entire issue by maturity date. Or it may represent a part of the outstanding maturity. If only a partial amount is paid back then the remaining balance redeems at maturity.[3] The purpose of the sinking fund is to reduce credit risk associated with the bond. However, the provision is still a disadvantage to the bond holder because it represents pre-payment and will thus require a higher yield to compensate.

The primary market

The primary marketplace is the procedure by which a company raises capital and their bond is introduced into the marketplace. This service is carried out by the large investment bank's placing an entire bond issue into the market in return for a fee. If the bank cannot place the entire issue with its customers then it will keep the remaining paper on its own books. The underwriting fee compensates the bank for taking on this risk.

There is a distinction of issuance technique according to the size of the deal. A single bond will usually be underwritten by a single bank that will then either guarantee a minimum price or try and place the paper at the best possible price.

Larger issues, particularly those aimed at a cross-border investor base, will be underwritten by a syndicate of investment banks. The group will collectively underwrite the issue and each member will place a proportion of the issue. The syndicate is formed by the bank winning the original mandate as a result of having established relationships with the borrower, special expertise in the area or a beauty parade.

There are a number of ego massaging terms to describe everybody's role within this group. Most prominent will be accorded to the mandate winner; named the lead underwriter lead manager, or book-runner.

A corporate bond is placed into the markets usually through the fixed price re-offer mechanism. Prior to this a temptation existed for some of the syndicate members to sell paper at a discount in the grey market (this is the market prior to the official launch of the deal). This will cause heartache for the lead manager, who recall, has to support the price. Under the fixed price re-offer banks are obliged to sell their allocation either at the initial, or above the offer price once it has been set.

[3] Repayment methods are quite general and include quite evocative phraseology including the word lottery whereby redemption is determined by drawing serial numbers randomly. The sinking fund call price is generally the par value of the bonds. The amount outstanding is known as the 'balloon'.

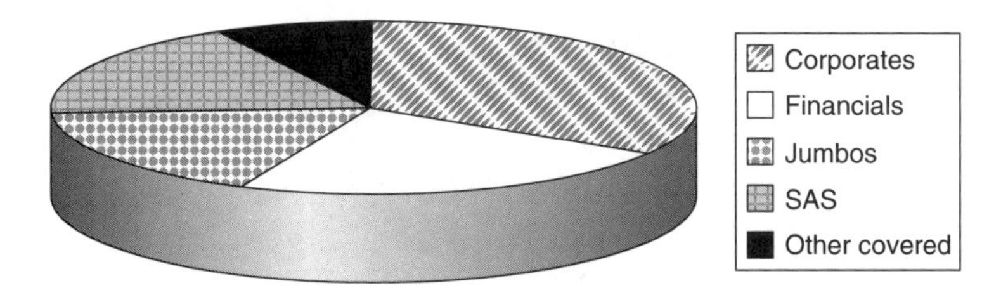

Figure 1.8 EU corporate bond (2002 supply). *Source:* CitiGroup.

A corporate bond will be priced using a combination of the government curve and a credit spread. It will be quoted with implicit reference to the same maturity government bond, or relative to the libor curve. If no government security has the same maturity then the yield will be interpolated between two bonds having a slightly lower and higher maturity. Figure 1.8 shows the supply by sector of the Euro primary market (note that this figure includes internationals).

The secondary market

Corporate bonds are almost universally traded on an OTC basis. This over-the-counter acronym should really be OTW – 'over the wire'. Some bonds are listed on designated exchanges. For example Eurobonds are listed on the London Stock Exchange and certain Asian borrowers appear on the Hong Kong and SIMEX exchanges. Within the US there are large listings of corporate bonds on the New York Stock Exchange. Some trading of bonds actually takes place within the exchange, although this is comparatively minor relative to the OTC market.

The amount of liquidity present within the marketplace varies greatly. As a rule only the large borrowers trade in a continuous manner. Often a placement will be made to an institution involving the entire issue who then hold it until maturity. This obviously makes the issue completely illiquid. These are the two extreme examples. The majority of issues, denominated in the major currencies, with a nominal out-standing of above 500 million dollars and of reasonably high-investment grade possess a healthy liquidity figure in terms of traded volume.

Liquidity is obviously highly dependent upon having a large and diversified investor base. This base can be divided according to the maturity of interest. The institutional investors comprise the large pension funds, insurance companies and mutual funds that hold sway over long dated issues. Activity at the short end of the curve is dominated by banks and corporates who are active for reasons of liquidity and hedging. Figure 1.9 shows the main investor base for US corporate bonds.

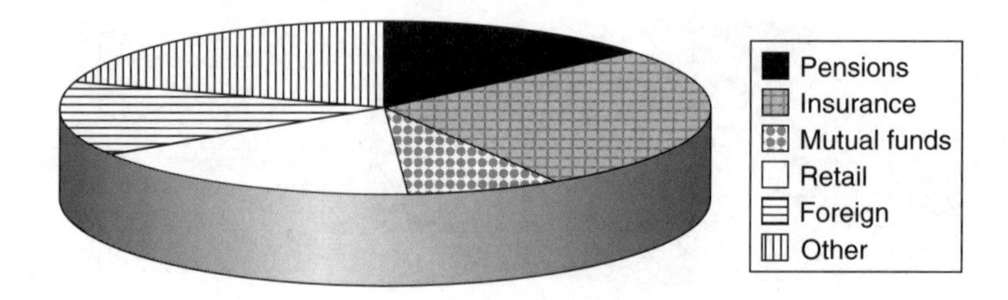

Figure 1.9 Holders of US$ corporate debt (March 2003). *Source:* Fed. Reserve.

Regulatory environment

Within an OTC marketplace it is vital to provide formal supervision. This is necessary as a foundation to investor confidence and the basis of liquidity. At the same time there must be a balance between any undue taxation policies which will serve to dampen the investor base. Get this delicate balance wrong and the business is forced elsewhere. An example of this is the Eurodollar market which developed as a consequence of tight capital controls within the US.

Types of bond

The main type of corporate bond is the so-called bullet structure which comprises a fixed maturity date and coupon. The coupon is paid regularly over the lifetime of the bond which is typically issued and redeemed at 'par'. This is a phrase used quite liberally by practitioners, and it took me several years in the marketplace before somebody gave me a definition other than 'par is par'. It simply means the trading value of the issue is the same as the notional value. So for example if €500 million notional was issued into the market and the value of the issue was €500 million then the individual bond would be said to trade at par. Even if the individual bonds were denominated in blocks of €10 000 they will still be quoted in terms of price relative to 100.

There are various gradations of corporate bond based on the ordering of the queue for creditors. These become important in the advent of a company default or insolvency. These grades can be described as senior, subordinated and junior. Obviously the senior debt has the highest priority. They rank above any other party who is owed money by the company including business creditors, but not the tax man!

Subordinated debt ranks behind both senior and secured and consequently carries a higher-credit risk. In some cases the subordinated bonds may rank after trade creditors. To compensate the bonds usually trade at the highest yields within the secondary market. Subordinates

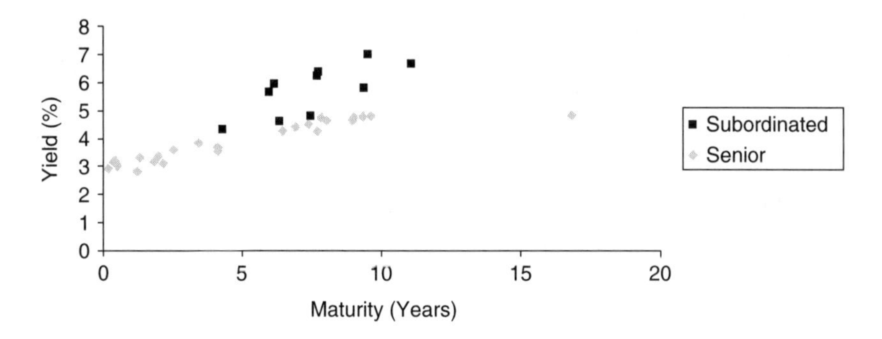

Figure 1.10 Ranking vs. yield (December 2002). *Source:* Bloomberg LP.

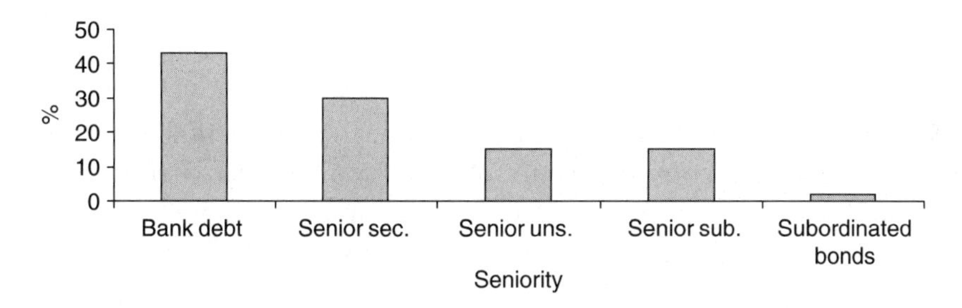

Figure 1.11 Debt cushion by instrument. *Source:* Standard & Poors US Loss Recovery Database.

are usually issued by a company which is relatively new to the bond market and further has less capital because of its youth. In order to enhance the appeal of its debt it will often issue the bond with additional features such as a step up coupon. Wherein the investor receives a larger coupon for a period of time, if the issue is not redeemed in the interim. Perhaps the most common subordinated instrument is the convertible bond which we discuss on p. 23.

In Figure 1.10, we show the effect of the seniority on the price of the bond.

Although it is ultimately the market that values the debt, Standard and Poor have a methodology to determine the coverage assigned to a bond in the event of default. This is known as the 'debt cushion' and it represents the amount of debt on the balance sheet contractually inferior to a given instrument. This is synonymous with the debt that will absorb first losses. We depict how this varies with instrument type in Figure 1.11.

Bonds can also be collateralized which adds an extra element of security to the holder. This collateral can either be in the form of fixed assets such as property or more typically financial assets. In the US, bonds that are secured with financial collateral are known as 'collateral cross bonds'. The nominal value of a collateralized issue will usually be lower than the pledged assets to provide an extra cushion. Further the collateral is held by the bondholder's custodian usually for the lifetime of the bond. In the event of default they become owners of this collateral. If this happens to be equity the voting rights are transferred.

A debenture is a particular type of insured bond which is secured on the general assets of the issuing company rather than specific fixed assets (in contrast with a secured bond). A company that has debentures in existence and subsequently issues secured debt may provide a negative pledge stating that the debenture ranks equally with the secured bonds issued. The purpose of this is to protect existing debenture holders.

In addition to the level of subordination, the debt will frequently be callable. This is an option feature of benefit to the borrower. If interest rates subsequently decrease then the environment will be more attractive to the borrower. To take advantage the existing debt would have to be purchased and then refinanced at the lower rate. The call provision allows this.

The callable bond will trade at a lower price than a bond of the same issue, maturity and coupon simply because the investor may have to part with their bond. Consequently the borrower is penalized in anticipation. We will give a little more elaboration on the call valuation because they represent an important source of information about the credit worthiness of the borrower. To be party to this you need to strip out the effect of the call on the bond. In equation form we have

$$\text{Price}_{\text{bond}} = \text{price}_{\text{underlying}} - \text{price}_{\text{call}}.$$

This equation states that the price of the bond of is equal to the price of a conventional less the price of the call. It is the underlying bond upon which we perform credit analysis. For example we can obtain the credit spread of the borrower through the yield implied by the stripped price. The usual method of obtaining the price of the call is with a tree where each node represents a possible term structure of interest rates (Figure 1.12).

A slight complication is the frequent use of call schedules. Rather than being callable at one specific time in the future the bond has a number of calls dates. The call level would usually decline with maturity, recognizing that the bond moves towards its redemption value as

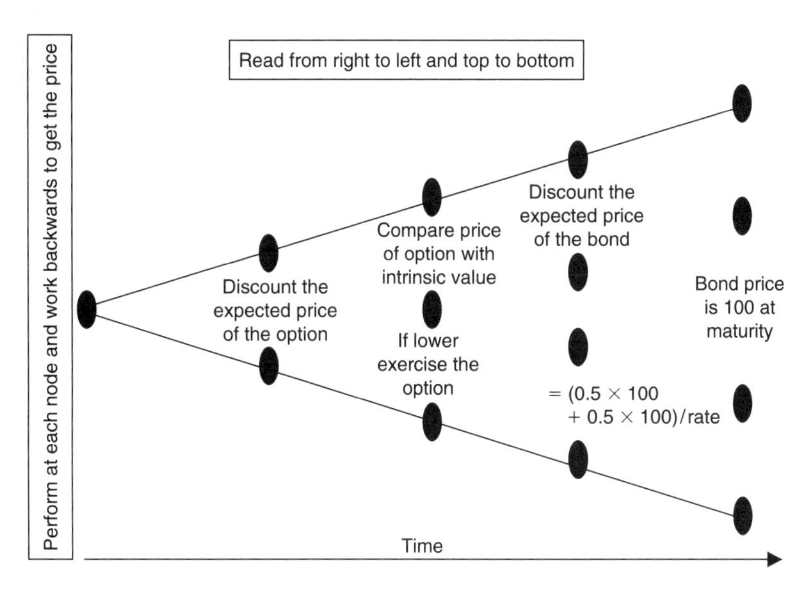

Figure 1.12 The steps in pricing the call.

Table 1.1 The call schedule. June 2010 € denominated.

Date	Value
06/01/2003	104
06/01/2004	103
06/01/2005	102
06/01/2006	101

maturity approaches. Table 1.1 shows a typical corporate bond call schedule.

Complimentary to the call, but less common, is the put bond. This allows the investor to sell the bond back to the issuer if its price goes below either par or the put price in the schedule set out in a table similar to 1.1.

The put provision will result in the bond trading at a slight premium to the ordinary bond. This is because the put is beneficial to the investor because she can sell at a slightly better price than the current market rate assuming it is below the put price:

$$\text{Price}_{\text{bond}} = \text{price}_{\text{underlying}} + \text{price}_{\text{put}}.$$

Information on the credit quality of the issue can be implied from the bond provided we can price the put option. This goes through in the same way we described for the callable bond remembering the change in sign in the above equation.

Fixed coupon bonds can be attached to a sinking fund arrangement instead of having bullet redemption. The term sinking fund arises because, historically, on issue a pool of cash is set aside to be used for bond redemption. Today this is an unusual arrangement. More common is a facility where a small percentage of the bond issue is redeemed every year. You might wonder why the bond can still be classed as a bullet? Simply, because the pay down is not contracted and will depend on the circumstances of the issuer. Consequently the chances are the bond will pay coupons and be redeemed according to a normal bullet schedule.

Sinking funds can apply to specific issues which are called, rather gratifyingly, specific sinking funds. Typically, however, the funds apply to an entire range of issues. These are known as aggregate sinking funds which are redeemed through a lottery method whereby the trustee selects the bonds on a random basis. The bonds can also be repaid by the issuer purchasing the notional value of the bonds in the open market.

There are two main types of sinking fund consisting of a category that pays off the same amount each year and funds which pay a progressively greater amount each year until the entire amount is redeemed. You may also possibly encounter a 'doubling option' provision enabling the issuer to repay double the amount originally specified. If the original specification allows the issuer to repay a larger unquantified amount it is known as an accelerated provision.

The main risk attached to holding bonds with a sinking fund provision is often the call risk. Credit risk, ironically, is often lower than the bullet because of the existence of the pool to repay the principal. The facility allows the issuer to redeem the bond, usually at par. So from enjoying a comparatively profitable bond, because the coupon may be higher than the prevailing market rate, the holder could suddenly end up with his capital in an unbenign interest rate environment.

1.5 Floating-rate notes

The floating-rate note (FRN) is a bond with a coupon which is periodically reset. The coupon is generally set equal to a short-term variable interest rate such as 6 month libor. Additionally the borrower will typically pay a spread which can be positive or negative depending on their credit worthiness.

These notes are typically issued by institutions requiring floating-rate debt to balance their floating-rate assets. High liquidity is required and because of this, banks and sovereigns compose the bulk

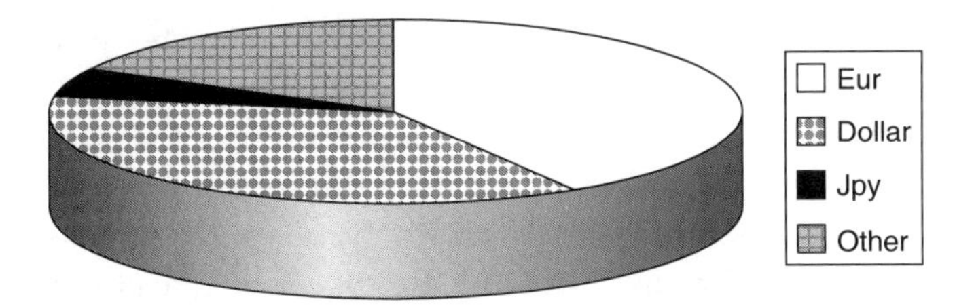

Figure 1.13 FRN volume by currency. *Source:* Deustche Bank.

of the market. Figure 1.13 shows the volumes of FRN outstanding by currency.

If this spread is very small then the FRN is a very safe instrument because it frequently resets to par. Away from reset dates there will be a rate risk equal to the duration of the next coupon date. Consequently if the market rate rises between resets dates the note will trade at slightly below par and if rates fall the paper will be priced at a premium to par.

There are various definitions of the margin which the reader should be familiar with. The first is the quoted margin which is the spread paid by the issuer, this is determined on the issue date and will be similar to the asset swap margin on the issuers existing bonds. If the issuer has no outstanding debt it will be similar to the margin quoted on comparable debt, that is FRNs of the same sector, maturity and rating.

The other type of margin is the so-called simple margin. This is a means of comparing the average return on the FRN with the reference rate. This measure is adopted by the money-market community who view FRNs as essentially deposit like instruments:

$$\text{Simple margin} = \frac{100 - \text{price}}{\text{maturity}} + \text{quoted margin.}$$

For example, if a 10 year bond trades at 98 and has accrued interest of 1.5 together with a quoted margin of –10 bps then

$$\text{Simple margin} = \frac{100 - 98 - 1.5}{10} - 0.0010 = 0.049.$$

Lets just sneak in one final margin before a coffee break, assuming you have been reading from page one. This is the discount margin used to price the bond and consists of an additional spread over libor which will be close but not quite the same as the quoted margin.

The reason behind the existence of this measure is simply that the credit worthiness of the borrower can change after the issue date. The extra piece is used to discount the flows, of libor plus the quoted margin, and generate the correct price.

We reproduce the rather ghastly formula below. You can think of this as just the standard formula for obtaining the price of a bond given the yield. The subtlety for the FRN however is the 'yield' comprises the existing reference rate and the discount margin. The cash flows are composed of the sum of the next coupon, comprising the libor reset and the quoted margin. Together with a stream of quoted margin payments. The remaining libor element is replaced by 'par' at the first coupon date. This is sufficient for valuation purposes, but to determine the credit risk we need to analyse it further. This is discussed in Chapter 5. Also notice that the FRN will price to par on reset days when the discount margin equals the quoted margin:

$$\text{Price} = \frac{1}{1 + (r + DM)^{\text{days/year}}} \times \left(C_1 + \sum_{t=1}^{t=N} \frac{QM}{[1 + (r + DM)]^{t-1}} + 100 \right).$$

1.6 Credit related instruments

Conventional and reverse FRN are illustrated in Figure 1.14.

Reverse FRN

This reverse FRN is representative of a general approach referred to as structuring. This can be interpreted as a joint approach to funding when the issuer of the underlying instrument works in unison with the bank originating the deal. The final so-called 'structure' is a combination of a vanilla instrument and some sort of derivative which enhances the yield from the investor's perspective and consequently makes the sale of the paper somewhat easier. Structuring is usually

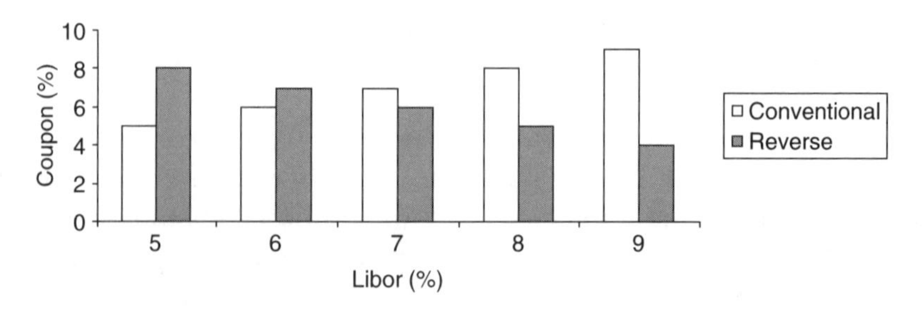

Figure 1.14 The conventional and reverse FRN.

applicable to issues that are difficult to place for a number of reasons including, a lack of credit worthiness. It can also be due to the issuer being an unfamiliar name in the market or simply poor timing. (Bear in mind that an awful for lot of structuring takes place within the secondary market whereby the bank works independently to try and create liquidity through making a relatively stale product more appealing. These tend to be less successful than the primary deals.) As a rule of thumb usually the more unpronounceable the structure the more difficult it is to find a buyer. Furthermore all structurers claim to live in Kensington, London and drive Aston Martins.

Generic examples of structuring include the FRN type instruments and the MTN borrowing programme we discuss in due course. (This is a specific schedule to provide financing for disparate issuers driven by windows of opportunity.) The programme typically includes a structured product facility. We can also think of the world of credit derivatives in terms of the structured product. In the context of the discussion this is an example of the bank working independently of the issuer to hedge specific credit exposures.

The payment on the note can be linked to one or more underlying assets or an index. We are particularly interested in the case where the reference is either an interest rate or credit related. These linkages can be in the form of either a price or rate level. They can also be in terms of the spread between two yields or the correlation between two assets.

The main motivation behind the structured product is the provision of a relatively attractive yield. However investors can also be worried about a downturn in the marketplace in which case they seek protection of returns. There are many brains within the capital markets only too willing to suggest a solution.

A further use of a structured product is to gain market exposure in an area which is difficult to replicate. This is particularly pertinent to credit where there may not be a bond, loan or private placement representative of the particular sector and credit.

The disadvantage of most structured products is the lack of a transparent market. Structures are dealt with exclusively on an OTC basis. Which can lead to wide bid-offer spreads inconveniencing the buyer in the event of an unwind. This can lead to some acrimonious situations particularly when the investor has been fed a stream of mark prices which hitherto have made the deal appealing.

More specifically we now focus on the reverse FRN and describe how the deal is actually arranged; which looks very complicated on first acquaintance. Let us not lose sight of the end goal, however, the structurer's first line of thought – why would anybody wish to receive on the deal? Answer – if the interest rate is declining then the owner of a conventional FRN would be the recipient of declining payments. Consequently if they require a decent coupon then they should purchase a reverse FRN.

We refer you to the Figure 1.15 where the coupon is 15 − libor. From a synthetic perspective we can think of the investor receiving a constant amount, that is 15 per cent and funding at libor.

A structurer tries to arrange a win–win situation which should really be referred to as a potential win–win–win situation because there are three parties. The bank no longer provides just advice but actually is integral to the structure. The idea is to keep the smile on everybody's face.

For example the investor is happy because she receives 15 – libor, if rates are below 15 per cent and then nothing if rates rise above 15 per cent. (Given that she projects rates to remain bound range this is an optimal way of exploiting the view.)

The borrower is happy because they pay either straight libor on their debt or libor − 10 bps if rates stay below 15 per cent. The bank is pleased because they receive margins of between either 10 or 15 bps. The Figure 1.16 outlines the deal from the bank's perspective, who arrange the structure through buying a cap and receiving fixed on twice the deal notional.

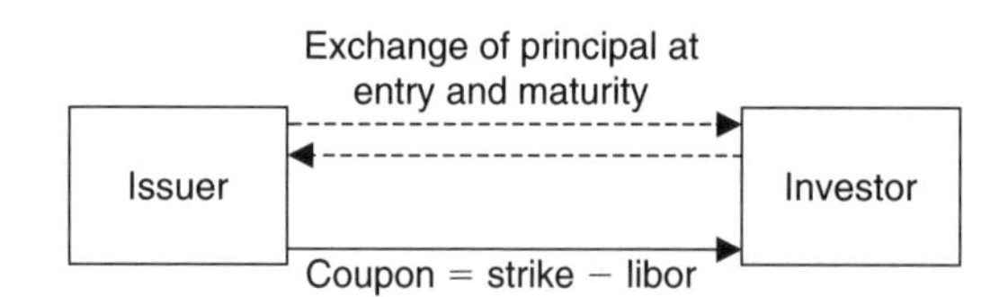

Figure 1.15 The reverse FRN from the investor's perspective.

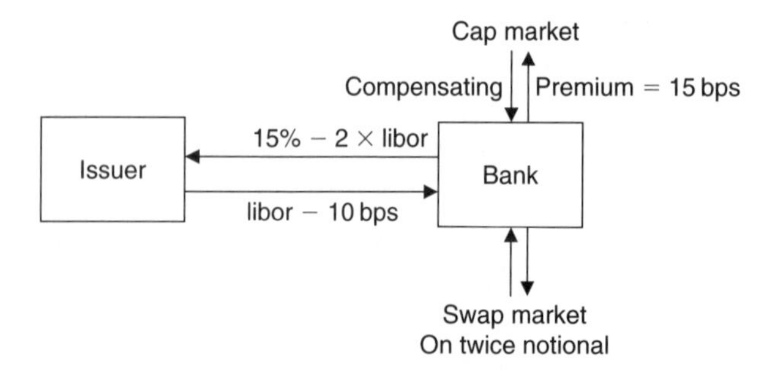

Figure 1.16 The reverse FRN from the arranger's perspective.

Capped FRN

This FRN pays an enhanced libor, potentially appealing to the institutional investor. The maximum coupon is capped hence the name. We give the example of a European borrower who would normally be able to issue a straight FRN at libor + 30, but with the enhancement induced by the structure are now able to fund at libor + 28. The investor receives an FRN on a good-quality credit paying a coupon of libor + 40 bps up to a maximum coupon of 6½ per cent. This extra coupon may make the difference between a successful transaction.

How is this piece of financial chicanery actually concocted? You will be glad to know that it represents one of the more straightforward structures. The issuer in addition to selling the straight FRN, sells a cap, usually to an investment bank (who prefers to don the appellation of arranger in these situations). A premium will flow from the arranger to the issuer and ultimately onto the investor. This enhances the coupon over and above the straight vanilla FRN issued by an equal-quality credit. If interest rates rise above the strike price of the cap it will be exercised by the bank. Instead of the issuer receiving on the premium and paying the investor, the issuer will now have to pay the bank the difference between libor and the strike. The investor only receives the strike and so looses out in this environment. Figure 1.17 illustrates the arrangement.

You can see from the diagram that the net cost of funding for the issuer is at libor + 28 bps representing a saving of 2 bps. This comes about because the premium the issuer receives is passed through to the investor, who is very pleased with life because, instead of receiving libor + 30, now get an extra 10 basis points. The bank is also quite happy because it is bullish on rates and has managed to hedge its interest rate exposure.

The cosy arrangement is dependent upon interest rates staying below the capped rate and indeed it will be sold under this qualification. Most structured notes require a fair degree of salesmanship.

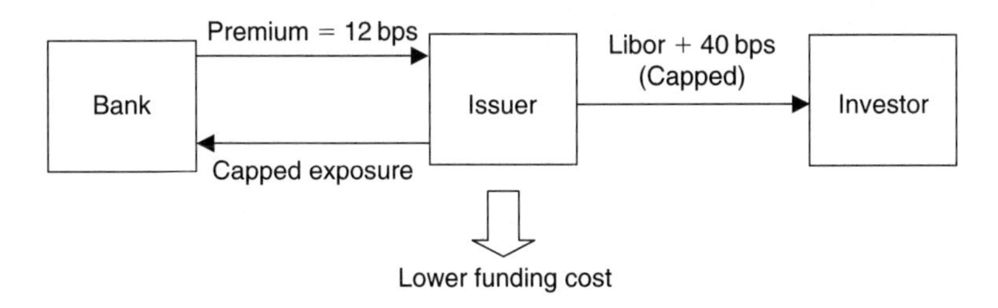

Figure 1.17 Capped FRN.

If rates increase above the strike price the issuer will fund at libor + 40, the differences between libor and the strike going to the arranger. The poor old investor receives a poor rate of interest which is the strike price on the cap + 40.

One of the key drivers determining pricing of the issue is the value of the cap. The premium for this instrument is typically high and our example of 12 bp per annum is representative. This is to be contrasted with the premium on a straight interest rate option of a few basis points. The reason for the superficial discrepancy is that the cap is required for 5 years. For a semi-annual exposure to libor the reset will be every 6 months. Consequently there are effectively 10 different exposures for a 5 year FRN issue to manage, buying a cap would lock in a ceiling but still enable the issuer to enjoy some upside participation.

Each one of these exposures is hedged with a caplet having the same strike as the cap. Given that the normal shape of the yield curve is upward sloping the premium for the longer-dated caplets will be very high because they are in the money options.

Collared FRN

The final type of embedded structure worth mentioning, because of its frequent deployment, is the so-called collared FRN. We are half way there in terms of comprehension, because 50 per cent of the structure is a capped FRN (recall that the issuer sells a cap to the arranger). If the issuer also buys a floor then the structure is termed a 'collar'. The motivation for issuing the collared FRN is to confer on the investor an enhanced coupon. (The investor must not be too bullish on rates because the collar does not allow participation.)

Moreover the investor anticipates a potential drop in rates which would make the floor feature considerably attractive because it acts as a lower band on the amount of interest received. Figure 1.18 shows the coupon our investor receives in comparison with the straight FRN.

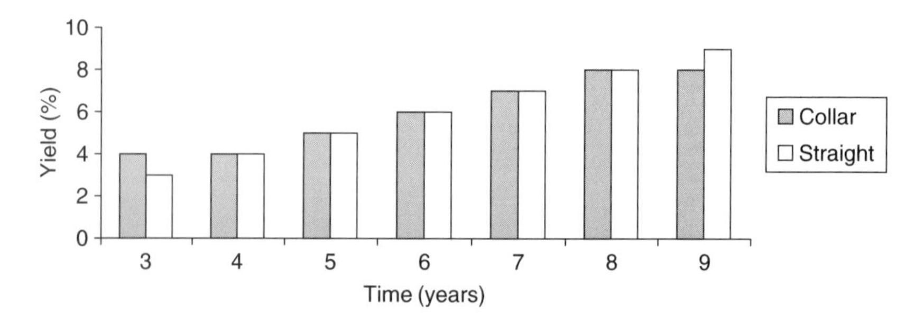

Figure 1.18 The effective interest rate on a collar.

For example instead of the investor receiving libor + 30, he may receive libor + 32. These extra two basis points represent the net premium of the collar. There will usually be a premium because the cap is worth more money than the floor. You may also hear of zero cost collars. This is of more benefit to the issuer who achieves a funding saving but is obviously not so beneficial to the investor, who does not receive any enhancement and would have to be quite bearish on rates to benefit from the 'kick in' on the floor.

Equity-linked bonds

There are two common types of equity-linked bond. The most common is the convertible bond. They represent a very popular way of financing for borrowers who do not have the credit standing to issue a straight bullet bond. They are correspondingly popular with investors because they combine the regular income of a bond together with equity participation. This takes the form of the right to exchange shares for the bond at a pre-specified price within a defined period. Figure 1.19 shows the total nominal value of convertible outstanding in comparison with the fixed income and equity market.

The other common type of equity-linked bond is the warrant. These are bonds issued with warrants attached and give the holder the right to purchase shares at a given price within a defined period. These are very similar in nature to straight equity options but come packaged with the bond. They are a more opportunistic feature, whereby the borrower exploits an issuance window. Consequently they are not widespread within the capital markets. (We will discuss in a little bit more detail within the Section 1.8.)

We now explain the convertible bonds in greater detail. As stated the convertible is a hybrid instrument which is partially debt and part equity. They usually appear on the balance-sheet as debt. The fixed income component consists of a defined maturity date and coupon.

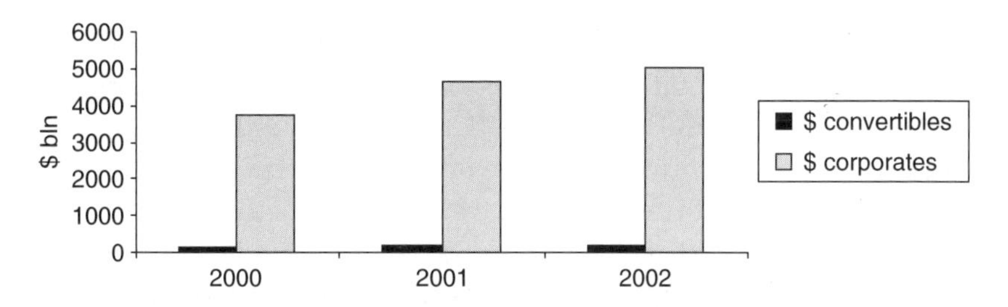

Figure 1.19 Comparison of debt outstanding. *Source:* Deustche Bank.

Table 1.2 A typical convertible bond.

Terms	Value
Issuer	Deutsche Lufthansa AG
Coupon	1.25%
Maturity	4 January 2012
Issue size	750 million
Face value	49.6032 shares
Number of bonds	1000 nominal
Share price	8.78
Current price	92.552
Conversion price	20.16

Source: Bloomberg LP.

We refer you to Table 1.2 which shows the common features of a convertible bond.

The mechanics of the convertible bond will now be described. Each bond upon issuance has a specified conversion price. This price represents the value at which the bond can be converted into the underlying shares. It is also a lot larger than the current share price. If the share price rises enough to reach the conversion price then the bond is converted into equity at the behest of the investor, no money changes hands and the investor now has shares. The coupon on the convertible bond will be lower than if straight debt was issued, this represents an advantage to the borrower.

The yield on the convertible will be higher than the dividend yield on the equity and this yield advantage is the benefit enjoyed by the investor. Formally the yield advantage is simply the difference between the current yield and the dividend yield:

$$\text{Yield advantage} = \text{current yield} - \text{dividend yield}.$$

This is also the comparable advantage of holding the bond instead of the underlying shares.

The yield that the bond actually trades at however will be less than the standard yield to maturity on a comparable bond, that is one of the same issuer, coupon and maturity. This is because there is effectively an option within the convertible. The option is of benefit to the investor and hence the price of the bond will trade higher than the comparable, consequently the yield will be lower. This is the main benefit to the issuer because the cost of funding would be lower than if they had issued a straight bond.

There are a number of measures within the market that the reader must be familiar with. Most prevalent is the notion of conversion price premium. This is the difference between the market value of the convertible and the market value of the underlying shares into which the bond is converted. To determine this we need the intermediate step of evaluating the conversion value, which is determined from the product of the current share price and the conversion ratio. This is the number of shares the bond can be converted into. For our example, detailed in Table 1.2, the conversion ratio is the face value of the bond divided by the conversion share price. Thus

$$\text{Conversion value} = \frac{\text{face value}}{\text{conversion price}} = \frac{1000}{20.16} = 49.6.$$

In order to determine the 'intrinsic' value of the option we multiply by the current share price:

$$\begin{aligned}\text{Conversion value} &= \frac{\text{face value}}{\text{conversion price}} \times \text{share price} \\ &= 49.6 \times 8.78 = 435.48.\end{aligned}$$

Then the premium is just the amount by which the price exceeds this value:

$$\text{Conversion price premium} = \frac{\text{bond price} - \text{conversion value}}{\text{conversion value}}.$$

Plugging in the numbers from the example:

$$\text{Conversion price premium} = \frac{925.52 - 435.48}{435.48} = 112.52\%.$$

The reader should not make the mistake of confusing the conversion price premium with the straight conversion premium. This is the amount by which the conversion price exceeds the current share price. Thus, rather confusingly, we have another equation featuring the word premium:

$$\text{Conversion premium} = \frac{\text{conversion price} - \text{share price}}{\text{share price}}.$$

Again from the example we have in Table 1.2:

$$\text{Conversion premium} = \frac{20.16 - 8.78}{8.78} = 129.61\%.$$

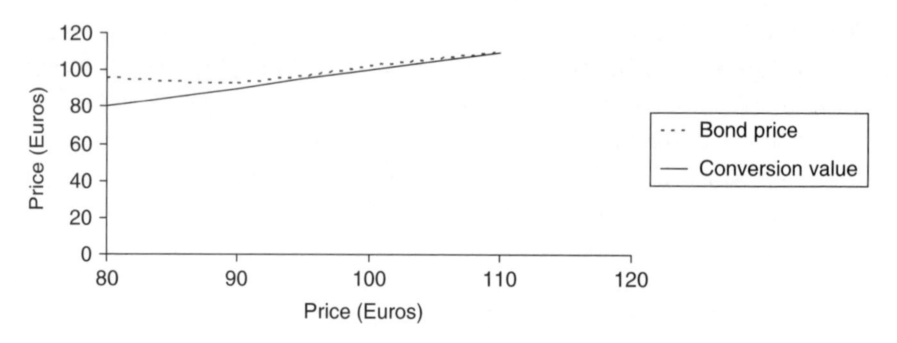

Figure 1.20 The conversion premium.

Perhaps a more intuitive way of thinking about the conversion premium is to break it down into its constituent pieces. We have done this in the equation below:

$$\text{Conversion premium} = \text{option value} + \text{coupon} - \text{dividend}.$$

This shows the value of the bond to the investor can be thought of in terms of what is received, that is the coupon, but the dividend is forgone, because we have not yet converted, that is why it is subtracted in the equation. The other piece is the value of the embedded option. The clearest way of illustrating how these components change with share price is with reference to Figure 1.20.

We can see from this chart that there are two main regions. We have the region to the right where the bond follows the share price and is said to be 'in the money'. The premium in this region is very small because there is no longer any upside potential within the bond. The region to the left is where the current share price is below the conversion value and here the premium will be appreciable in anticipation of the share price rising.

1.7 Asset-backed securities

These are fixed income instruments which have specific financial resources pledged as collateral to pay the interest and redemption. These resources should be looked upon as a pooling arrangement rather than a one to one matching with the so-called asset backing to the resulting instruments.

The backing can consist of many different types of receivables. Commonly encountered are mortgages, consumer loans, credit card receivables and commercial loans. In common with much financial architecture the phenomenon of asset-backed securities was introduced within the US back in 1970 and indeed the North American market is still the largest.

The seeds of securitization were sewn by the Government National Mortgage Association (or GNMA). This government sponsored agency began issuing so-called mortgage pass through certificates. This is an asset-backed security representing participation in a pool of mortgages.

The mechanism works through each of the residential mortgage owners paying their monthly interest and sometimes redemption payment into a central vehicle. A number of securities will subsequently be issued into the marketplace and purchased by investors. If we follow the path of an individual monthly mortgage interest payment it will not always go to the same security. Indeed sometimes it may represent a very small component of the coupon for the first asset issued and sometimes it may be a small component of the redemption payment for the second issue. The point is that the investor has absolutely no interest in the dynamics of a single person's mortgage actions, however pooled together into many thousands it will be a relatively stable asset base which grows in a fairly predictable manner. It is the stable characteristics that the investor is buying into.

Implicit within the last paragraph, is the mechanism of securitization. This is virtually synonymous with asset-backed securities. We have described a pass through arrangement whereby the investor bears all the risks associated with the collateral. These risks can be rather unpalatable and consequently the arrangement as it stands might not be able to successfully issue the proposed securities into the marketplace. To avoid this possibility the backing may be consolidated.

This is typically known as *credit enhancement* because the risk is typically credit in nature. For example in our pool of mortgages some of the lenders may default. (However the mechanism could also mitigate pre-payment risk; some property holders may redeem early causing the investor a headache because instead of receiving a large coupon on a 10 year bond, for example, unexpectedly receives his capital in an unfavourable yield environment. The objective of enhancement is to mitigate this type of scenario, which has nothing to do with credit.)

So far we have discussed asset-backed securities purely from the investor's perspective we wish to complement this with the motivations for the issuer.

If an issuer has made a number of commercial loans, the bulk of which are financed at libor plus a credit related spread. The repackaged loans can occasionally be funded at a lower rate because of their enhanced credit worthiness. This allows the package to be sold off at a comparable value to that derived at origination. The benefit then is

Table 1.3 The balance sheet pre- and post-securitization.

Holding	Value (€ M)	Capital requirement (€ M)
Initial portfolio	5000	400
Securitized amount	500	40 (on balance sheet)
Senior securities	400	None
Junior securtiites	100	None
Final portfolio	4500	360

a transformed capital position, enhanced liquidity and perhaps most importantly less dependency on its traditional revenue stream.

Securitization can be represented as transference of risk to the capital markets. The implication here is that the organization originating the collateral upon which the obligations are made has moved capital and its associated risk off the balance sheet. We draw a distinction between a true sale, whereby assets are physically transferred and risk transfer which is more common in Europe, this is not accompanied by any movement of capital – these are commonly referred to as synthetic. This is key to understanding what has developed into a fairly disparate activity predominant within the European marketplace.

Everyone knows the example of the release of regulatory capital is a major motivation for banks to engage in securitization, but other businesses adopt the method in order to target a lower cost of funding and ultimately an increase on shareholder return on equity (Table 1.3).

The company can also change its debt/equity ratio (or leverage) through these means. We illustrate how it is possible to achieve this in Table 1.3, depicting the reduction of debt on the balance sheet and the resulting saving in regulatory capital. (Applied at 8%.)

One question that may have occurred to the reader is where does the burden of credit analysis now lie? As you know, a commercial bank systematically evaluates the credit risk associated with the borrower prior to making a lending decision. In the landscape of asset-backed securities the lending is effectively advanced by the issuing entity through the sale of the asset-backed structure into the capital markets. The bank receives the proceeds upon transferring these assets into the entity (in the case of a true sale). It is the job of the rating agencies to subsequently evaluate the credit worthiness of both the collective pool of receivables and the resulting structure.

All public mortgage and asset-backed securities are rated by one or both of the large credit rating agencies such as Moody's, and Standard and Poor's. This is now a specialist service, distinct from their standard business of providing measures of company credit worthiness.

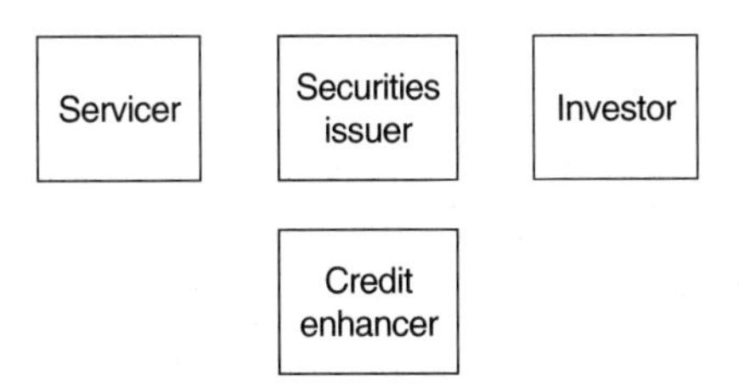

Figure 1.21 The main elements of an asset-backed structure.

Within a securitization structure it is normal for the issued securities to be of good to high-investment grade (many issues launched in Europe are rated AAA/Aaa). The focus of the agencies is to evaluate both the resulting security structure and the characteristics of the asset backing. Usually a pass through arrangement will not provide sufficient protection to the investor and evaluation will be performed on the additional enhancement.

The amount of additional enhancement is determined by establishing the risk present within the collateral through stress testing which quantifies the effects of various loss scenarios, driven by either credit or market related events.

Once additional enhancement is required the question arises as to what forms are available. We refer you to Section 4.9 in Chapter 4.

In order to further discuss we need a diagram of the common elements within a securitization structure. We refer you to Figure 1.21.

With reference to Figure 1.21 the original assets are sourced through the originator/servicer. The risks are transferred (or sometimes sold) to a special independent legal entity which can either have trust or company status. The main feature of the vehicle that comes into existence is the enjoyment of a completely different credit character distinct from the originating company. This is the so-called the SPV or special purpose vehicle.

The SPV being a separate legal concern, can now issue securities into the marketplace, which are evaluated by the rating agencies. We also see in this diagram an external credit enhancer. This can take the form of a cash collateral account segregated for the benefit of the company or trust. It is set up at the time of issue and used on the occasions when there are insufficient receipts within the pool to cover the required outgoings. The funds within the account are usually borrowed from a third party bank and will be returned once the issues have been repaid.

On this theme another mechanism is the so-called 'collateral invested' account representing an ownership interest in the trust. This works in the same way as the cash collateral account and makes up any shortfall needed to pay the investors. If funds are drawn down during a particular period they will usually be repaid later if the spread recovers.

Further reserve funds can be built up into separate ways. Either a portion of the profits upon issuance is placed on deposit, or the excess servicing spread is pooled (if any). These represent proceeds generated from the difference between the incoming payments and the debt servicing payments.

1.8 International bonds

The International (often called the Eurobond) market is now one of the largest and most important sources of capital. It continues to grow and develop new structures in response to the varying demands placed upon it by the investor community (Figure 1.22).

The International marketplace can only be used by a good credit including some governments, large corporates and supranationals. Investors are predominantly institutional but the private client is also important, looking to invest in the Eurobond market due to a lack of development within their domestic market. Indeed many instruments are designed to be tax efficient specifically to appeal to the private investor.

The distinguishing characteristic of the Eurobond is the nature of issuance. They are placed across borders by an international syndicate of banks. This method of issuance is distinct from the auction system characteristic of government bonds. The bond is subsequently traded OTC by the market participants in a number of international financial centres. A further characteristic of the market is the lack of any one central authority to provide regulation. They are, however, usually registered on a national exchange enabling some types of institutional investor access to the market who might otherwise be frozen out. Possibly because of local legislation banning the holding of non-exchange traded assets.

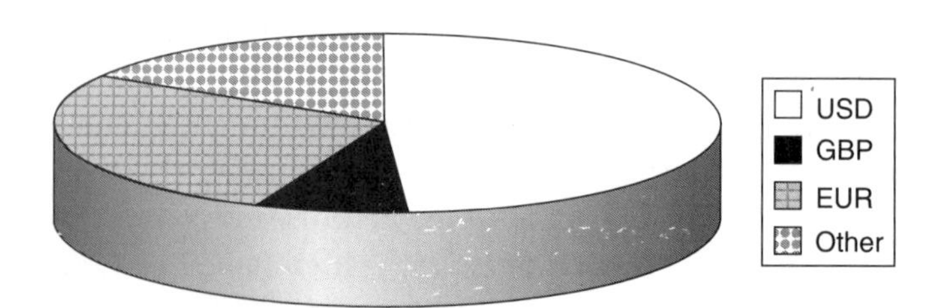

Figure 1.22 International bond volumes by country (May 2003). *Source:* Deutsche Bank.

The major currencies of issuance are the dollar, euro, sterling and yen. The term 'euro', originally used as a prefix, was coined to represent dollar deposits within Europe in the 1960s. These received a preferential rate due to the perception of higher risk. Now we have a situation where 'euro' refers to any currency on deposit outside of the country of issue. For example sterling on deposit in Japan would be called eurosterling. The currency of issuance does not necessarily match the currency in which the borrower is domiciled, indeed the currency will be chosen on the basis of how attractive that debt will be perceived by the investor community within that currency.

Interest on Eurobonds is paid gross of any tax. They are bearer bonds and have no central register. However, they are usually held in a central repository for settlement purposes. These features were key to the development of the market.

The majority of Eurobonds are conventional bullet structures with a fixed coupon and maturity date. The latter typically from 5 to 10 years, many bonds are considerably longer dated. This is particularly true of the eurosterling market, thus meeting the considerable demand of institutional clients which have long dated pension obligations.

The bond is typically unsecured and consequently depends upon the borrower's credit worthiness in order to appeal to the investor base.

The Eurobond market gave birth to the FRN. Here the coupon payment varies and is dependent upon a reference rate typically either libor or euribor. There will be an additional spread, dependent upon the credit quality of the issuer. For example borrowers with a poorer credit than AA (which is representative of the swap market) will be referred to as libor plus borrowers, conversely issuers with a better credit than AA will be able to borrow at libor minus. Typically spreads range from 10 to 200 basis points.

Common non-vanilla structures, especially within the sterling market are perpetuals, which pay a regular coupon but do not mature, and conventional bonds with an embedded call or step up feature. We have discussed these arrangements and will not go into detail here.

Also important within the Eurobond market is the zero coupon bond which pays no coupon but is issued at a discount to par. The effective interest is implied by the return on the difference between par and the issue price. This return is locked in so effectively represents an income. However for tax purposes it is categorized as a capital gain and taxed at a preferential rate. These bonds have correspondingly become less important within the US and UK who have adjusted their tax legislation. Correspondingly the return counts as income and not capital gain. Table 1.4 illustrates a typical deal.

Table 1.4 A typical Eurobond deal.

Detail	Example
Borrower	European corporate
Form of notes	Senior notes available in temporary global note and bearer form
Ranking	Pari passu with all outstanding unsecured senior debt
Announcement date	16 June 2000
Issue price	99.3140
Final maturity	25 October 2010
Currency	Euro
Amount issued	650 million
Interest basis	Act/Act
Fixed rate of interest	5.75%
Re-offer	99.3140
Fees	0.325%
Market of issue	Euro MTN
Repayment type	Bullet
Lead managers – books	Societe General, Deustche Bank AG
Co-lead managers	ABN Amro, BNP Paribas Group
	CDC Ixis Capital Markets, J.P. Morgan Secs.
Co-manager	CM CIC, Credit Agricole Indosuez
	Credit Lyonnais, Dresdner Kleinwort Benson
	HSBC, Natexis Banques Populaires
	Nomura International PLC
	Schroder Salomon Smith Barney

Source: Bloomberg LP.

It is common for conventional Eurobonds to be issued with warrants attached. These are issued in fixed denominations and allow the holder to buy shares at a pre-specified price up to and including a pre-specified date in the future.

The warrant is an embedded option conferring the right but not the obligation to purchase at the exercise price. This will be below the current share price of the issue. If during the exercise period the shares remain above the exercise price, then the warrant cannot be converted and will expire worthless. Occasionally the warrant is detached from the host bond and traded within a secondary market.

The idea of the attachment is to make the issue attractive to the investor, because without such inducements it may prove impossible to place the bonds at an attractive yield for the borrower. This coupon will be lower then a conventional bond without this feature. If the warrant is subsequently exercised then the issuer either receives cash or shares. The issue is said to be non-dilutary if the issuer does not have to create additional shares.

From the investors perspective the so-called high gearing represents a chance of appreciable return for relatively small outlay. Further they will have an exposure to the share price without taking on direct ownership. If the share price increases they will exercise and benefit. However if the share price performs adversely they still receive a constant income from the bond.

The issuance process

Eurobonds are issued through an international banking syndicate. This group is formed by the winner, known as the lead manager, of a bidding process. The borrower will invite a number of banks to bid at a price which they think is reflective of the market conditions and the appetite for the paper.

The success of the operation is not necessarily judged purely in terms of the cheapest possible funding but rather in terms of the market perception and credibility of the issuer. There is often a trade off between these two components. For example the credibility concern is potentially a higher priority for new issuers who may subsequently tap the market. The company's choice of lead manager will reflect not just the quality of the bid but also their reputation within the market place.

After successful bidding, the lead manager upon formal appointment will be invited to form a group of other banks known as the syndicate. The lead manager will underwrite the issue, this guarantees that it will hold any potential shortfall if the paper is under-subscribed. This is precisely the situation that all parties wish to avoid because it causes reputational damage. Additionally the bank ends up with substantial quantities of paper valued below par on its trading book which will subsequently be difficult to place.

One insurance mechanism is referred to as a fixed price re-offer scheme. The syndicate will agree on an issue price, the commission schedule, and how the issue will be distributed among the syndicate. The banks attempt to sell their allocation into the marketplace at the pre-specified price. The re-offer mechanism prevents the bank being able to sell back to the lead manager at a discount; consequently the lead manager has greater control over the offering process.

An important indicator of a potential price is determined from the 'grey market'. This is a period before the official launch announcement when the bond will actually trade prior to the official appearance. This serves as a useful guide to the lead manager who can gauge the level of activity and hence institutional demand for the paper. This may lead to changes in the re-offer price.

There are three important dates in the calendar of the new issue. These are the announcement date, the offering day and the closing day. Prior to the announcement, the lead manager and issuer will have had discussions confirming the specifications of the subsequent issue. This will include, for example its nominal size, target coupon and price. At this stage they remain provisional. During these meetings the lead manager will also appoint the trustee, principal and agent. Confirm the members of the syndicate group and delegate responsibility for the legal documentation and prospectus.

The new issue is formally confirmed on the announcement date. Details on the maturity of the issue, intended size of the deal and the coupon range are disclosed. A formal invitation is further sent to each of the potential syndicate members detailing the timetable of dates for the issue and the legal documentation containing their obligations.

The next phase is the offering day. Between the announcement date and the offering day the syndicate will have clarified the final terms and conditions of the issue. Usually the specifications on a bond will change from the announcement date. Particularly if there has been a large change in the market conditions. (Any smaller movements will be addressed through a change in the price of the bond relative to par at issue.) Once the final details of the bond have been clarified, the syndicate members usually have a fixed period, usually a day, to accept or reject the terms.

The offering day comes at the end of this period when the bonds are finally offered to the market. Prior to this the syndicate will have purchased the bonds from the issuer at the announcement price. The deal would have been allotted according to the documentation provided by the lead manager. Each of the members will have concluded a 'book-building' or placement process.

The period between the offering day and the closing day is referred to as stabilization, the issue will now trade in the secondary market. The price of the bond will be supported by the lead manager in unison with the other syndicate members. Finally the closing date itself represents the transfer of funds from the syndicate members for settlement.

Syndicate members

Visibility is all important within the banking community and in an area where the overall profitability of a transaction can be relatively small it becomes of paramount concern.

The underwriting lead manager has the most prominent role. The issuer of the bond will base their decision typically on the basis of a beauty parade in conjunction with a bid. This route is not always taken and the issue may be awarded to the investment bank which enjoys an existing relationship or a bank that has a particular expertise within the specific sector.

After a mandate has been granted the lead manager takes on a number of responsibilities. The main function is to underwrite the deal. Consequently if the bond cannot be placed within the market, the lead manager will take paper onto its own book. This really is a worst-case scenario and much of the due diligence beforehand tries to eliminate this eventuality.

The lead bank will subsequently form a syndicate of banks sharing the responsibility of placing the issue. Next in order of status will be the co-lead manager. This function arose somewhat historically because of its capability to distribute across a geographic boundary. For example a European bank may not have a significant client base within the US.

The other members of the syndicate are known as syndicate banks. An issue will not always be placed by a syndicate. This depends very much on the size of the deal, for example some of the large international bonds issued by the US agencies have a notional size over $1 billion necessitating a large distribution mechanism. Comparatively small issues under $100 million would be placed entirely through a single manager.

A further important function of the lead manager will be to analyse the marketplace and determine the appetite for a new issue on a particular credit. Further responsibilities assigned to the lead manager include forming the prospectus of the issue. This specifies details of the bond issue, financial and general background information on the issuing company. The lead manager will also be accountable for any legal issues involved with the transaction.

Pricing

The all-important price of the deal will be expressed as a percentage of 100. A price is established by the lead manager. This involves determining the coupon on the bond such that within the prevailing interest rate and credit environment the price of the bond is par. These details are circulated on the announcement date and if on the pricing date the actual market environment has changed then it will be reflected in the price of the bond which will trade away from par.

In pricing the deal there is somewhat of a conflict of interest. This arises because the lead manager is trying to maximize the bank's profitability but also is trying to ensure the lowest possible borrowing for the issuer. If the bond is issued at too high a price as soon as the bond trades it will sell off leading to a poor impression of the issue. This will adversely affect subsequent offerings. Too low a price and the borrower will be aggrieved because they will end up paying a higher-borrowing cost than the market rate.

The preliminary coupon on the bond is established using a standard methodology. The maturity of the bond will mainly be a function of the investor appetite and is gauged in discussion with the bank's client base. The yield is then obtained by looking at the comparable securities, that is those with the same credit rating and sector as the issuer. If there are no comparables then the yield on a government security having the same maturity is established and a credit related spread is added. The resulting coupon will be the yield provided the bond is issued at par. Eurobonds as we have described commonly incorporate other features which affect their valuation. To price the deal with an embedded option would follow the same process as described above with the option stripped out.

Fee structure

The fee structure for Eurobonds is relatively generic. The fees are not accounted for separately but rather are reflected through an adjustment to the final price. The amount increases with maturity, nominal amount and decreases according to the credit quality of the issuer. The breakdown will include a component for underwriting which is paid to the lead manager and a participation fee which is divided among syndicate members. Typical size ranges from 25 basis points to 80 basis points depending on the nominal size of the issue.

Valuation and subsequent management

The valuation of Eurobonds is performed by quoting a spread from the relevant government bond. The vast majority of bonds will have an associated benchmark government issue. If this is not the case then the spread will be added to a yield interpolated between the neighbouring maturity government bonds. It is quite commonplace for the issue also to be quoted relative to the libor curve. The credit spread will be referenced relative to the swap rate equal to the bond's maturity. Table 1.5 shows the comparable quotation methods.

One of the other major factors responsible for the growth of the International bond market is the existence of a very liquid currency

Table 1.5 The methods of quoting a bond valuation.

Issuer	Coupon (%)	Maturity	Benchmark	Govvie. Spread	Swap Spread
Deutsche Telekom Intl.	7.125	June 05	UKT8H 05 (the government issue sharing the same maturity and currency)	103 (basis point spread relative to benchmark yield)	79 (basis point spread relative to swap rate at same maturity)

Source: Bloomberg LP. (12 June 2003).

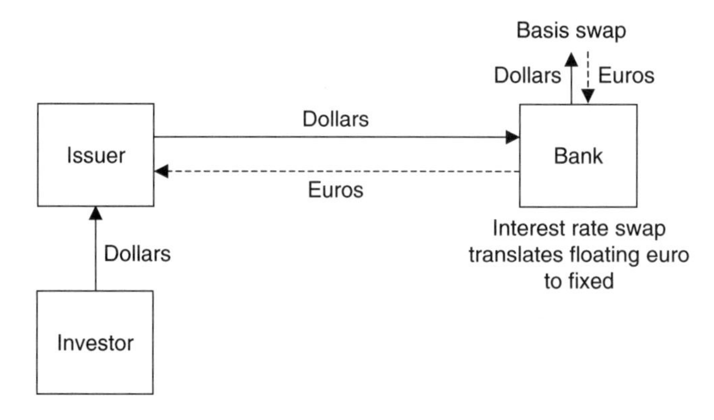

Figure 1.23 The principal exchanges on a currency swap.

and asset swap market. This is of enormous benefit to the issuer who knows that their debt will appeal in another country, because perhaps it fills a sector gap in the market. (Perhaps they knew this because of the due-diligence provided by their investment bank.) This introduces a slight problem however, because for accounting purposes they will be taking on unwanted currency exposure. Our investment bankers come to the fore once again and suggest the currency swap as a means of mitigating this exposure. Figure 1.23 shows such an arrangement. The other beneficial consequence for our borrower is that the financing can be significantly cheaper than if they had issued straight into the foreign currency.

Usually the borrower will not want a fixed coupon bond on its balance sheet. This represents an extremely risky instrument. Consequently an asset swap will be performed which exchanges the interest rate profile of the bond so the net position is the creation of a synthetic FRN which has considerably lower market risk. Figure 1.24 shows an asset swap.

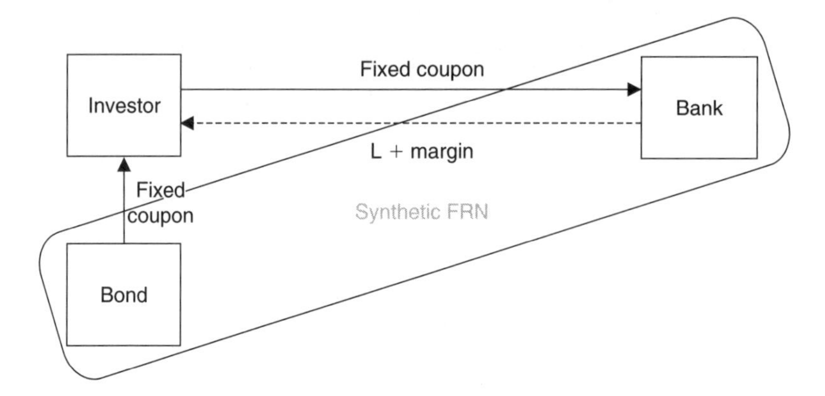

Figure 1.24 The asset swap.

Clearing systems

We have left this section towards the end of our discussion, because unfortunately it is a little dry but with your motivation now fully established its time to do a quick tour. There exists a specialized clearing system either Euroclear or Clearstream which is partly responsible for the settlement and warehousing of international bonds.

The clearing system exists in order to avoid the physical handling of bearer certificates.[4] For example when the bond is purchased by the investor, either within the primary or secondary market place, the certificate representing ownership is passed on to their custodian bank for safe keeping. The clearing system is designed to manage the process. It achieves this in two ways. The first is to allocate a unique code to each international bond issue. This code is known as the international securities identification number or ISIN. The second step is the opening of a securities clearance account and a cash account for the investor.

After the investor has traded, the bonds are credited into the securities clearance account and the resulting proceeds will be deposited into the cash account.

[4]When issued Eurobonds are said to be in temporary global form. The document associated with this represents the entire issue. This document is then exchanged to the permanent global form which is held by the clearing arm of the bank on behalf of either Euroclear or Clearstream. The definitive form is the certificate held by investors conferring legal ownership of the debt. The definitive form is typically a bearer certificate (they can be registered) consisting of a printed certificate displaying the details of the issue. These bearer certificates are physically deliverable. To tie this in with our description of the clearing system, if the investor buys a bond in the secondary market, for example, then a bearer certificate is transferred into their account registered with either Euroclear or Clearstream at their custodian bank.

Regulation and taxation

The main legal consideration for a potential issuer is the prohibition of distribution to residents within the US. This is a requirement from the US Securities Act and dates back from 1933. London is the principal centre for the issuance and trading of bonds hence the marketplace will be subject to certain pieces of UK national law.

With regard to taxation the primary consideration is that Eurobonds are not subject to withholding tax in the country where the borrower is resident for tax purposes. This is generally regarded as one of the most important factors responsible for the enormous growth of the Eurobond market.

We can contrast this with the taxation regime of a domestic bond held by a normal resident. In this situation the bond holder will effectively receive lower interest payments than the advertised coupon because the investor is subject to withholding tax on the bond. The tax rule also benefits the issuer who can pay a lower coupon in the Eurobond market. The comparable domestic issue would have to have a higher coupon to compensate the investor for the extra taxation.

The absence then of any withholding tax is a significant advantage. This is further enhanced with issuance in bearer form, allowing anonymous holding through an external discretionary account.

International Securities Market Association

The International Securities Market Association (ISMA) is a regulatory body based in Zurich comprising a membership of the banks dealing in international securities. As such it provides a framework for the Eurobond market, establishing uniform practices necessary for creating liquidity. Such measures include the procedures for settling transactions and standard methodologies for yield calculations. ISMA also provides the coordination between national governments.

MTN market

Markets and features are shown in Table 1.6.

1.9 Commercial paper

Companies finance their activities through the issuance of longer-dated bonds. Shorter dated capital often referred to as working capital is obtained directly from banks. An alternative source of funding is

Table 1.6 The MTN programme.

Market	Feature
$MTN	Not widespread because $MTNs require the issuer to register over and above the *Shelf registration* requirement with the SEC. This is common and allows the issuer access to a wide investor base and greater flexibility in terms of future issuance. Non-US issuers require a *SEC registration or a 144*. The latter does not allow exposure to such a wide investor base. Some EMTNs however are 144 registered.
MTN	Medium term note issued into the domestic currency and market of the issuer. This is often referred to as a 'quasi private placement'.
Euro-MTNs	Non-domestic issue, which falls into the international market and modelled on the CP programme. The documentation has to be annually registered. Because there is always an upfront cost to perform any issuance, the EMTN will only be worthwhile for regular borrowing on a large scale. However the benefits include a wide investor base, multiple currencies and maturities.

available through the commercial paper market. This is utilized by borrowers with a high-credit rating and is rather similar to the money-market product.

The borrower receives funds which are at a discount to the face value and then pays back the normal amount at a short period in the future, usually from 30 to 90 days and certainly not more than 9 months. (This is because within the US security legislation is such that debt instruments with a maturity less than 9 months do not require registration, so administrative costs are avoided.) They are always issued in bearer form.

The commercial paper note does not have a coupon and for this reason it trades at a discount to par. The interest is implied through the discount level. The primary markets for commercial paper are dominated by the US dollar. The Euro commercial paper market is becoming increasingly important. The buyers of the paper are mainly institutional and, on the whole, dominated by money-market unit trusts in the US. Pension funds are important investors within Europe.

The market mechanism is one of direct borrowing with little secondary market activity. Consequently buyers hold the CP until maturity. This is chosen to match their investment requirement. The CP market is characterized by two categories of borrowers falling in either the financial or non-financial bracket. Not surprisingly borrowing is prevalent in the financial category. This is a consequence of both banking

Table 1.7 Commercial paper programme.

	US programme	Euro programme
Currency	US $	Euro
Maturity	1–270 days	2–365 days
Interest	Zero coupon, discounted issue	Zero coupon, discounted issue
Quotation	Implied discount rate	Implied discount rate
Settlement	T + 0	T + 2
Registration	Bearer form	Bearer form
Issuance	Bank or corporate	Bank or corporate

Source: Bloomberg LP.

and financing activity within large corporates being dominated by the need for liquidity and short dated interest rate exposure. The market is dominated by borrowers with a high-credit rating, however there is increasing activity among lower-rated organizations which have a supporting arrangement. This is known as credit supported commercial paper. The backing can either be in the form of assets or a letter of credit.

Commercial paper is normally issued within a programme. This is typically from 3 to 5 years for European paper and longer for the US. An upper limit to the amount that can be borrowed is predetermined. Subsequently the borrower can issue up to this quantity for short periods. At the end of each period the paper is redeemed and then reissued with the proceeds of the new issuance being used to redeem the maturing paper. There is a slight risk of a potential shortfall, due to perhaps the deterioration in the borrower's credit, hence the need for a standby line of credit from a bank which will be drawn against in this contingency.

Commercial paper can be issued through two routes. One is known as direct issuance, whereby companies issue directly to the investor with no intermediary involved. This is quite a common arrangement which is cost effective because no fees are involved. Direct issuance typically takes place within a rolling programme.

The alternative route is to use the bank as an intermediary; this is the dominant form within the US (Table 1.7).

1.10 High-yield bonds

This market developed in the US during the 1980s. The engine for growth was the viability of acquisitions financed through the issuance

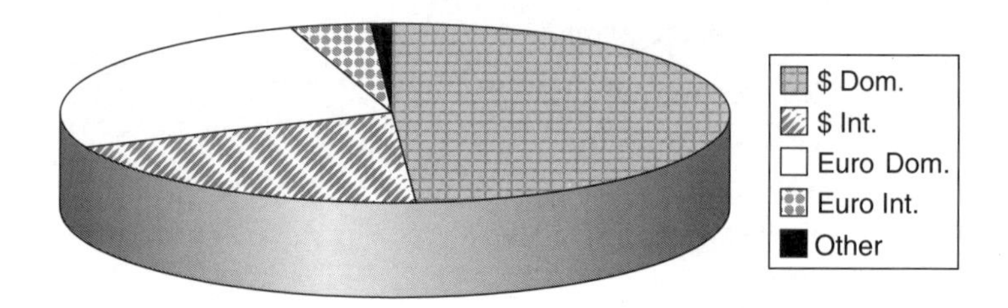

Figure 1.25 Global high-yield volumes. *Source:* Deutsche Bank (May 2003).

of high-yield debt. This activity was very prominent right through until the 1990s, which signalled a downturn in the marketplace. Recently, however, the market has seen record levels of activity enabling it to reach a level of maturity. Further the model has been exported to Europe.

The US high-yield bond market is now a viable source of finance for both unrated and companies that are rated below investment grade. The major currencies for high-yield issuance consist of the dollar and euro. Sterling is also an important marketplace. We should also note that the definition of European high yield includes companies that issue dollar debt but generate significant earnings from European activities.

The European high-yield market continues to try and catch up with the US in terms of the issuance and notional outstanding. Figure 1.25 illustrates the comparative volume of high-yield issuance throughout the past decade. The European market is still very young however and currently dominated by the so-called 'fallen angel' consisting of former investment grade bonds that have been downgraded. Very few bonds are actually issued as Euro high yield.

One of the major reasons behind the initial growth of the European market has been the arrival of the euro. Although this physically arrived at the beginning of 2002 it has long been a viable trading currency within the financial marketplace. Equally important has been the demand for financing. This has been led historically by the telecom and technology sector tapping this market to pay for their infrastructure requirements. The other side of the coin representing demand is dominated by the pension funds. The tentative move towards private provisioning within Europe will only make this component of demand more important.

The majority of bonds issued into the US market consist of plain vanilla securities with a fixed coupon and maturity of about 10 years. Many of the bonds also incorporate a call provision which is active over a short initial period relative to the maturity of the bond. The idea

Table 1.8 The maximum volatility of the asset class (02–03).

Asset category	Volatility (%)
Euro Broad Investment Grade	4
Government Bonds	4
MSCI Europe	27
Euro High Yield	18

is that the issuer will be able to refinance on the back of an improved credit rating.

Less common are non-vanilla bonds which benefit the investor. This is because the issuer, as a consequence of their indifferent credit worthiness, has to post-additional features on their debt in order to appeal to the investment community.

Perhaps the prevalent example of a so-called sweetener is the *step up* security. The initial coupon starts low in comparison to a higher value which kicks in at a later pre-specified date. The higher coupon will be payable up to maturity of the bond. Why stop at one step up when you can have several? Many bonds particularly within the sterling marketplace exhibit a series of coupons each one progressively higher and separated by about 25 basis points.

A *split coupon* security pays no coupon for the initial part of its life and thereafter becomes a fixed coupon bond for the remainder. The bonds are issued at a discount. The grace period allows the company to build up financial well-being until it has to pay coupons.

A *payment in kind* security gives the issuer the option of paying the coupon either in cash or with similar securities. The choice is usually confined to a limited period at the start of the issue. The bond will trade differently if similar securities are chosen for settlement and/or no cash interest is paid during this period.

Less commonly encountered is the *exchangeable variable rate* note. This pays a floating coupon after a pre-specified date; prior to this the coupon is fixed.

One of the important considerations, from the perspective of the institutional fund manager is the extent to which an asset enhances portfolio performance but does not simultaneously introduce a lot of extra risk. Within this context and with the proviso that risk is a mean variance measure, the last decade has revealed high yield to be an attractive asset class in comparative terms (Table 1.8). This conclusion is illustrated in the accompanying graph as given in Figure 1.26.

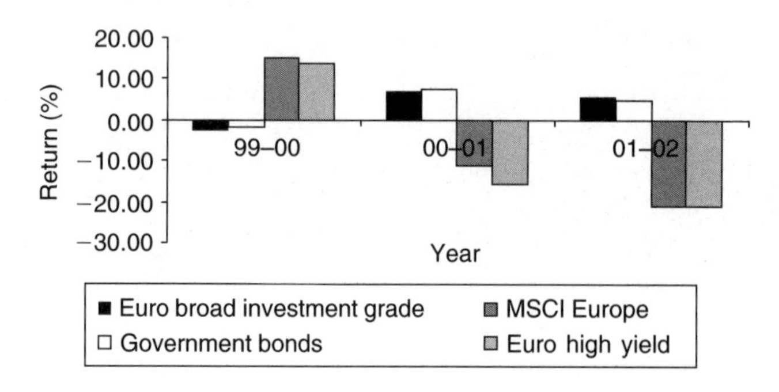

Figure 1.26 High-yield comparative performances.

1.11 Credit risk

A vanilla bond issued by a high-investment grade corporate will have two distinct components of investment risk. The major risk borne by the bondholder will be the price volatility caused by variations in the time value of money. Additionally there will be a risk due to the possibility of the issuer defaulting. For the example we neglect liquidity risk and assume that the inflation premium is included as a component of the risk free rate.

The remaining two sources of risk each have their own independent behaviour. The extra spread over the risk free rate is simply the market's estimate of default probability.

We can give a graphic illustration of these two components at work with reference to Figure 1.27.

This may on first appearances look rather like a picture that Nasa would be proud of. But a closer inspection reveals all the risk characteristics of a corporate bond. First we will explain what the axes represent. From the middle and sloping down to the right is the return on the bond, running into the page is the time horizon, in units of years. The vertical axis represents an effective probability.

Two separate humps broadly characterize the diagram. The larger hump to the left represents the influence of market risk. To begin with, the market return is distributed equally about zero. If we observe very closely it can be seen to approximate a normal distribution. As time progresses the mean component of return on the bond begins to dominate, even though for any one year there is still a distribution about this mean. We can also see that the actual thickness about the mean tends to decrease as the maturity on a bond gets closer. If we just had a government bond that would conclude the story.

The credit risk manifests itself within the small hump to the right. The saying is that a picture is worth a thousand words; well consider

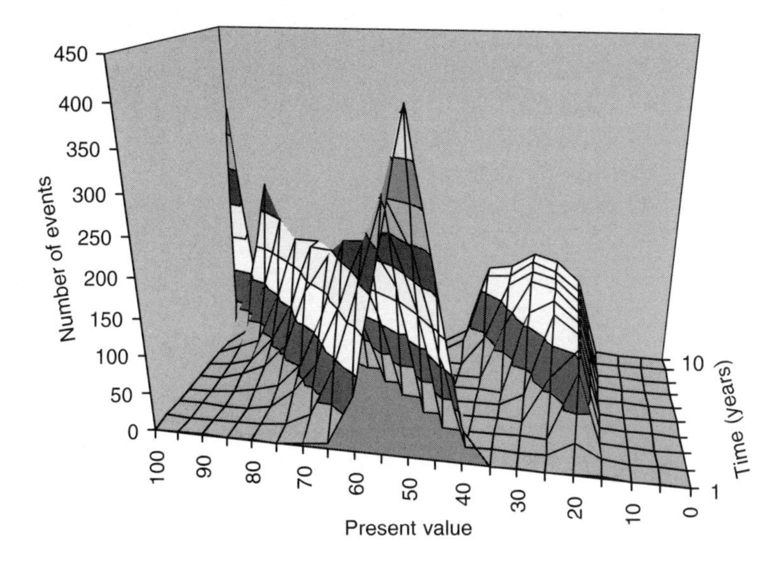

Figure 1.27 An illustration of the default process for a 10 year corporate bond.

yourself lucky because you have both. The picture repays a careful study; this is rather like a kaleidoscope which at first is confusing because your eye and mind are not quite coordinated. Initially the picture is missed but then with a bit of patience the shape materializes.

The hump is quite narrow to begin with because the chance of the borrower defaulting is quite small post-issuance. This is quite intuitive because young companies tend to be fairly liquid to begin with and coupon payments to the bond holders will have a very high priority. As time advances the probability of default will grow. This is because even if the marginal probability, which represents the chance of default in any one particular year remains constant, the so-called cumulative default probability, which is the measure most relevant to a long-term bond holder increases with time.

We will come back to this diagram a little bit later to discuss how the risks are represented mathematically. But this is asking a little bit too much to begin with. The actual details are quite complicated; we need to build up slowly.

The first thing we are going to look at is the pricing of a 1-year zero coupon bond issued by a non-government. We study a good-quality credit which does not have any liquidity risk. We choose a zero coupon bond because it highlights rather well the actual finances at work as opposed to tedious bond maths.

We can price the bond exactly in the same manner as we would a government bond, but the rate at which we use to discount the cash flow requires an additional spread implicitly containing the market

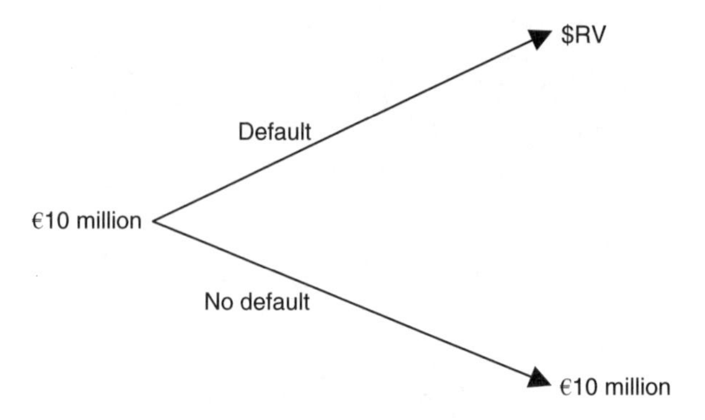

Figure 1.28 The default process for a 1 year zero.

perception for the issuer default probability. This increased rate is represented by a spread over a government security of the same maturity. The maturity aspect is important because the spread itself is a so-called term structure. Whereby acknowledging that the spread is maturity dependent and generally increasing with time. This is totally consistent with the fact introduced within Figure 1.27 that the cumulative probability of default increases with time.

We can write down the effective discount rate below:

$$\text{Credit discount rate} = \text{risk free rate} + \text{credit spread.}$$

The credit spread can be thought of comprising information on the actual default intensity and the recovery rate given a default. Consequently we can write the credit spread as

$$[\text{Credit spread} = (\text{default intensity} \times \text{recovery rate})]$$

Although this is technically correct in practice nobody ever tries to disentangle these two separate processes. It is the classic joint observation problem. Instead the market is just content to measure credit spreads as observed within the market itself.

Another equivalent method of determining the price of the bond is perhaps more natural because it actually addresses default as a contingency. This method states that the bond in a year's time could have defaulted. Further because default is a binomial process, we can display the cash flows with a diagram (Figure 1.28).

We can see that at the end of the year the bond has either defaulted in which case we lose some of our original investment, but not all of it, a percentage will be recovered. Or it has not defaulted. We denote the value of the bond at default by $RV.

So we have two ways of pricing the bond. On the one hand we can discount the non-defaulted cash flows of the borrower by a rate which encompasses spread information. Or we can discount cash flows at the risk free rate, with the proviso that the cash flows are those after default. If there is going to be any sanity in the world these two approaches better come out the same way.

You should also get into the habit of thinking of credit as a risk distinct from libor risk. For example libor risk is typically modelled by a tree where each node represents a possible value of the rate in the future. A proper way of representing credit would be to go about it the same way, but before we race ahead lets add a little bit more in the way of foundation by considering the situation where the underlying libor risk is a variable but the credit situation can be represented by either a default or non-default state.

We look at a 2 year zero under the two approaches. First up, the approach using defaulted cash flows. In this situation we assume that at each node the bond price is the expected value given the two possible outcomes of either default or no default. As with all pricing trees we start at the far right representing maturity, because we know the value of the bond. Do not forget the tree is just representing the libor risk only. That is why it appears in both representations. The credit risk however is represented within the cash flows for the first picture and then in the discount rate for the second picture.

At maturity we would normally expect to get 100 back, but because this is a credit bond it might have defaulted so the cash flow we get at maturity is an expected value. For example a default probability of 5 per cent and a recovery rate of 95 per cent will give an expected maturity value of 99.75. This value will be the same at all three of the nodes. In the example shown in Figure 1.29 the default probability is 2 per cent and the recovery rate is 50 per cent.

We then move back to the 1 year horizon. The value here will be the expected value of the bond given its subsequent evolution; remembering to discount this value. This gives the same expected value as the implicit spread method demonstrated using the rate highlighted as shown in Figure 1.30.

Having, hopefully, convinced you that the method of adding an extra spread to discount undefaulted cash flows is entirely equivalent to discounting defaulted flows, generated through a probability calibrated to the spread, at the risk free rate. We rather turn the tables and tell you that the capital market mentality is to think in terms of spread as a synonym for the default. Consequently we should be concentrating our efforts into being able to explain the behaviour of the credit spread from a modelling perspective.

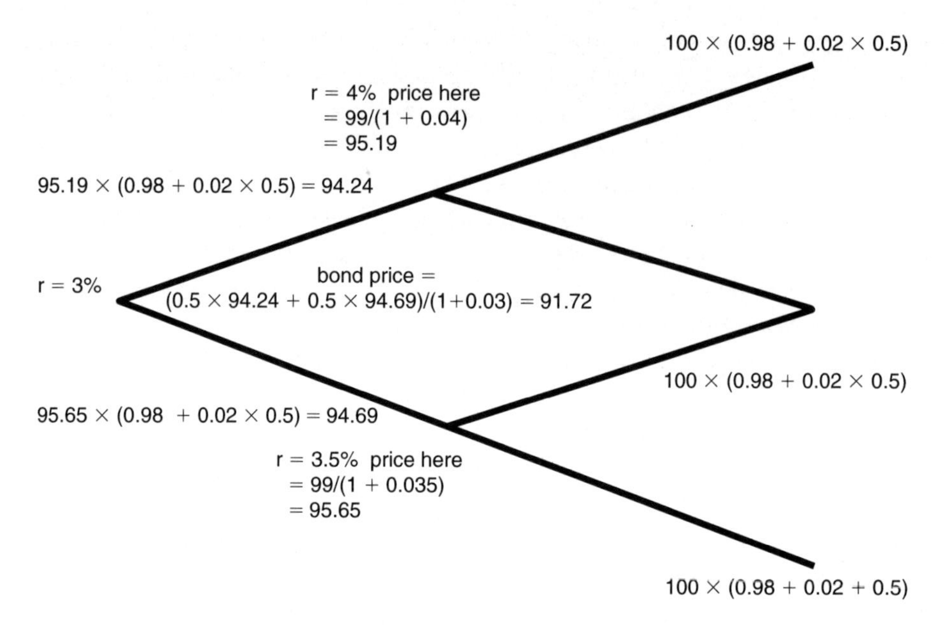

Figure 1.29 The defaulted cash flows.

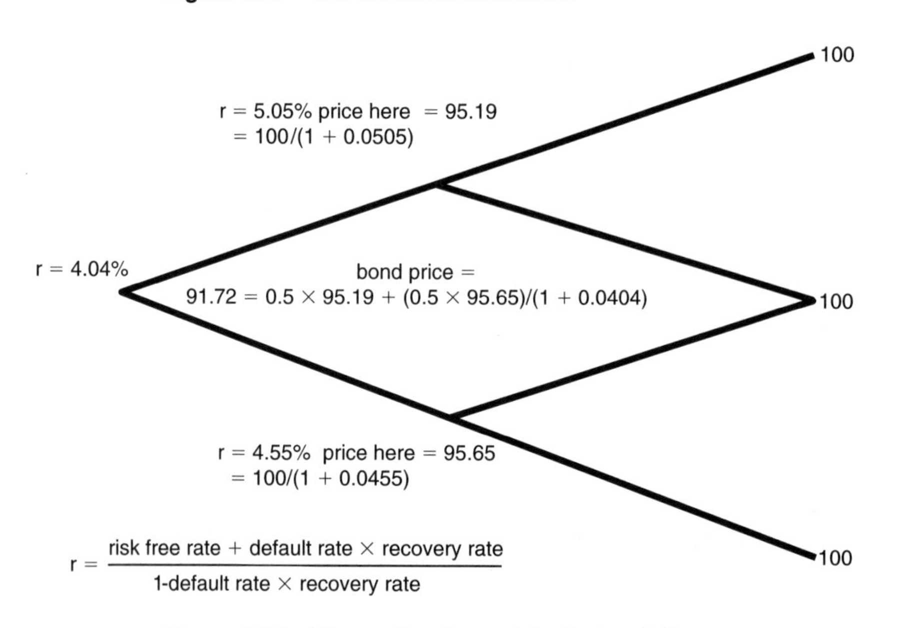

Figure 1.30 Discounting the undefaulted cash flows.

There is a huge amount of effort devoted to the pursuit of term structure modelling which can accurately address the behaviour of credit. It is very difficult, more so than straight market risk because of the character of credit. In Figure 1.31, we illustrate the spread behaviour of a credit bond.

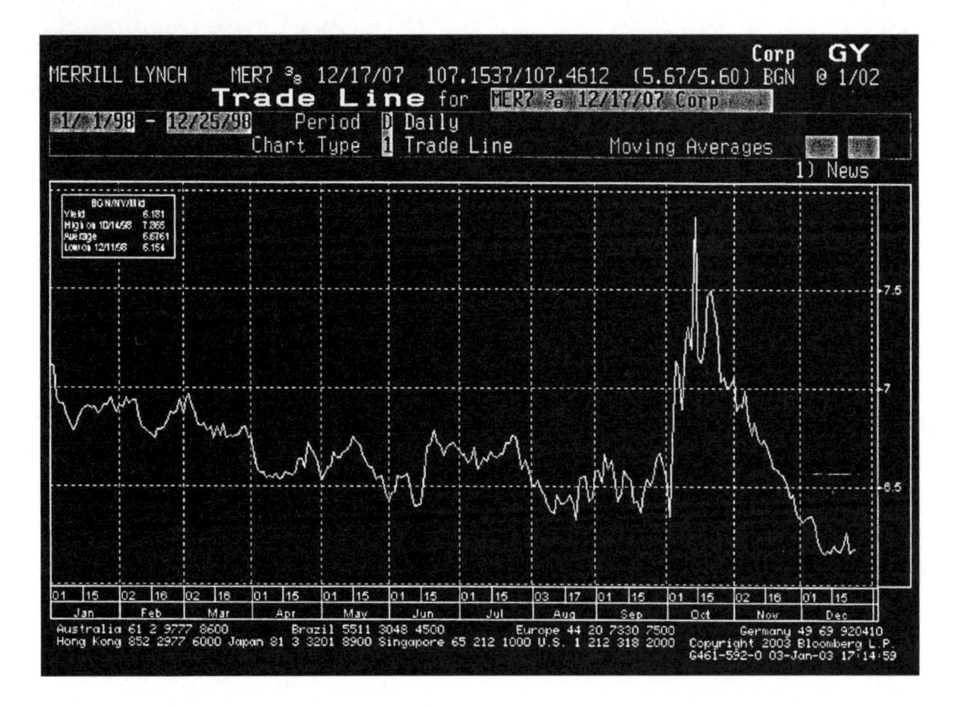

Figure 1.31 The yield of Merrill Lynch paper through the 98 period.
Source: Bloomberg LP.

The sharp peak is typical of the behaviour of credit spreads and in extreme cases it becomes what is termed a jump. Whether the yield between these points has any meaning is open to question. However there is a standard methodology deployed to account for spread behaviour which we will elaborate on.

We begin by thinking in terms of a default intensity which represents the probability of an issuer defaulting in that particular year. We define the default intensity, λ, as the ratio of the number of defaults that are observed to the number of issues at the outset, or equivalently

$$\text{Number of defaults} = \lambda \times \text{number at outset}.$$

We can think of extending this idea to a shorter period, all we have to do is to multiply by the period in question because of the definition of intensity (expressed in number per year). Thus for a period other than a year we have

$$\text{Defaults in period } \Delta t = \lambda \times \text{number at outset} \times \Delta t.$$

This can, in the limit of very small periods, be solved to give

$$\text{Number surviving} = \text{number at outset} \times \exp(-\lambda \times \Delta t).$$

The negative sign arises because we require the survivors not the defaulters. For example with a default intensity of 5 per cent and 1000 loans we would have, 96 per cent remaining after three quarters of a year. You should know that the quantity called 'expected time to default' is the reciprocal of the intensity and represents the case of 37 per cent remaining.

This is standard but we are simplifying, and an important property of default is the fact that it varies with time. To capture this situation we make the default intensity a function of time. This means the probability of default, over a period of a year, at time s in the future is given by $\lambda(s)$.

This is a forward default probability and it is necessary because we need to be able to calculate losses in the future. Do not think of this as a predictor, but rather the market expectation based on the current environment.

We can determine the number surviving as a product of the number at the beginning of the period with the probability for that period. The property of exponentials allows us to sum their arguments. This gets us to the expression

$$\text{Number surviving} = \text{number at outset} \times \exp\left(-\sum_{\text{year}} \lambda(t) \times \Delta t\right).$$

We can now think instead of a 1 year period of shrinking it to a very small timescale. Technically the sum becomes an integral and we divide by the number at the outset to arrive at the probability of default. This will be given by

$$\text{Survival probability} = \exp\left(-\int_{0}^{\text{future}} \lambda(t)\mathrm{d}t\right).$$

Now we add another extra layer of modelling to accommodate the fact that the default intensity does not just have a deterministic dependence on time but is stochastic in nature. With this in place the relevant equation becomes

$$\text{Survival probability} = E\left[\exp\left(-\int_{0}^{\text{future}} \lambda(u)\mathrm{d}u\right)\right].$$

where the upper case E operator means that we have to average all the possible paths over time that the default intensity may take. Now we do not necessarily have to start at time zero, we can think of actually starting at some point in the future. The relevant statistic of interest to us would be the probability of survival for the forward period, but to get here the company must have survived so we actually require a conditional probability. This conditional probability is given by

$$\begin{bmatrix}\text{Probability of surviving} \\ \text{until } T \text{ given survival at } t\end{bmatrix} = \frac{\text{probability of surviving until } T}{\text{probability of surviving until } t}.$$

But we know each of these they are given by equation immediately above. So we can write in the result

$$\text{Survival probability} = E\left[\exp\left(-\int_t^T \lambda(u)\,du\right)\right].$$

To give a straightforward example of conditional default, if we have a nice straightforward issuer that has a default intensity of 1 per cent per annum, then the chance of it surviving in the second year will not be the 99 per cent but rather a figure just below this given by

$$\text{Survival in second year} = 0.99 \times 0.99 = 98.01\%.$$

Thus we can see that the survival probability is a little lower, because it has to have survived the first year obviously in order to get to the second.

Let us go back again to the general case and examine how we actually start using these equations. We state that default must be a type of jump. Mathematically it means that the default process must be driven possibly by a Poisson.[5] This gives us a jump, but furthermore the probability of this jump is just given by the arrival intensity. Now we want to calibrate this arrival intensity with the market somehow. We can do this by appealing to our 'Nasa diagram' in Figure 1.27. (Recall the zero coupon bond is the simplest type of exposure and will hopefully enable us to see the wood from the trees.) To calibrate, we need to get the intensity from the spread. We discussed in our binomial

[5]A Poisson is another type of random process distinct from the Gaussian you may be more familiar with. They are both stochastic but the standard market behavior of assets including stocks and bonds are accounted for by the Gaussian. This describes their evolution in terms of a shock and a drift. The shock is given by the drawing of a random number but distributed either normally or log normally. Credit risk however is presumed to be a jump type process, which is an actual discontinuity in price. The figure below represents the evolution of an asset following a Gaussian type process which can be contrasted with the Poisson process, as exemplified in Figure 1.31 representing a bond throughout the 98 credit crisis.

tree example of Figures 1.29 and 1.30, that discounting by a spread is equivalent to discounting the defaulted cash flows at the risk free rate. This means we have

$$\frac{100}{(1 + \text{risk free}) \times (1 + \text{spread})} = \frac{100 \times \text{intensity} \times \text{recovery} + (1 - \text{intensity}) \times 100}{1 + \text{risk free}}.$$

We can cancel the factor incorporating the risk free rate and also divide both sides by 100 and collect the intensity onto one side to give

$$\text{Intensity} = \frac{-[1/(1 + \text{spread})] + 1}{1 - \text{recovery}}.$$

As the spread is small we can expand the one over term, this will just come out at the spread. To a very good approximation then we arrive at the default intensity of

$$\text{Intensity} = \frac{\text{spread}}{1 - \text{recovery}}.$$

Now all we need to do is get the spread and we can use the above equation. The spread is implied from the price of a credit risky corporate zero, the value of this bond assuming a continuously compounded rate, will be

$$\text{Price} = E\left[\exp\left\{-\int_{\text{now}}^{\text{then}} [\text{forward default free(intervening)} + \text{spread(intervening)}]\, d\,(\text{intervening})\right\}\right].$$

This now looks very similar to the equation for the survival probability but with the spread replacing the intensity. Consequently we can use it to calibrate the intensity from the spread; making an assumption on the recovery rate. Although one expression is in terms of probability and the other in price, both are adjusted consistently in the forward period allowing direct association between spread and intensity for all times.

We have all the equations now let us examine how the surface is produced. We need at least two random processes. The first describes the rate used to discount the bond. We are going to 'freeze' the risk free rate of borrowing and just examine the spread driven by a random

Table 1.9 The data for the example.

Characteristic	Value
Risk free rate	5%
Credit spread volatility	1%
Recovery	50%
Risk free volatility	0

process. This is an integral component of the 'risk free' bond price. We reproduce the price of a zero coupon bond below:

$$\begin{aligned}\text{Price} = 100 &\times \exp[-\text{rate vol} \times (\text{maturity} - \text{time}) \times \text{surprise} + \text{rate} \\ &\times (\text{maturity} - \text{time}) + \tfrac{1}{2} \times \text{rate vol}^2 \times \text{time} \times \text{maturity} \\ &\times (\text{maturity} - \text{time})].\end{aligned}$$

This price has been plucked from the realms of standard 'interest rate' methodology and assumes an HJM process in the overall rate. This single factor model is equivalent to stating the whole term structure behaviour can be explained by 'one shock'. We refer you to a good text .We are going to use the data provided in Table 1.9.

To get the surprise we refer you to Section 4.10 in Chapter 4, this describes how you can generate a number from a Gaussian given that you only have access to a standard uniform random generator.

Substituting these values into the formula above, we produce the price of the bond at the second year in an undefaulted state as

$$\begin{aligned}\text{Price} = 100 \times \exp[-0.01 \times (\,10 - 2) \times \text{surprise} - 0.07 \times (10 - 2) \\ - 0.5 \times 0.01^2 \times 2 \times 10 \times (10 - 2)].\end{aligned}$$

Where 0.07 is composed of the sum of the initial risk free rate and the spread. At the 2 year point for example, this gives €51.48 for a particular realization of the surprise (=1.20).

But the bond could also default and we use a Poisson process calibrated by the adjustment to the risk free rate.This is synonymous with the possibility of a jump dependent upon the spread. It is a good assumption, generally if an issuer is going to default then it is reflected in the marketplace through wider spreads. We use the same HJM motion to model the spread process (remembering to subtract the risk free rate). We produce the standard form for the spread below:

$$\begin{aligned}\text{Spread (mat., start, time)} = \text{start value} + \text{spread vol} \times \text{surprise} \\ + \text{spread vol}^2 \times \left(\text{mat.} - \frac{\text{time}}{2}\right) \times \text{time}.\end{aligned}$$

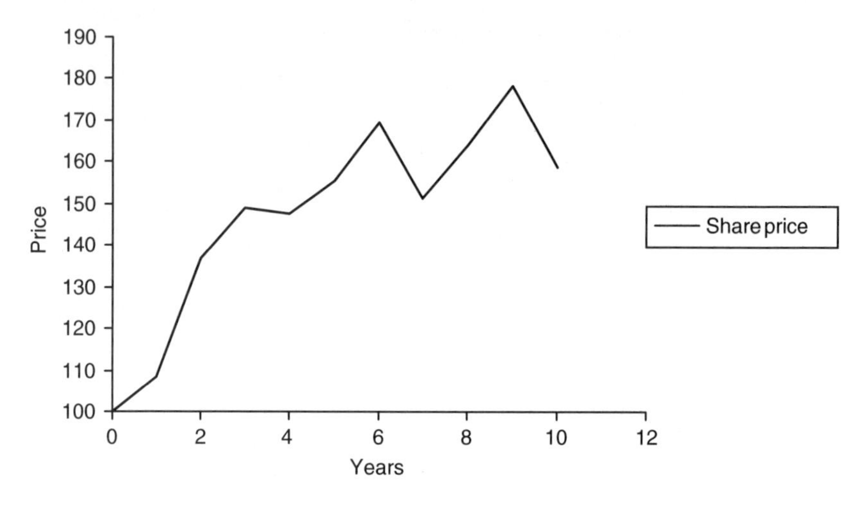

Figure 1.32 A Gaussian process.

Once again we can substitute the values from the table to get, using the same value for the surprise above

$$\begin{aligned}\text{spread}(10,0,2) = {} & 0.02 + 0.01 \times \text{surprise} \\ & + 0.01^2 \times \left(10 - \frac{2}{2}\right) \times 2 = 0.034.\end{aligned}$$

Finally we simulate default or Poisson by a straight comparison of the spread with a level which would constitute a default in this case we took 20 per cent.

1.12 Risk management of fixed income portfolios

We now start looking at approaches to managing the credit risk in a portfolio context. A portfolio is a very complicated entity. Consequently, we start at the very basic level and begin with an examination of the credit risk for just one bond.

Even a humble bond presents a number of challenges to the provision of a comprehensive risk treatment. We are going to step back from credit for a moment because there is a general framework for managing risk; anticipating that credit risk can be addressed within this architecture. So before continuing with credit we need to understand this general edifice.

This general framework divides the labour necessary to produce a risk report. The basis of this distinction is the separation between the general behaviour of the market and the characteristics of the asset. This is a quite natural division because on the one hand we have the market which we usually described by a set of rates. The description must capture how much these rates are likely to move and also the relationship between their co-movement. On the other hand we have a financial asset within the portfolio which changes value mainly as a result of the underlying market change. So quite a natural risk paradigm is displayed in the bullet points below:

- Identify a set of metrics which characterize the marketplace.
- Find out how your instrument depends on these metrics.
- Capture movement in the metrics and their interaction.

We apply this methodology for both the single bond and then a portfolio bonds. First off, then we have to identify metrics, this is not straightforward as there is a great deal of flexibility in this choice. They can be completely abstract or they can actually be observable in the market. For example if I had a 5- and 10-year government bond within my portfolio then a natural set of risk factors will consist of the 5- and 10-year yields. But I could equivalently choose the principal components of the curve. The main constraint when choosing a set of risk factors is that they are mathematically independent variables. Consequently it should be possible to isolate the change in the portfolio value due to the change in one risk factor.

Since our portfolio consists of just one credit bond the risks inherent in holding the bond will consist of the general market risk together with the further risk due to the credit exposure. We will call these factors M and S respectively. These are the risk metrics. Aside from worrying about how these factors actually move we can now examine the second bullet point which is how the bond changes in value due to a change in either of these factors. Well any graduate new to the trading floor can price a bond dependent upon a credit spread (drawing upon the concept of yield to maturity). We reproduce the graduates work in the equation below for a 10 year bond:

$$\text{Present value} = \sum_{\text{time}=1}^{\text{maturity}} \frac{\text{coupon}}{(1 + M + S)^{\text{time}}} + \frac{100}{(1 + M + S)^{10}}.$$

We can now think of this value changing because of either a movement in the general market conditions, or it could change due to a variation in the credit worthiness of the issuer. The upshot is that we have an expression which isolates a change in the holding due to either component of risk. Although, generally, spreads and the underlying market will change together, this situation will be examined at a later stage. The power of the equation is that it allows the risk manager to isolate changes in the market from the nature of the instrument.

The calculation of the variation in the present value due to a changing spread is no different from the standard duration calculation but with the spread replacing the yield. We reproduce this formally for the change in present value due to movements in spread:

$$\frac{\text{Value change}}{\text{Spread change}} = -\frac{1}{(1+M+S)} \times \left(\sum_{\text{time}=1}^{\text{maturity}} \frac{\text{time} \times \text{coupon}}{(1+M+S)^{\text{time}}} + \frac{10 \times 100}{(1+M+S)^{10}} \right).$$

The reason for introducing this simple case is to illustrate credit risk within the context of a familiar example. Note we can apply this methodology more generically because the bond could be exposed to other sources of risk such as optionality (if it is callable for example). We consequently specify the price of a bond as it depends on many risk factors:

$$P = P(R_1, R_2, \ldots, R_n, t).$$

and then the sensitivity to these risks as

$$dP = \sum_{\text{risk}_i} \frac{\partial P}{\partial R_i} \times dR_i + \sum_{\text{risk}_i}^{\text{risks}} \sum_{\text{risk}_j}^{\text{risks}} \frac{\partial^2 P}{\partial R_i \times \partial R_j} \times dR_i \times dR_j + .$$

An expression of the form $-(1/P)\,(\partial P/\partial R)$ is known as a partial duration, or option adjusted duration, or spread duration depending on the context of the risk factor (the negative sign arises because price decreases with yield). We will give a few examples of the use of the equation above in a few examples you may be more familiar with and depict the output in Figure 1.33. First let us look at a 2 year zero coupon bond, if the yield is continuously compounded then we have

$$P = \exp(-2 \times \text{yield}).$$

The derivative of an exponential is just an exponential so we will have

$$\frac{dP}{P} = -2 \times \text{yield} \times \frac{dy}{\text{yield}} + 4 \times \text{yield}^2 \times \left(\frac{dy}{\text{yield}}\right)^2.$$

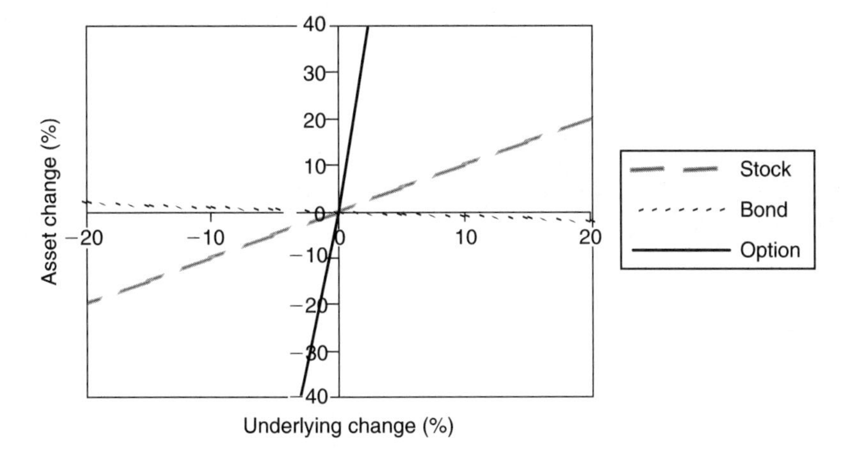

Figure 1.33 Dependence on the underlying.

Table 1.10 The details of the bond.

Trade details	Value
Deal date	9 May 2003
Coupon	6%
Maturity	9 May 2005
Libor	4.1%
Credit spread	62 bps
Nominal	€10 000 000
Rating	A

Thus the partial duration is 2 years. We can also do the same for an option, and write the change in the option price as

$$\text{Value change} = \delta \times (\text{underlying change}) + 0.5 \times \Gamma(\text{underlying change})^2.$$

Thus the change in option value is related to the change in the price of the underlying by the option delta and gamma. For these reasons the expansion is often called the 'delta–gamma' approximation. This approach is widely used within Risk Metrics™ for example.

Before we branch into further theory lets do a concrete example on our portfolio, consisting of one corporate bond. As a starting point we need to calculate the sensitivity of a 2 year corporate bond to changes in the spread of the issuer, the pricing is given by the equation for the present value.

If we substitute the figures in from the details in Table 1.10 we find the sensitivity of the bond to a 1 bp change in the issuer spread is given by −1901 €.

This in itself is quite valuable because it allows us to compare the credit risk within our portfolio of corporate bonds. The problem with this measurement however, is that the risk may be higher simply because the exposure is larger. It would be better for comparison purposes to look at the credit sensitivity on a nominal of 100 for each bond.

OK so what use is the sensitivity beyond this? We go to the next step which is to re-introduce how much rates are liable to move. Recall to evaluate how credit risky a bond is we have separated the effort into a purely instrument specific measurement which is the sensitivity equation. We are now determining how much the spread is likely to move. This is the volatility of the rate. We now need to get how the volatility of the price, because that after all as a portfolio manger is all you care about, is related to the change in volatility of the rate. We can do this for any number of positions, each exposed to a relevant spread.[6]

The change in value for the portfolio will be the sum of the individual changes in cash-flow value, but the change in cash-flow value will be the product of its sensitivity and the change in yield at that particular maturity. Thus we can write

$$\text{Portfolio price change} = \sum_{\text{asset 1}}^{\text{assets}} \text{weight} \times \text{sensitivity} \times \text{rate change}$$

for the portfolio price change for a movement in the rates. To get the volatility we need an expression for the volatility of the price changes, thus we can write

$$\begin{aligned}\sigma^2(\text{Portfolio price change}) = \sum_{\text{asset 1}}^{\text{assets}} & \text{weight}^2 \times \text{sensitivity}^2 \\ & \times (\text{rate change} - \text{average})^2 \\ & + \text{cross terms.}\end{aligned}$$

We can write this in matrix form as

$$\sigma^2(\text{Portfolio price change}) = \text{sens} \otimes \Omega \otimes \text{sens}^{\mathrm{T}}$$

[6]Generally within the fixed income sphere, risk managers settle on an economical approach to describe the entire yield curve. This is typically composed of a discrete set of risk free rates (usually taken as the overnight rate and then the 3, 6 and 9 month deposits together with the 1–10, 15, 20, 25 and 30 year par rates) and a characteristic credit spread. Any bond that falls into an intervening period is priced using interpolated rates. Consequently we use the sensitivity expression for any bond, but with the proviso that the rate may be interpolated if the bond does not mature on the standard grid.

Table 1.11 Data used in the example.

Date	AAA	AA	A	BBB	libor
27/12/02	20	42	98	164	4.38
20/12/02	18	46	70	150	4.47
13/12/02	21	43	71	150	4.51
06/12/02	19	41	69	148	4.61
29/11/02	14	38	70	144	4.68

Source: Bloomberg LP.

Table 1.12 Standalone credit risk.

		Sensitivity calculation	
Year	Payment (€)	Present value (€)	*t* × present value (€)
1	600 000	572 956	572 956
2	600 000	547 132	1 094 264
2	10 000 000	9 118 864	18 237 728
Totals		10 238 952	19 904 948

where

$$\text{sens} = [\text{weight}_1 \times \text{sens}_1, \text{weight}_2 \times \text{sens}_2, \ldots].$$

We now work through an example of a two bond portfolio, comprising an A and AA issue, commencing with just one bond, evaluating the risk then adding another. All will be revealed. The data was obtained from the 'Fair Market' curves from Bloomberg. So we would first place our bonds into the appropriate category and determine the volatility and correlation from the series as shown in Table 1.11.

Coupon bearing bond with standalone risk

We produce the detailed steps necessary to calculate the credit risk. In Table 1.12, we have determined the present value and an intermediate step of the maturity weighted average of the present value.

The spread duration is then

$$\begin{aligned}&\text{Spread duration}\\&= \left(\frac{1}{\text{price} \times (1 + \text{yield} + \text{spread})}\right) \sum_{\text{time}}^{\text{all flows}} \text{time} \times \text{value of flow}\\&= 0.95 \times \frac{19\,904\,948}{10\,238\,952} = 1.86.\end{aligned}$$

Table 1.13 Details of the other bond.

Trade details	Value
Deal date	9 May 2003
Coupon	5%
Maturity	9 May 2007
Libor	4.1%
Credit spread	36 bps
Nominal	€10 000 000
Rating	AA

This gets us to the sensitivity of the bond to changes in the issuer's quality. Itself, quite a valuable number because it does not contain any assumptions regarding the behaviour of this so-called 'spread'. To complete the risk management picture we must introduce the assumptions on the evolution of the credit (typically historical information is used providing the issuer is of sufficient liquidity to ensure that this approach is viable). We determine the volatility, from the Bloomberg data, of the spread to be 0.95 per cent per annum. To translate this to a price volatility we just multiply by the duration $= 1.86 \times 0.95\% = 1.77\%$. We now add another bond into our 'portfolio' with the details specified in Table 1.13.

Combining the two bonds

Combining the two bonds are discussed in Table 1.14.

Gamma term

Thus far we are underestimating the risk due to spread movements; this is because we are neglecting the changes in value of the portfolio due to the non-linear nature of the relationship between the value and the spread. We can address this through the modification introduced into the equation below:

$$\text{Portfolio price change} = \sum_{\text{asset 1}}^{\text{assets}} \text{weight} \times \text{sensitivity} \times \text{rate change} + 0.5 \times \left(\sum_{\text{asset 1}}^{\text{assets}} \text{weight} \times \text{gamma} \times (\text{rate change})^2 \right).$$

But we need the volatility of the portfolio for purposes of risk, we can write this in matrix form as

$$\sigma^2(\text{Portfolio price change}) = \text{sens} \otimes \Omega \otimes \text{sens} + 0.5 \times \text{Tr}(\Gamma \otimes \Omega)^2.$$

Table 1.14 The two bond calculation.

Steps	Values
Correlation (between spreads)	69%
Volatility 1st spread	0.95%
Volatility 2nd spread	0.58%
Covariance	
Diagonal	0.0001, 0.0000
Cross term	0.00004
Sensitivity (=weight × value × spread duration)	
1st issue	€9 503 890
2nd issue	€18 181 405
Portfolio volatility	
Step 1	$\begin{pmatrix} 0.0001 & 0.00004 \\ 0.00004 & 0.0000 \end{pmatrix} \otimes \begin{pmatrix} 9.503.890 \\ 18181405 \end{pmatrix}$
Step 2	$(9503890 \quad 18181405) \otimes \begin{pmatrix} 1549 \\ 973 \end{pmatrix}$
Step 3	€ $\sqrt{32410807097}$
Portfolio VAR (=1.65 × volatility)	1.45%

Table 1.15 The 'convexity' adjustment.

Including gamma			
Year	Payment (€)	Present value (€)	$t \times (t+1) \times$ present value (€)
1	600 000	572 956	1 145 913
2	600 000	547 132	3 282 791
2	10 000 000	9 118 864	54 713 183
Totals		10 238 952	59 141 887

Again before proceeding with gamma we need the intermediate steps outlined in Table 1.15.

The spread gamma is then

$$\Gamma = \left(\frac{1}{\text{price} \times (1 + \text{yield} + \text{spread})^2}\right) \sum_{\text{time}}^{\text{all flows}} \text{time} \times (\text{time} + 1) \text{ flow value} = 0.92 \times \frac{59141887}{10238952} = 5.33.$$

We can then determine the 'correction' to the price volatility on our standalone bond by incorporating this term, let us examine a 50 bps

Table 1.16 The correction to the VAR for convexity.

Steps	Values
Gamma (=weight × value × spread convexity)	
1st issue	€27,287,184
2nd issue	€84,924,865
Portfolio volatility	
Step 1	$\left[\begin{pmatrix} 27{,}287{,}184 & 0 \\ 0 & 84{,}924{,}865 \end{pmatrix} \otimes \begin{pmatrix} 0.0001 & 0.00004 \\ 0.00004 & 0.0000 \end{pmatrix}\right]^2$
Step 2	$\sum_{\text{1st diagonal}}^{\text{all diagonals}} \begin{pmatrix} 9\,414\,350 & 5\,518\,659 \\ 17\,175\,512 & 11\,511\,336 \end{pmatrix}$
Step 3	€ $\sqrt{0.5 \times 20\,925\,687 + 32\,410\,807\,098}$
Step 4 VAR(= 1.65 × volatility)	Portfolio 1.45%

widening in spreads. This is quite a large movement, but you will see that the gamma term only manifests itself under these types of conditions:

$$\text{Value change} = \text{price} \times \text{spread duration} \times \text{yield change} + \tfrac{1}{2} \times \text{price} \times \text{convexity} \times (\text{yield change})^2.$$

substituting the values:

$$\text{Value change} = 10\,238\,952 \times 1.86 \times \frac{50}{10\,000} + \frac{1}{2} \times 10\,238\,952 \times 5.33 \times \left(\frac{50}{10\,000}\right)^2.$$

This turns out to be (€94,357).

How do we combine the two assets? We have worked through the linear term in Table 1.15. We lay out the steps for greater accuracy in Table 1.16.

Higher-order risk and tail risk

Even though the above calculation adds greater accuracy, you need to be aware of the assumptions when it comes to using the expression. These are particularly pertinent when it comes to the credit context. For example of great concern to the credit portfolio manager will be the distribution of returns, unlike the case of market risk (equity, *fx* and interest rate) these are heavily 'skewed'. This is because it is possible

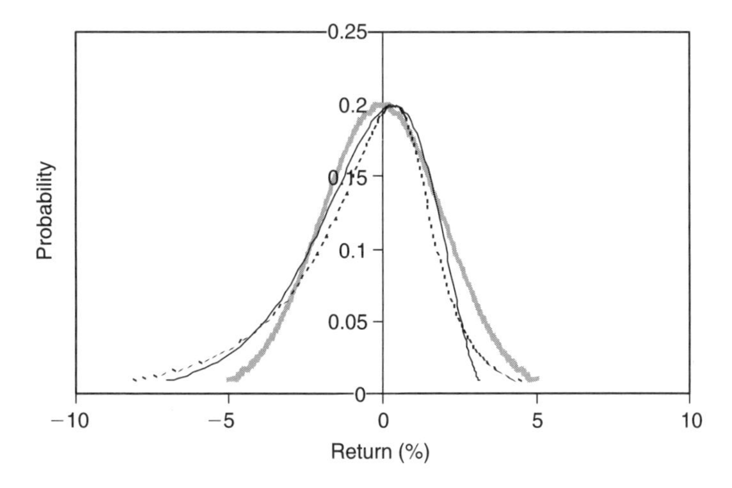

Figure 1.34 Three separate distributions differing in their 'moments'.

to have a very large loss with a small probability. This must be addressed by any realistic fixed income credit risk management tool. Lets us take a short break from the narrative to introduce a few terms from the world of statistics. In Figure 1.34, we can see three curves or 'distributions' for three different portfolios.

We can consider this to represent a plot of the total number of observations in a certain band against the returns on our portfolio (all made on the same timescale.) The word distribution means that the total probability for all outcomes is one. This is the area under each curve. All of the shapes have this as a fundamental property. They can differ however, in a number of properties which further characterize a distribution. The first of these is the mean, which is the central point. We consider each portfolio to have the same mean. Usually for a set of daily returns this is zero. If we consider longer time scales there will be some drift, or accumulation. The next is the width of the distribution, or standard deviation – again we propose that each of our portfolios has the same 'width'. So how do they differ? Let us introduce the next term; 'Skew', this tells us the distribution is not symmetrical around the mean. We can see in Figure 1.34 that our second and third portfolio have the same skew, this should be contrasted by the first portfolio which is just a standard bell shaped. We can see already that it is very dangerous to just consider the so-called lower 'moments' of the distribution. Finally the last characteristic of a distribution is the 'kurtosis' which is a measure of how much probability resides in the tail. The third curve differs from the other two by having a positive 'kurtosis'. Note that the units of skew and positive are absolute numbers, while

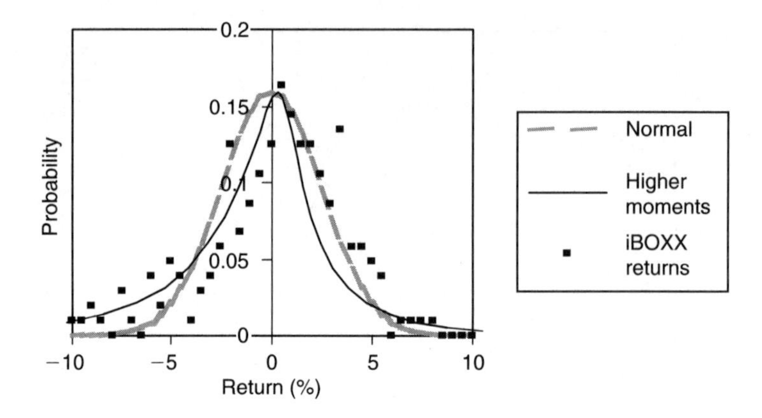

Figure 1.35 Sources of credit risk and their representation.

the standard deviation is measured in the units of the particular study. They are defined mathematically as

$$\text{Skewness} = \frac{E\left[(\Delta PV)^3\right]}{\text{volatility}^3} \quad \text{and} \quad \text{kurtosis} = \frac{E\left[(\Delta PV)^4\right]}{\text{volatility}^4} - 3.$$

Back then, to the main narrative. What is the origination of the higher 'moments'? If we consider the previous expansion techniques, specifying the value as it depends on the risk factors, then there are two sources. The first is the non-linear nature of this relationship. If the series expansion just ended at the linear term we would not encounter any skew or kurtosis in the representation of the real distribution we are trying to model. The non-linear term however, introduces just such an effect.

Of overwhelming importance is the formation of higher moments through the actual distribution of the spread. This is usually anything but normal. For example for a typical credit index illustrated in the chart (Figure 1.35) the magnitude is many times larger than the effect caused by the convexity in the relationship.

A word on total risk

One major benefit of expansion techniques is their usefulness in determining the total risk within a portfolio. Generally if we have a portfolio composed of investment grade fixed income bonds then the main source of risk will not be credit, but rather traditional libor and *fx*. Our expression, expanding the value in terms of risk factors is quite a natural way of dealing with these extra components. It is just a question of interpretation.

If our portfolio is composed of 50 bonds, issued by 40 distinct entities, denominated in 10 different currencies, for example, then how do we derive the total risk? The factors will be comprised of a number of characteristic spreads, 10 foreign exchange rates and then 10 libor curves, one for each currency. We initially can write an expression involving a change in the portfolio value for a change in one of the rates:

$$\Delta\text{value} = \Delta\left(\sum_{\text{currency 1}}^{\text{all currencies}} \exp(\log fx(\text{currency})) \times \text{value}(\text{spread}, \ \text{libor}(\text{currency})) \right).$$

We have written the exchange rate dependence in a funny way to make use of the fact that it is log-normally distributed. The order we have presented is quite an intuitive one, there are typically more spreads than currencies. Thus for each currency (and thus libor sensitivity) there will be a number of spreads; leading to distinct risks.

First we can simplify the *fx* sensitivity using the property of exponentials, that the derivative with respect to the variable is just the exponential of the variable:

$$fx \text{ sensitivity} = \left(\sum_{\text{currency 1}}^{\text{all currencies}} fx(\text{currency}) \times \text{value}(\text{spread}, \ \text{libor}) \right).$$

We can now complete the task by evaluating the sensitivity with respect to spread movement, which we have already done on page 58. Then finally with respect to a movement in the 'risk free' rate which we take to be libor. We have also done this for fixed coupon bonds – their sensitivity to a rate change will be the same regardless of whether the change is coming about because of a widening of spreads or a change in the underlying libor rate. Notice however this will not be the case for a FRN, here the sensitivity to libor is much lower. Generally the sensitivity is dependent on the nature of the underlying asset.

As we already know the sensitivities we can collect our results into a matrix form for the total sensitivity. We display this below:

$$\begin{array}{l} fx_1 \times \text{value} \\ fx_1 \times (\text{sens}(\text{spread}_1) + \text{sens}(\text{spread}_2) + \cdots) \\ fx_1 \times (\text{sens}(\text{libor}_1)) \\ fx_2 \times \text{value} \\ fx_2 \times (\text{sens}(\text{spread}_3) + \text{sens}(\text{spread}_4) + \cdots) \\ fx_2 \times (\text{sens}(\text{libor}_2)) \\ \qquad\qquad \vdots \end{array}$$

Table 1.17 Types of credit spread.

Spread	Elaboration
Swap spread	Loosely termed as the spread of the par rate to the government yield at the same maturity. More rigorously the asset swap margin.
OAS spread	The constant spread added to the implied libor pricing curve.
Yield spread	Excess yield to maturity spread over the relevant maturity government.
FRN quoted margin	Spread over libor payed on an FRN issued by a credit.
Asset swap margin	Spread added to the coupon of a bond which prices the bond exactly using the implied libor pricing curve.

Here the issuers are categorized into the appropriate currency. Thus if the first of our 10 currencies had three spread sensitivities then the first ellipses in the above expression would stop at three. The third row of each distinct currency has the total libor sensitivity which will be the total sum of each of the individual contributions at the issuer level, because the sensitivities are the same we can add the components.

To get the total risk we need the evolution of the rates, this is obtained from the covariance matrix and will have the structure specified below:

$$\begin{array}{cccccc}
\mathrm{vol}(fx_1) & \mathrm{cov}(fx_1, \mathrm{spread}_1) & \mathrm{cov}(fx_1, \mathrm{spread}_2) & \mathrm{cov}(fx_1, \mathrm{spread}_3) & \mathrm{cov}(fx_1, \mathrm{libor}_1) & \cdots \\
\cdots & \mathrm{vol}(\mathrm{spread}_1) & \cdots & \cdots & \cdots & \cdots \\
\cdots & \cdots & \mathrm{vol}(\mathrm{spread}_2) & \cdots & \cdots & \cdots \\
\cdots & \cdots & \cdots & \cdots & \cdots & \cdots \\
\cdots & \cdots & \cdots & \cdots & \mathrm{vol}(\mathrm{libor}_1) & \cdots \\
\cdots & \cdots & \cdots & \cdots & \cdots & \mathrm{vol}(fx_2)
\end{array}$$

In general there will be some diversification benefit because the correlation between credit spreads and libor generally is not unity.

A word on types of spread

Finally it is worth depicting the various ways of measuring credit risk. We have been using the yield spread, but an equivalent framework could be set up using asset swap margins for example. Indeed many practitioners consider this as the natural way of addressing credit risk within the fixed income framework (Table 1.17).

1.13 Credit Metrics™

Credit Metrics™ was formed in response to the unique challenges posed by the nature of credit within a portfolio context. It had its foundation within the Morgan Guaranty Trust Company in the 1980s. It is now an independent consultancy owned by JP Morgan Chase and co-sponsored by five of the leading banks.

Credit Metrics™ was 'released' in the same spirit as Risk Metrics™. That is to make the underlying methodology freely available. At the time it was perceived as a very novel way of running a venture particularly when that business is often concerned with very proprietary approaches. However the strategy is one of conferring leadership in an area which is one of the leading challenges in the financial marketplace. After all this is clearly an area that needs leadership.

The philosophy can be viewed as a portfolio approach, as opposed to traditional 'bottom up' credit analysis, and as such the heart of credit metrics is the assessment of the changes in value of a portfolio, consisting of potentially quite disparate asset classes, due to changes in the credit quality of the issuers. The application, Credit Manager™ which is the technological manifestation of this approach, addresses both credit migration and default within a portfolio context.

The technology presented a systematic quantitative portfolio approach to credit risk management, enabling the user to measure concentration risk within a portfolio. (This can be described as the risk due to exposure to one or more groups of obligors by sector or location.) It is not sufficient just to be able to measure concentration exposure. The next step is to manage the amount of additional risk. This can be achieved through a programme of appropriate diversification; credit metrics will suggest a number of ways to modify the portfolio which reflect existing credit lines and limits.

We wish to refer you to the Section 6.3 in Chapter 6. This goes into detail about the inherent difficulties of portfolio credit risk modelling, however just to recap on the two thorny problems. The first is the distribution of credit returns, which I would hazard a guess and say that every man and his dog knows by now that these are not normal (Figure 1.36).

If you need a brief refresher on the shape of this profile, then in the diagram below we have the credit returns on a portfolio. Notice that they extend much further out than the returns due to market risk which are highlighted as the broken line. This can be put into a slogan that credit returns are characterized by a fairly high chance of making a small profit together with a fairly small chance of losing a large investment.

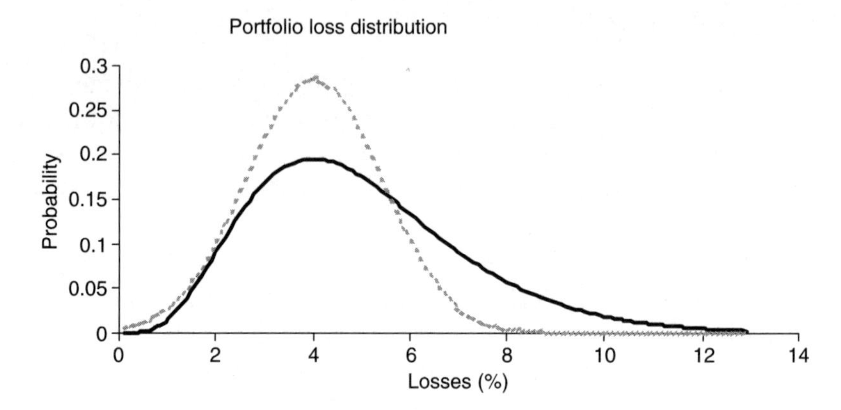

Figure 1.36 The losses of a portfolio.

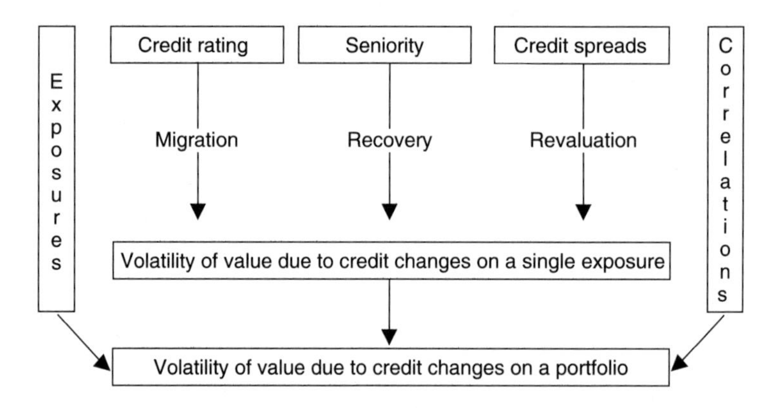

Figure 1.37 The credit metrics route map. *Source:* Credit Metrics™.

The other major bugbear when it comes to looking at credit in a portfolio context is the difficulty of assessing correlation. This is comparatively easy for market risk on highly liquid instruments because there is ample data available. This contrast is painted by most authors in black-and-white with the implication that market risk is done and dusted and credit risk is tough. The reality though is shades of grey. Correlation within a market context is still historic which must be qualified as a basis for the future. For less liquid instruments even this directly inferred number is questionable. Credit correlation as applicable to a fixed income 'marked to market' business, can be measured quite well and adequately captures the risk due to changes in spreads, but default correlation is perhaps the greyest arena.

We press on now with a programme of understanding and applying Credit Metrics. The route map provided by the group is reproduced as shown in Figure 1.37.

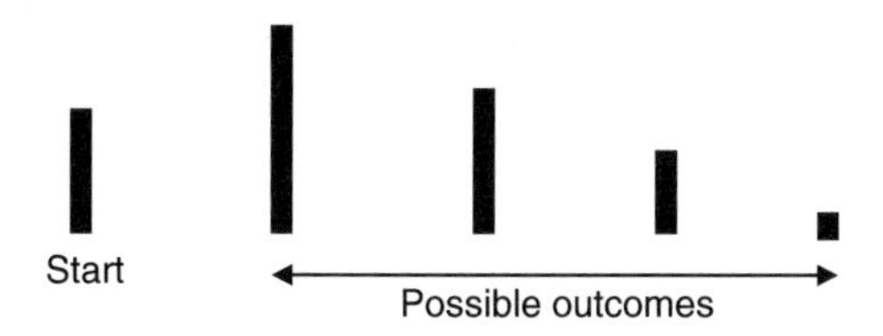

Figure 1.38 The standalone bond and its possible states.

Table 1.18 Migration probabilities. *Source:* Standard and Poors, 2002.

	Rating Outcome				
	AAA	AA	A	BBB*	D
AAA	89.37%	6.04%	0.44%	4.16%	0%
AA	0.57%	87.76%	7.30%	4.36%	0.01%
A	0.05%	2.01%	87.62%	10.26%	0.05%
BBB	0.03%	0.21%	4.15%	95.24%	0.37%
D	0	0	0	0	1

*We have aggregate probabilities between investment grade and default partially for pedagogical purposes and further due to the lack of spread data on Euro denominated speculative grade credit.

Table 1.19 The 6 year bond using credit metrics.

	Revaluation for the AA bond				
State	Probability (%)	Relative spread (bps)	Accrued (€)	Bond value (€)	Total value (€)
AAA	0.57	−13	5	102.23	107.23
AA	87.76	−13	5	102.23	107.23
A	7.30	38	5	98.59	103.59
BBB	4.36	121	5	93.00	98.00
Default	0.01	Very large	0	0	0

We give a brief example on the application of this framework consisting of just one bond. It is a AA bond with a maturity of 10 years and a coupon of 5 per cent. We want to know the impact of credit risk on its value in 1 year? The starting point is to consider the states that the bond could migrate into, there are four possibilities. It either gains value, loses (due to spread widening), stays the same or defaults. These outcomes are depicted graphically as shown in Figure 1.38.

We then use the standard data from the agencies to furnish us with the probabilities for evolution. We reproduce just such a Table 1.18.

The next step is to revalue the bond in each of the states. This was achieved using the Bloomberg Fair Market curves on trade date 30/12/2002. We took the starting yield from the 10 year maturity AA curve and the ending yield at the 9 year tenor from the curve representing the evolved state. This enables us to revalue the bond, by a simple duration calculation. We then add on the coupon to get the total valuation displayed in the final column of Table 1.19.

Finally to determine the expected value of the bond we weight these terminal values by the probability of landing in the state:

$$\text{Expected value} = 0.0057 \times 107.23 + 0.8776 \times 107.23 + 0.073 \times 103.59 + 0.0436 \times 98.$$

You will encounter a more realistic example incorporating the combination of different asset classes within Section 2.13 in Chapter 2.

1.14 Credit indices

The choice of index

Certainly a book on fixed-income portfolio credit investing would not be complete without a full discussion on the role of indices. These form an integral part of the investment process. The goal of the vast majority of institutional fund managers with appreciable corporate bond mandates is to outperform the relevant bond index. This raises a distinct number of issues. The first would be an appropriate choice for the index, this will be heavily influenced by the particular style of management employed to outperform the index. The choice will then be made on the basis of a wider number of considerations which we itemize as follows:

- The benchmark should obviously be representative of credit as a distinct asset class. There is a widespread misconception that government bond indices should be an appropriate credit index. This is based on the observation that a large number of corporate issues are, after all just bonds in the same sense of government bonds. Unfortunately corporate bonds are exposed to a distinct set off risks which are absent from government bonds. This must be reflected by the index.
- The credit index should reflect the investable universe over which the fund manager can make a selection. This is just as controversial. As it is very difficult to outperform a relatively wide credit index, it is more common to adopt a credit index with comparatively tightly defined characteristics and then perhaps to select issues based on more general criteria. We discuss this point in more detail in the next section. This is generally referred to as the relevance of the benchmark which should reflect the objectives of the underlying management style.

- It is very important for the index to be replicable; synonymously the portfolio manager can capture the underlying index with a small tracking error using an appropriate number of bonds. This introduces the importance of sufficient liquidity at the constituent level and additionally the pricing information should be available within the public domain.

There are other more general considerations that are not credit specific, these include the following:

- A 'rules based' calculation governed by transparent formulae. The criteria for membership of the index should be similarly transparent. Further the components should not change too frequently or in a haphazard manner.
- The benchmark should be investable, meaning that the constituent assets are instruments that are traded widely within the investment community.
- Reliability is also a key feature of any benchmark. Further the index should be published on a timely basis and should reflect the performance of the set of assets that it represents.

The use of a credit index

As we have mentioned earlier one of the major advantages of an index is its ability to represent particular characteristics of the investable 'universe' of bonds. These characteristics will allow the formation of a smaller number of assets drawn from the 'universe' and used to compile and construct a benchmark for the basis of performance measurement. This aspect is particularly important to enable an objective assessment for the investment manager. For example a typical bond universe will consist of approximately 70 000 bonds with maturity greater than 1 year; a broad-based index will restrict that number considerably. Depending on the criteria, the index can range from 500 liquid bonds to more than some 4000 for the least liquid categories. The general approach is termed index 'stratification'. We can think of a broad index running along three dimensions. We display each of these dimensions within the Figure 1.39.

A good credit index will have a selection criteria based on liquidity. This will narrow the range of securities included. (Beware of broad credit indices which incorporate less liquid securities by way of introducing model-based pricing. This generates a price based off comparable securities. It is of questionable worth, however, and more often than not rather opaque. Another fundamental problem with proxy pricing is

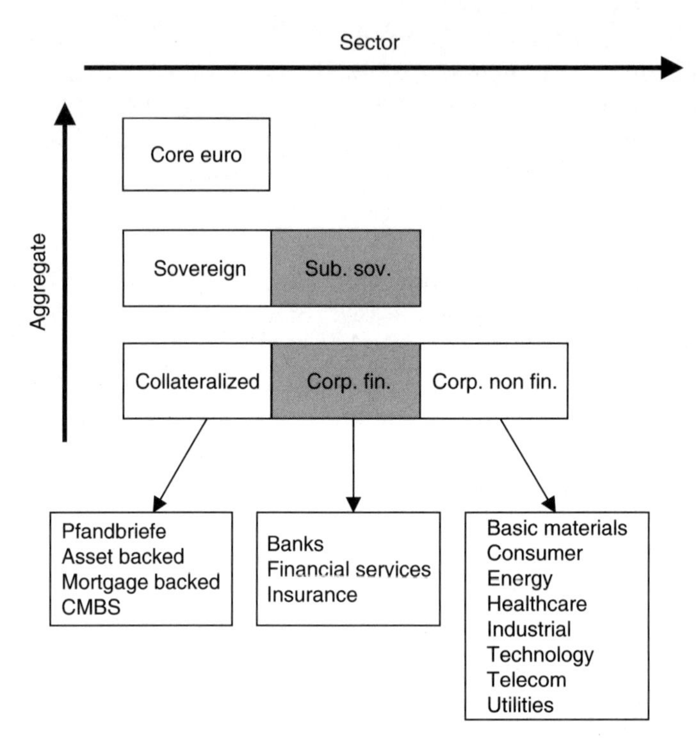

Figure 1.39 Two dimensions of the credit index for the Euro denominated market.
Source: Deutsche Bank.

the reduction in volatility of the index.) The resultant index will more accurately reflect the conditions prevailing in the market. Further any changes on more narrowly defined criteria such as rating or sector movements will also be transparent (Figure 1.40).

An index will provide the typical source for historical risks and returns; sub-indices will provide a platform for understanding the detailed market behaviour in the past. A particularly important application is so-called 'performance attribution', which decomposes the historic return within a portfolio into a number of distinct categories. Including curve movement for the straight risk free element of the yield and then spread movement. For dedicated credit portfolios the performance can carry more information on the nature of the changes in spread.

The index will also provide a basis for back testing and evaluating various types of modelling. If employed in this capacity it is very important to know how the index was constructed in the past and a comprehensive set of descriptive information on the constituents of the index should be available at each point in the past.

One of the main quantitative applications of credit indices is to serve as a benchmark for portfolio optimization. Regardless of whether the

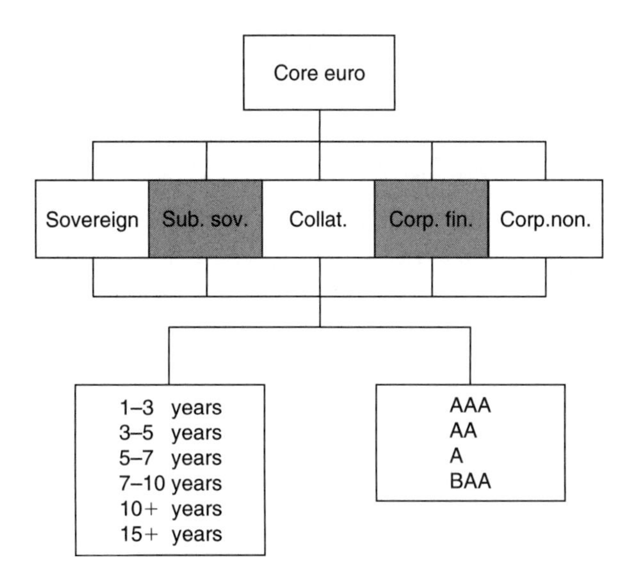

Figure 1.40 The maturity and rating dimension of an index for the Euro denominated market. *Source:* Deutsche Bank.

approach is linear or quadratic, the underlying data required for this approach will consist of a large number of securities upon which an optimized portfolio can be constructed. This initial underlying 'universe' will consist of the largest pool of possible issues. Consequently rather a broad credit index is used in a first instance. The benchmark should thus be employed as the basis of the selection criteria for the optimizer.

The next step would then possibly be a linear approach, if the objective is to find a portfolio which maximizes either yield or return up to some pre-specified horizon. The more common approach is the so-called quadratic which aims to reduce tracking error relative to the benchmark while simultaneously maximizing return. This activity is more data intensive because a risk matrix is required. Typically, this will be based on historic data for each of the issues within the benchmark. Common to both flavours of optimization will be the need to introduce constraints. Almost any criteria can be applied but they generally consist of either rating or sector criteria reflecting the need for all bonds in the resulting portfolio to be of good investment grade. This is useful, for example, when a comparison with a broad benchmark has been made, a portfolio manager might be under weight a particular sector. The constraint will then be introduced which sets a lower limit on her exposure. In addition there will potentially be specific constraints adopted on perhaps present value or liquidity criteria.

A good index system

There is currently a bewildering choice of potential benchmarks proffered by a large number of vendors. It is incumbent upon us to introduce some criteria for benchmark selection particularly within the realms of European credit, which in contrast to the US, has not quite evolved towards an industry standard.

It is a common misconception among bond investors that any rule-based index will display consistency of risk-return profiles for related holding periods. This is certainly not the case and while volatility levels will be in some accordance, the levels of return can be appreciably different. The source of this discrepancy is usually the introduction of proxy pricing for illiquid bonds incorporated as index constituents. This may seem attractive until the considerations of actually trading these bonds are entertained. By way of conclusion the portfolio manager should perform diligence on an index and ensure it is a liquid rule-based aggregate that is representative of the market.

There exist a large number of classical prescriptions as to what constitutes a good benchmark. However it must be borne in mind, particularly with regard to credit investing, of equal import to the quality of design is the quality of the data. Together with the infrastructure supporting the provision of the service.

Many vendors regard the provision of an index service as highly proprietary, consequently constituent data and methodology are only available on a commercial basis. Further a custom index creation facility, allowing the user to tailor the benchmark according to their risk/return appetites, may be sold as a differentiating capability. These developments have been a hindrance to market progression in general. Given the dramatic decrease in the cost of mediating information it is now becoming viable to compete only on bespoke index services rather

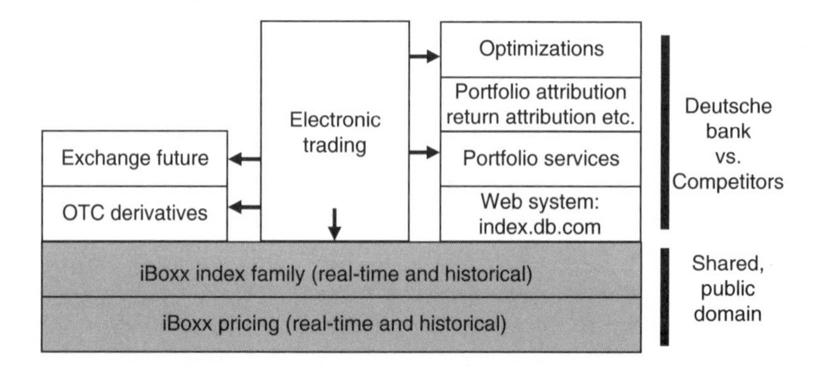

Figure 1.41 The current and future of credit index. *Source:* Deustche Bank.

than the actual intrinsic index calculation. This has fuelled the general movement towards a single provider of credit-based indices (Figure 1.41).

Perhaps one of the most important points constituting a good index system is the availability of quality prices. This is particularly true of corporate bonds which are traded in an OTC market, where prices are usually driven through positioning by desk axes.[7] Consequently to derive an index from a single source would be of questionable value. The most responsive pricing should be a multiple contribution system from the main liquidity providers within the marketplace. To ensure consistency the prices should be taken at a similar time and then the quoted index level will represent an average of the individual contributions.

There has been a sea change in the way that indices are used reflecting what is considered to be relevant subsequent to the introduction of the euro.

In summary the use of indices among the institutional community has increased dramatically. Further there has been a strong movement away from both the traditional domestic government bond and the European currency-based indices towards broad-based credit indices.

Prior to the advent of the euro the international investment community used global treasury indices for their benchmark. In order to recognize the currency risk inherent when investing from abroad, the returns were calculated either on a hedged or unhedged basis depending on the mandate of the investor. The component countries within the index constituted the main G7 borrowers together with Belgium, Denmark, Netherlands, Finland, Austria, Sweden, Spain, Norway, Portugal, Australia and New Zealand. The domestic investment community focused on a number of country specific indices. For example German investors measured their manager relative to the REX or REX + indices.

The major change has been the focus away from currency towards credit. Very little new money is now invested into the old-style government bond indices. There is not a dominant supplier of an index post-euro and a number of broad-based credit indices have emerged from a handful of vendors. The competing indices are all rule-based credit indices including both speculative and investment grade fixed income Euro-denominated bonds with maturity greater than 1 year.

Swap-based indices

Other contenders for representative benchmarks for credit consist of the swap indices. It might seem somewhat strange to use the idea of a

[7] Trader's parlance for being long or short the bond.

Table 1.20 Comparison of benchmarks.

Government	Swap-based indices
Divergence of issuance	Credit product
Difficult to hedge with	No repos
Poorly correlated	Less well correlated with sub-investment grade

bilateral arrangement as an index, but have no such fears. The marketplace is highly liquid and the equivalent instrument consists of buying a bond of AA (high-investment grade) with coupon equal to the relevant maturity swap. The index is a constant maturity in the sense that the bond does not redeem and so the total return will be fully characteristic of investment grade quality credit. We can see in Table 1.20 the advantages of such an index comparative to government bonds.

The vendors of this product include Lehman Brothers who provide 'Bellwether Swap Indices' consisting of the 2, 3, 5, 10, 20 and 30-year monthly returns. Resulting from investing in the hypothetical bond with a coupon equal to the relevant swap tenor.

1.15 Optimizers

We certainly could not write a chapter on fixed income credit without discussing a topic which is represented widely within the industry. This area is referred to as optimization. Strictly, we use it in the narrower sense of the mathematical-based approach. As opposed to the collective meaning, because in a sense all financial service companies are seeking to 'optimize' their investments. It is just that not many subscribe to particularly quantitative ways of performing this.

We would anticipate the use of such quantitative tools to be used quite widely. Especially within the investment management community where asset selection is one of the key choices confronting the manager. However all too often lip service is payed, hiding the real reservation over the assumptions that go into the components. In order to equip you for the debate we discuss two flavours of optimizer. We begin with the linear. The purpose behind optimization is usually to maximize a return on the portfolio subject to the constraints that the manager finds himself under. These can be quite wide in scope including, for example duration, maximum weight in a sector or maximum weight in a particular stock. This flexibility in addressing the real situation of the mandate explains the attraction of these tools.

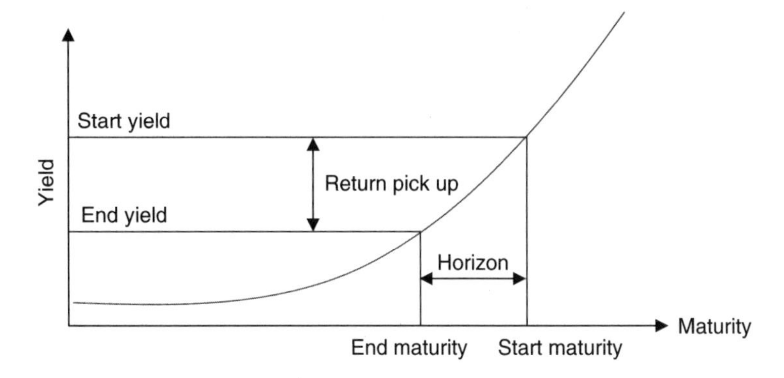

Figure 1.42 The components of the roll-down return.

However, this must be qualified somewhat by the other major input which is the return on the bond. Where do we get this? There are three choices:

- Forward price return } Passive
- Roll-down return
- User defined Active

The forward price is based upon the assumption that the return on a deposit is independent of the 'strategy'. For example I could deposit at today's rate or I could withdraw at some time in the future and redeposit at the forward rate. Either way the return is the same. One consequence is that you cannot make allocation decisions based on information in the market because all strategies are equivalent. We are left to exploit the second way of furnishing returns.

The next best assumption is based on the market not moving. The ensuing returns are referred to as 'roll downs'. This is somewhat unlikely but it is still better than a pure predictive scenario. This time all strategies are not equivalent, thus we can use the approach as the foundation for allocation. The reason for the admission of arbitrage is that the trade cannot be 'locked in' because the relevant rates are not the forwards. Consequently there is sensitivity to risk.

The easiest way to describe the components of a roll-down return is to appeal to the graphic as shown in Figure 1.42.

With reference to the diagram, the bond starts out to the far right and then ends at the horizon period for which we are seeking the return. The maturity of the bond at horizon will of course have decreased. Generally yields are upward sloping, consequently there will be a gain in the return because the price will be higher. This component must be

Table 1.21 Comparison of benchmarks.

Issue	Coupon	Maturity	Yield	Roll	Carry	Price	Clean end	Return (%)
G.E. Capital	5.50	26 September 2003	4.33	10.10	1.38	101.66	101.52	1.18
LBK-Thuringen	4.25	29 September 2003	4.34	10.08	1.06	99.85	99.99	1.19
KFW Intl Finance	6.25	15 October 2003	4.30	9.99	1.56	102.88	102.56	1.18
G.E. Capital	4.00	28 October 2003	4.25	9.92	1.00	99.60	99.79	1.17

Table 1.22 The linear optimization output.*

Issue	Duration	Return (%)	Holding (%)	Weighted return (bps)
G.E. Capital	2.3	1.32	5	6.6
KFW Intl Finance	2.2	1.28	0	0
G.E. Capital	2.3	1.30	0	0
Rabobank	2.3	1.33	5	6.65

*Constraints: duration 4; holding 5%.

added to the other elements of return including the accrued interest on the bond, which is always positive. This is simply the interest that accrues due to the bond bearing a coupon. Finally we have the 'pull-to-par' which is the change in value due to the effect of maturity. (This is a distinct effect and is dependent upon the bond yield.) This effect can either work for the portfolio manger or against depending on whether the bond is priced above or below par. If above there will be a loss because the bond must redeem at par. In Tables 1.21 and 1.22 we examine the total return for a variety of bonds, and a sample of the optimized output, sharing the characteristic of being priced of the same Bloomberg Fair Market Curve.

Marginal measures of risk

Rather than the explicit use of quadratic optimizers, many managers control risk through the use of 'risk plots' illustrated in Figure 1.43. These display the portfolio relative to contours of equal risk. These are formed by isolating the risk contribution of each position into a product of its sensitivity and the exposure. The contour then represents the exposure which would give equal risk contributions. This allows two ways of managing the risks annotated as shown in Figure 1.43.

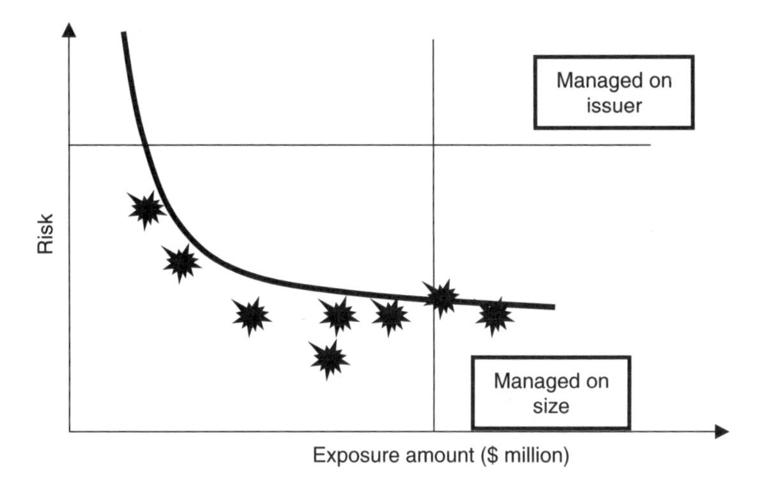

Figure 1.43 Ways of managing credit exposure.

1.16 KMV model

The rationale of this approach is based on the information available concerning the creditworthiness of the company implied through it's equity price. Given that the stock market represents one of the most liquid, sensitive and transparent arenas it makes some sense to try and create a systematic approach to gathering this information.

We should also mention at this juncture that the equity markets are an obvious place to look for correlation assessments for the same reasons. However beware the correlations determined will be on equity returns, not default correlations *per se.* There is a difference which we explore in Section 6.4.

The basis of the KMV approach is to treat the firm's equity as a call option on the company's assets. That sounds unnecessarily complicated, and in my experience the problem of explanation arises because the majority of students have switched off once the word option is introduced. Better to start with an example of a family company selling tomatoes financed with a bank loan and their own equity. The company has done rather well and they wish to retire on the proceeds, consequently they need to release the equity. The potential new owners would look at the overall balance sheet of the company as a basis for their decision on how much to pay. In particular if the total value of the assets, including crops, machinery and land exceeds the bank loan then this will be the price to pay. If however the family business has not done so well and the assets are less than the original bank loan it is better for the family to liquidate the company and write off the debt (and delay that retirement). Thus the company will have defaulted on its debt.

We can see that optionalilty enters through the price of the assets at some future date relative to the amount of debt. Further the equity value of a company depends on how much the net assets exceed the debt. This is exactly equivalent to treating the equity as a call option on the firm's assets (or equivalently the debt as a put option). With a strike price equal to the firm's debt.

How does this formalism help us with our original goal of extracting information about the creditworthiness of the company from the equity market? The observables comprising the equity price, equity volatility and the quantity of debt are inputs to the option model. The firm's assets value can be inferred from this equation and then we are in position to analyse its creditworthiness. Now we are familiar with the idea let us examine a little more formalism. We could write an equation for the value of the equity based on Black Scholes substituting in the relevant parameters consisting of the underlying, exercise price, volatility, time-to-expiry and risk free rate. However a few concerns should now be forming in your mind. Hopefully, high among these will be a recognition that the underlying is the asset value of the company (i.e. the positive side of the balance sheet in its entirety), this is not what the market values directly, furthermore the 'thing' that is observable presumably has a different volatility. Having convinced you that there is some subtlety when it comes to applying the model. Let us proceed with the assumptions needed to employ any option formulae given that we can only indirectly observe the requisite inputs.

A graph is very helpful here and we reproduce the graph as shown in Figure 1.44.

We start on the left with the initial value of the company. This evolves over time as a stochastic process with some drift. In particular the

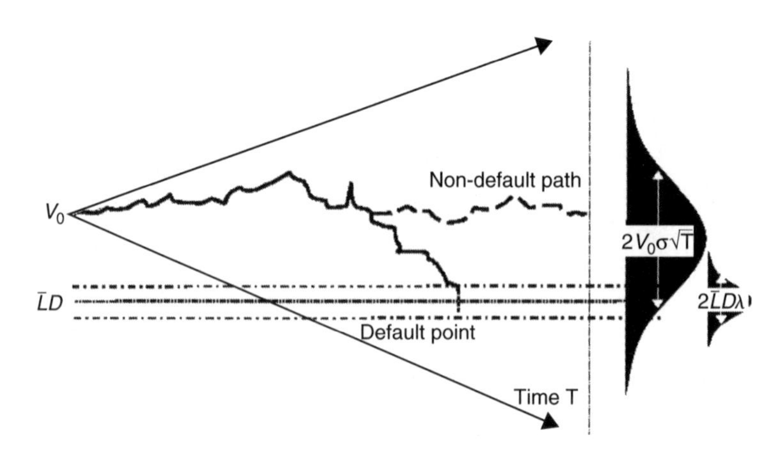

Figure 1.44 Structural model schematic chart. *Source:* Credit Grades.

randomness is represented by a Brownian motion (which is the simplest tractable process). The debt of the company is considered fixed, even though in practice this could possibly fluctuate in value – particularly if it is long dated traded debt.

The above paragraph constitutes the basis of the model, there is one further refinement, necessary because as it stands it will produce unrealistic credit spreads. A second random process must be introduced. This can be identified with the recovery rate assuming the company folds. However this has no time dependence. The evolution of the asset value and the default recovery are depicted in Figure 1.44. The asset value lives in a cone whose apex is at time zero, while the recovery amount lives in a set of tramlines. Of particular interest is whether the asset dips below the lower tramline. The company has then defaulted. We know the solution of the random processes; this means we can represent this probability mathematically:

$$\begin{aligned}&\text{Intial asset price} \times e^{\sigma \times W_t 2 - \sigma^2 \times t/2}\\&\quad > \text{average recovery rate} \times \text{debt per share} \times e^{\lambda \times Z - \lambda^2/2}.\end{aligned}$$

Where σ, W are the volatility of the assets and Brownian motion respectively. λ, Z are the volatility of the recovery rate and process respectively. We introduce another process, which is really the difference between the two, this creates a simplification:

$$X_t = \sigma \times W_t - \lambda \times z - \frac{\sigma^2 \times t}{2} - \frac{\lambda^2}{2}.$$

The chance of going through default can be rewritten as a condition in X only. Well we have seen a lot more equations and finally we are in position to calculate default probability. This is none other than the chances of hitting the barrier for the first time given the initial value is a long way from it, in recognition of the fact that most companies start off well capitalized. The probability is well known for a Brownian motion and we reproduce the result for the survival probability:

$$\text{Survival probability} = \Phi(\text{asset vol} + \cdots) - \text{factor} \times \Phi(\text{asset vol} - \cdots).$$

This is a difference in cumulative normal distributions which should remind you of Black Scholes, indeed we should expect to encounter cumulative distributions because the probability of the assets falling below the debt is required. However the formula is not much use until we can use the equity volatility directly (this is why the remaining arguments are represented by ellipses).

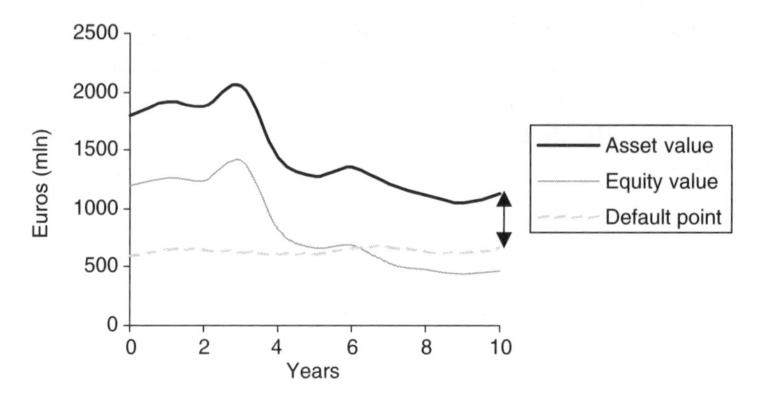

Figure 1.45 KMV distance to default.

In order to do this we magic out of a hat, a notion known as the distance to default. This is quite an intuitive concept. It is simply how far the asset value would have to fall (measured in standard deviations) before the company defaulted. Figure 1.45 will help to clarify this. The arrow in the figure has a length equal to the product of the asset level, asset volatility and the distance to default.

We can see the distance is larger when the default frequency is very low. When the distance is small the default frequency is correspondingly higher, conceptually, the following formula would characterize the Distance to Default:

$$\text{Distance to default} = \frac{\text{asset value} - \text{default point}}{\text{asset value} \times \sigma_{\text{asset value}}}.$$

It is worth dwelling for a few moments on this expression because it encapsulates the major drivers of default into one expression. Intuitively it might be expected that a well capitalized company with low quantities of debt would not be a candidate for default. However due consideration must also be given to the asset volatility, this is dependent on the companies business. Generally a company with larger asset volatility will be at greater likelihood of defaulting than another firm with the same asset value and leverage. We give an example calculation as shown in Table 1.23.

We now move onto deriving the asset volatility from the stock volatility. They can be related through the equation below:

$$\sigma_{\text{stock}} = \sigma_{\text{asset}} \times \frac{\text{asset level}}{\text{stock}} \times \frac{\partial\ \text{stock}}{\partial\ \text{asset level}}.$$

Table 1.23 The steps in deriving the distance to default.

Distance to default	$2.9 = \dfrac{156 - 42}{156 \times 25\%}$
Market capitilization	156 000 million
Default point	42 000 (debt due within a year)
Asset volatility	25%

We can now deploy two boundary conditions, the first is that as the asset nears the default threshold the value of the equity approaches zero, this means near the default boundary:

$$\text{Distance to default} \approx \frac{1}{\sigma_{\text{stock}}}.$$

But we also have the other extreme where the company is doing very well, under these happy conditions most of the company's value is reflected in the equity. Thus we have

$$\frac{\text{Stock}}{\text{Asset level}} \rightarrow 1.$$

We can find an expression for the asset value and distance to default which satisfies both of these conditions; we also require the equality that the total assets are composed of the equity plus average debt recovered. The expression then is

$$\text{Distance to default} = \frac{\text{stock} + \text{recovery} \times \text{debt}}{\sigma_{\text{stock}} \times \text{stock}} \times \log\left(\frac{\text{stock} + \text{recovery} \times \text{debt}}{\text{recovery} \times \text{debt}}\right).$$

This gets us to an expression relating volatilities to something measurable:

$$\sigma_{\text{asset value}} = \sigma_{\text{stock}} \times \left(\frac{\text{stock}}{\text{stock} + \text{average recovery} \times \text{debt}}\right).$$

Finally the expression for the survival probability is given by

$$\text{Survival probability} = \Phi\left(-\frac{A_t}{2} + \frac{\log(d)}{A_t}\right) - d \times \Phi\left(-\frac{A_t}{2} - \frac{\log(d)}{A_t}\right).$$

where

$$d = \frac{\text{intial stock price} + \text{average recovery} \times \text{debt}}{\text{average recovery} \times \text{debt}} \times \exp \lambda^2$$

and

$$A_t^2 = \sigma_{\text{asset}}^2 \times t + \lambda^2.$$

That is more than enough equations lets rapidly move on to an application of the above. We wish to determine the default probability of a company, and we know from the equation above that this will depend on time. Let us take the parameters specified in Table 1.24.

We can determine the annualized probability of default, which is a more natural means of assessment. This is given by $\mathrm{P}(t) = -\log(P(t))/t$. We reproduce the results as shown in Figure 1.46.

Table 1.24 The characteristics of the company.

Characteristic	Value
Stock price	200
Initial stock price	100
Stock volatility	25%
Debt per share	400
Debt recovery	50%
Barrier volatility	20%

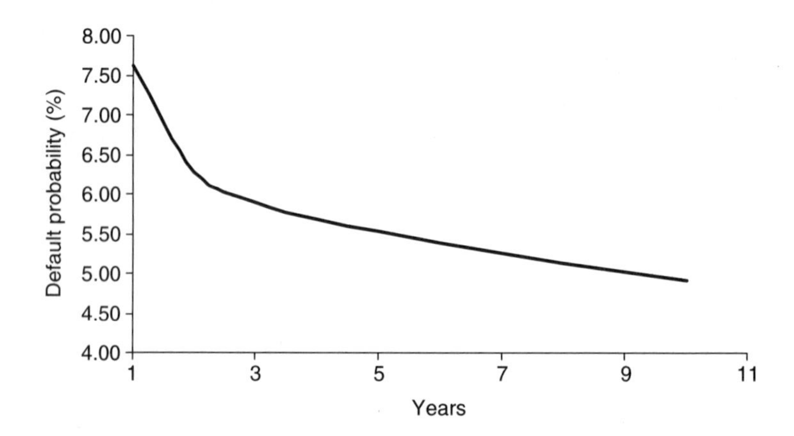

Figure 1.46 The default probability using a structural approach.

1.17 Rating agencies

A chapter on fixed income credit management would certainly not be complete without a discussion of the rating agencies. Their importance in the capital allocation process is writ large. This is because banks are becoming increasingly less important as a source of finance and large companies are correspondingly looking more towards the debt capital markets to reach their funding requirements. This change of landscape carries the implication that the analysis employed by the hitherto credit officers within the banking world is now replaced by an entity, acting on behalf of the investment community, which must evaluate the credit worthiness of every bond issue. This entity is called the rating agency.

The three major agencies are Moody's Investors Services, Standard and Poor's often referred to as simply S&P, Fitch IBCA/Duff and Phelps. Their role is to provide a quantitative evaluation (or in other words to rate) the range of securities found within the debt capital markets. The rating agencies assign a letter which is an assessment of the long-term credit quality of the debt. The highest recorded rating is interpreted as 'the capacity to pay interest and repay principal is extremely strong.' You can see from this wording that the actual end result of their work is just to tell the investor what chance they have of getting interest on the debt together with the chances of receiving the principal at maturity. Thus I bet you can guess the status of the 'D word' which is the 'obligor is in payment default.' Consequently the lower the grade thc greater risk that the investor will not receive both their interest and principal payments. All debt rated higher than BBB is referred to as investment grade, while issues below this are referred to as speculative or non-investment grade. A phrase which is dropping out of use is 'junk status' referring to sub-investment grade bonds. You will usually be confronted with two quotes. For example BBB-/BAA3, the interpretation here is the quote represents both the rating accorded from S&P and then Moody's which we expect to be very close but often there is a discrepancy. We reproduce in Table 1.25 the comparison and then an interpretation.

The credit quality of a company is obviously a volatile metric. Consequently ratings are subject to some revision through time and indeed the agencies publish their findings on a continuous manner in recognition of this fact. There is more terminology to address the fact that new information which could have an impact on the company's credit worthiness. But the impact has not been quantified. Then the issuer is said to be on credit watch. The issuer then appears on either

Table 1.25 The comparative long-term investment grade ratings.

Moody's	S&P	Elaboration
AAA	AAA	The obligor's capacity to meet its financial commitment on the obligation is *extremely strong*
AA1	AA+	
AA2	AA	Differs from the highest only in small degree. The obligor's capacity to meet its financial commitment on the obligation is *very strong*
AA3	AA−	
A1	A+	
A2	A	More susceptible to adverse changes in circumstances and economic conditions than higher grades. The obligor's capacity to meet its financial commitment on the obligation is *strong*
A3	A−	
Baa1	BBB+	
Baa2	BBB	Exhibits *adequate* protection parameters. Adverse circumstances are more likely to lead to a weakened capacity of the obligor to meet its financial commitment on the obligation
Baa3	BBB−	

Source: Bloomberg.

Standard and Poor's or Moody's rating review list. There is a further distinction between long and short-term ratings.

The question arises as to how successful agencies are in terms of performance. We would anticipate that the actual level of default is inversely correlated with the investment grade. Figure 1.47 bears this out with the triple-A category defaulting less than 2½% over a 20 year period.

It must be stated that the rating agencies are better measures of relative rather than absolute risk because over time the default rate is subject to a drift. Thus the default rate of 2½% for A would depend upon the prevailing economic cycle to some extent.

The costing for the rating agencies service is met directly by the issuer. This may seem a somewhat cosy relationship which could be advantageous for both parties in order to potentially produce an artificial rating in order to lower the funding cost for the borrower. However in the longer term this would not benefit any party; because the credibility of the rating agency would be damaged and the borrower would not have a 'rubber stamped' issue. It is overwhelmingly important that the objectiveness of the agency is upheld. If the investor community were to lose confidence in the agency then the issuer would no longer believe they could lower the funding by obtaining its ratings.

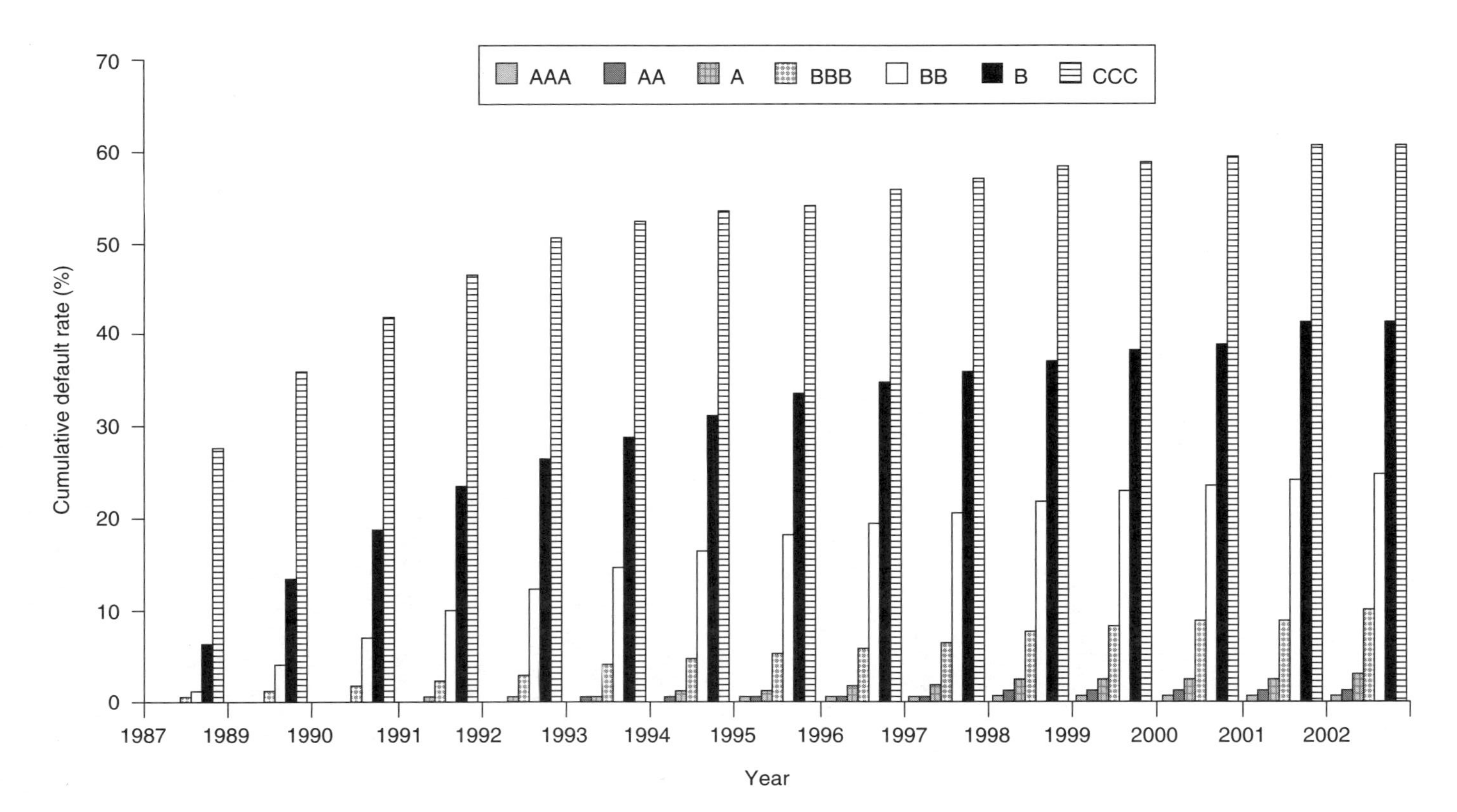

Figure 1.47 Global corporate default rates by rating. *Source:* Standard and Poors.

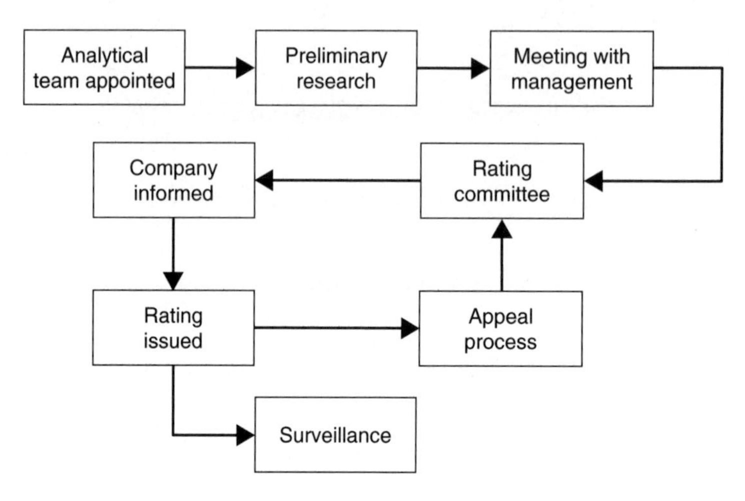

Figure 1.48 The rating process. *Source:* Standard and Poors.

The rating process

In Figure 1.48 we illustrate the systematic steps performed by the agencies in order to 'rate' an obligor or capital structure.

References

Deutsche Bank Index Quant System, *Deutsche Bank Research*, March 2001.

Mark, iBoXX and the Seven R's of Indexing, *Global Investor*, December 2001.

Bos, Kelhoffer and Keisman, Recovering from Record Defaults, *Credit*, September 2002.

Duffie and Singleton, Modeling Term Structures of Defaultable Bonds, *Review of Financial Studies*, 1999.

Rennie and Baxter, Financial Calculus, *Cambridge University Press.*

Gupton, Finger and Bhatia, Credit Metrics™ – Technical Document, *Risk Metrics Group.*

Mina and Xiao, Return to Risk Metrics: The Evolution of a Standard, *Risk Metrics Group.*

Risk Metrics™ – Technical Document, *Risk Metrics Group.*

Greenfield, The Lehman Brothers Swap Indices, *Risk*, September 2001.

Pan, Equity to credit pricing, *Risk*, November 2001.

Crosbie and Bohn, Modeling Default Risk, *KMV*, January 2002.

Kocagil, Escott, Glormann, Malzkorn and Scott, Moody's RiskCalc™ for Private Companies: UK, *Moody's Investors Service*, February 2002.

Finger, Finkelstein, Pan, Lardy, Ta and Tierney, Credit Grades™ – Technical Document, *Risk Metrics Group*, May 2002.

Brady, Corporate Defaults Peak in 2002 amid Record Amounts of Defaults and Declining Credit Quality, *Standard and Poor's*, January 2003.

Jarrow and Turnbull, Pricing Derivatives on Financial Securities Subject to Credit Risk, *Journal of Finance*, Vol. 50, 1995.

2

Loan portfolio

Loan portfolio management

2.1 What is loan portfolio management?

Introduction

Banking used to be based on the premise of borrow at four, lend at ten and golf course by four. To a certain extent it still is. However, the current business model is no longer as easy to specify. Indeed the key to understanding the disparate visage of activities is the lack of viability of a business model predicated on the spread between the deposits (banks liabilities) and the subsequent loans (the banks assets). The margin has been under attack from both sides. On the one hand the rate obtainable on deposit is no longer attractive when compared to other forms of investment, thus restricting the supply of capital. Furthermore the rate which can be charged on loans is limited by the capital markets as an alternative source of funding. This has pressurized our rather traditional bank manager to either seek out alternative sources of income or find new areas of activity.

Within this chapter we are concerned with the current commercial lending environment. This was historically driven by the wish to use the balance sheet as a source of income. Such loans were made on the basis of rather traditional credit analysis with the goal of placement at an attractive margin. The resulting loan tended to remain on the balance sheet for its duration. This was a consequence of accrual-based accounting, reinforced by the absence of any liquid secondary market and the need to preserve the confidential nature of the relationship with the borrower.

The majority of organizations still originate bilateral loans which remain on their balance sheet. Attractive margins can still be booked provided flexibility of funding is available to the borrower.

However, something of a revolution is steadily transforming this environment, challenging many of the hitherto standard market practices. These can be detailed in no particular order as the establishment of a liquid secondary loan market in some locales, the move to market as opposed to cost-based accounting and the development of alternative approaches to managing loan portfolios. These alternatives have their origins within the fixed-income marketplace.

Perhaps the most notable development, however, is the growth of the credit derivatives market as a viable medium of transferring the risk associated with the loan. To add further fillip, the regulators have been at work deciding on how much capital must be allocated against a loan book. This obviously has implications on the attractiveness of either an existing loan or a proposed new business line.

At the current juncture the many ramifications are still working their way through the system and it is still too early to generalize on loan portfolio management. However, many of the concepts and tools are now in place and we give a summary of how organizations are managing such a key area of their business.

2.2 The loan market

Syndicated market

The so-called syndicated loan market is one of the largest, with a capitalization of over $2 trillion, most flexible sources of finance within the economy.

Over the past 20 years the market has developed substantially. In 1980 approximately only $100 billion was financed. The main driver behind this growth has been the provision of credit to the corporate sector as a means of funding their acquisition deals. This can be contrasted with the pioneering days when the main borrowers were sovereigns and financial institutions.

These corporations borrow in size and the term jumbo is emotive phraseology describing a multi-billion dollar deal. The reader may recollect deals involving Vodafone and Mannesmann. These were representative of any number of jumbo transactions used within the telecoms sector.

Should I finance from the loan market or the bond market? Let us see how the numbers stack up (Figure 2.1).

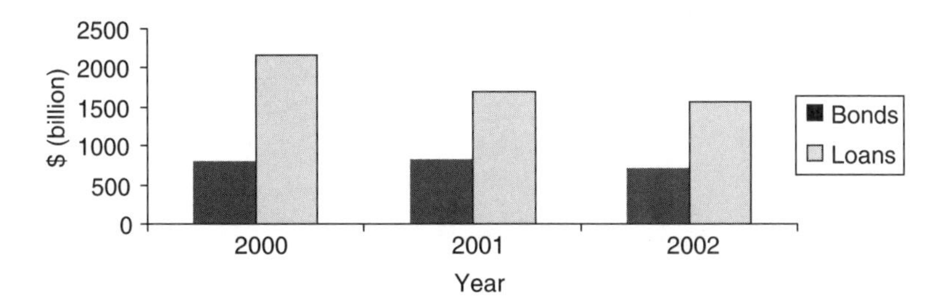

Figure 2.1 Notional issuance of syndicated loans and corporate bonds (major currencies and US inv. grade). *Source:* ABN Amro and Deutsche Bank.

Figure 2.1 shows a comparison between issuance, you can see that loans are preferential to bonds as a source of finance. But that the bond market is relatively important. Aside from the syndicated market there are many reasons for the dominance of the traditional loan. Simply many borrowers do not have the credit worthiness to access the capital markets, indeed for most of the past 10 years the bond markets really have been open to high-quality borrowers rated AA or better. Recently the market has expanded down the rating scale to accommodate borrowers in the BBB category, this development has been fuelled with the introduction of the euro which has reclassified all investors as credit analysts rather than currency analysts. The longer-term development of the high-yield bond market in Europe will probably add to the erosion of the loan market as a funding area.

It is premature, however, to speak of any demise because loans will tend to remain attractive simply because they offer more flexibility than a standard bond issue which post-issuance has very limited flexibility unless the borrower is willing to countenance the level of penalization associated with incorporating such clauses on the bond. The bilateral market will also remain popular for the more mundane reason that the borrower can remain confidential.

You can see from Figure 2.2 that the US$ is by far the most dominant market; this simply reflects that the main user of the syndicated loan is the US corporate, further the dollar has been adopted as the currency for international transactions. The capital is used for either acquisition or project finance, with corporate finance activity dominant.

The secondary market

The arrival of the institutional investor as a source of demand has promoted the development of a secondary market for term loans. For example, prime funds are required to mark their portfolios to market.

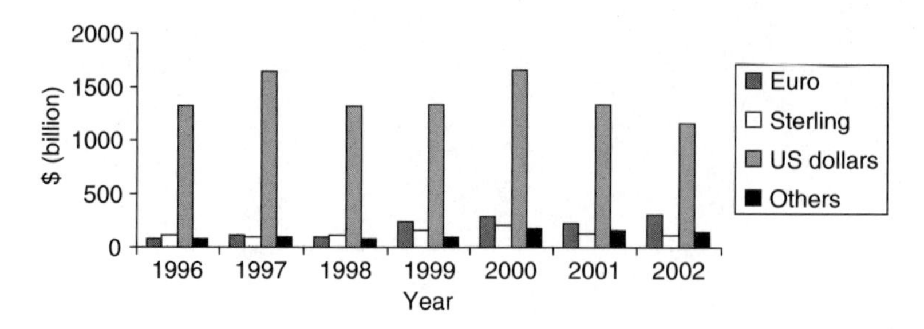

Figure 2.2 Notional issuance of syndicated loans with denomination.
Source: ABN Amro.

Thus their NAVs will be impacted by current loan trading levels, hence the importance of a liquid exit point, because adverse market performance may necessitate a loan sale. Conversely a profit may be booked.

2.3 Definitions

The syndicated loan can be defined as the provision of finance by two or more banks under contractual arrangements with terms and conditions governed by a common document. The interest charge on a loan is at a variable rate of interest periodically reset either 1, 2, 3 or 6 months, up to the discretion of the borrower under terms negotiated through the *agent*. This is the representative member of the banking group appointed to act on behalf of the syndicate.

The syndicated loan is a multi-bank transaction; each bank is independent in the sense that it has no contractual arrangements conferred through syndicate membership. One consequence of this is that if a member bank cannot extend finance, other members have no legal duty to make up the difference.

Within the syndicated credit market there are three main types of a loan.

Term loan

This is the extension of finance for a specific amount of money which has to be repaid in full by the term date. The borrower has the right to draw down funds in either a single amount or in tranches during the availability period. Repayment of the finance may follow an agreed repayment schedule referred to as the amortizing-term loan. Alternatively it could be paid in a single final amount – the so-called bullet loan. Amounts that are repaid as scheduled, or earlier, may not be subsequently redrawn. It is this restriction on the borrower's behaviour that forms the source of distinction between the term loan and the revolving credit facility discussed next.

The term loan can include a multi-currency option which permits the borrower to choose which currencies are drawn.

Revolving credit facility

This facility makes available funds for an agreed period of time, but in contrast to the term loan the borrower has the right, but is not under obligation, to draw down, repay or redraw some or the entire loan at their discretion. This so-called revolving feature is available throughout the life of the facility.

Standby facility

This rather perversely is a vehicle which the borrower is not expected to use, but rather it is a standby; usually to other instruments, such as commercial paper. If the preferred source of funding ceases, then the standby facility can be drawn down. This can happen, for example, due to illiquidity in the primary market.

US syndicated market

We spend some time discussing the US leveraged loan market because it could possibly serve as a template for the development of the European loan market. Over a decade ago the US loan market was based upon relationships, while this is still an important driver of the market structure a number of developments have arisen which has caused some convergence between the loan and bond markets.

The word convergence is used in the sense of a developed capital markets mentality which perceives transparent pricing and relative value comparison as the norm. The engine driving this change has been the entry of the institutional investor. Within their mindset a loan is an *asset* not a relationship and they judge a loan in terms of risk-return characteristics, relative value comparison with the other liabilities of the issuer and the liquidity.

An important step facilitating this process has been the advent of loan ratings. This becomes an important milestone on the road to transparency because agencies perform the role of due diligence, which would hitherto be undertaken by the lender prior to extending credit. Each of the major agencies Standard and Poors' (S&P), Moody's and Fitch IBCA have an extensive service that rates leveraged loans. Latterly we have witnessed indices developed for the investor in order to track their portfolio against standard benchmarks.

What actually is the asset? Typically it is the long-dated tranche of a term loan. Recall that a term loan consists of a drawdown facility with a scheduled repayment. The usual arrangement under advance of the loan is to offer a number of tranches with a different maturity; usually each tranche will have a 50 basis point spread increase over the previous tranche. The components sold to the institutional client consist of what are colloquially referred to as alphabet loans. Starting from A and usually ending up at D. The normal arrangement is for the B–D loans to be sold to institutional clients while the shorter-dated A loan are held by the banks.

We should say a quick word on the phrase 'institutional investor' which comprises a disparate number of groups. The dominant players are prime-rate funds. These are mutual funds that invest in loans. Activity will also include the leveraged funds, which execute 'arbitrage' strategies between the loan and the bond markets. (We use the term arbitrage in a very qualified sense because there is no true arbitrage between a bond and the loan market.)

Finally collateralized debt obligations (CDO) activity has been large; this is a widespread heterogeneous business. This can be described as repackaging loans into bankruptcy remote vehicles, which subsequently issue debt according to investor appetite. The loans serve as collateral. There are two types: the collateralized loan obligation (CLO) is mainly a tool deployed by banks to manage their loan book. While the term arbitrage CDO describes the situation where a manager controls the collateral within the CDO (this is described in a lot more detail in Section 4.7). This can be contrasted with the balance-sheet CDO where the collateral backing is fixed. The motivation is the source of distinction, arbitrage CDOs are investment vehicles whereas balance-sheet CDOs are usually organized by banks to move capital off the balance sheet.

2.4 Relative value analysis

This type of analysis has become increasingly significant. But the importance can be overestimated because there is no true relative value execution in the sense of the bond market. Here it is common for an investor to sell the proceeds of one issue and buy another to establish a positive cash flow. The position is held through to a horizon in which the yield environment will have hopefully changed in accordance with the expectation of the investor. Within the loan market it is simply not possible to execute any similar ploy, because of the relative liquidity of the product. (You can see that many of the terms in the loan marketplace are carried over from the bond markets without being truly applicable.)

The term relative value is used in a more restrictive sense to facilitate a comparison between a loan and the bond. This is particularly important when the loan is originated because it will be priced quite close to where the bond trades in the secondary market, although of course there are usually exceptions.

It is worth pointing out the main structural differences between a bond. The loan is a floating-rate asset and so carries little interest-rate risk. The deal is also a senior secured obligation. Typically the loan carries no pre-payment provision. Consequently if the credit improves the borrower may pre-pay without any ensuing penalty.

International bonds by comparison are usually unsecured and issued with a fixed-bullet structure and a penalty clause for any redemption. Referred to as a 'spens clause'.

You should note that the loans are always priced relative to par and at origination the spread is determined such that market value of the deal is equal to the notional amount of the loan.

2.5 Term sheet of a loan

Example of term sheet of a loan is given in Table 2.1.

2.6 The syndication process

There are three distinct phases to a syndicated transaction. The first of these phrases is the pre-mandate phase, followed by the post-mandate and finally the post-signing phase.

Pre-mandate

This period lasts from 1 month until possibly up to 1 year. During this phase the following events will occur:

- The identification of the borrower's requirements.
- The credit arrangement process adopted by the banks.
- The bidding strategy and the internal arrangement on the part of the banks necessary to supply the credit.
- Finally the syndicate will offer the loan and subsequently accept the mandate.

Table 2.1 The term sheet of a syndicated loan.

Detail	Example
Borrower	European corporate
Current risk	D-(Sr.) C-(Sub.) [S&P] Caa1 (Sr.) Caa2(Sub.) [Moodys]
Closure risk	B-(Sr.) CCC+(Sub.) [S&P]
Deal date	B2 (Sr.) Caa1 (Sub.) [Moodys]
Commitment	GBP 2 500 000 000
Loan type	Term loan
Signing date	06 September 2000
Expires date	05 March 2006
Purpose	Takeover
Secured	Yes
Distribution	Syndication
Fees	Upfront 75 bps
Spreads	LIB + 225 bps (initial pricing, dropping to LIB + 200 bps, tied to net interest to EBITDA grid thereafter)
AIS (Drawn)	225
Underwriting fees	60 bps for GBP 175 m, 30 bps for GBP 90 m
Upfront fees	75 bps for GBP 175 m, 75 bps for GBP 90 m, 60 bps for GBP 35 m, 50 bps for GBP 20 m
Comment	Arranged to support NTL's $13 billion merger with Cable & Wireless Communications
Mandated arranger	Chase Manhattan Bank, Morgan Stanley Dean Witter & Co
Arranger	BNP Paribas, Banca Commerciale Italiana, Bank of America, Bank of Scotland, Bankgesellschaft Berlin, CIBC World Markets, Citibank, Credit Lyonnais, Deutsche Bank, Fortis Bank, HSBC Banking Group, J.P. Morgan & Co., Royal Bank of Scotland, Scotiabank Europe PLC, WestLB
Co-arranger	Abbey National PLC, Bayerische Landesbank, Girozentrale, Dai–Ichi Kangyo Bank Ltd, Dresdner Kleinwort, Wasserstein, Fleet National Bank, Hypo Vereinsbank, Lloyds Bank Plc, Rabobank

Source: Loan pricing corporation.

The period is driven by the needs of the borrower, and the extreme example is taken from acquisition finance where the syndicate is assembled within 2 or 3 days. For project finance it is usually a much more protracted timescale.

Post-mandate

The major achievement during this phase will include launching the deal, consisting of completing the information package, signing and book closure. This phase is usually just over a month, typically 6–8 weeks. This to some extent is the most critical point of the deal because all parties have committed themselves to raising finance and consequently risk enters the picture, at this stage it is predominantly credibility risk that will be incurred.

Post-signing

This is a period lasting up to the maturity of the loan itself which may be anything from 6 months to many years. There is some terminology associated with this phase, including discretionary events describing actions on the part of the borrower including notification of drawdown, the selection of interest period and currencies. Non-discretionary events include payment of fees, interest and the repayment of the principal.

Duties and roles

There are clearly defined roles within the cycle of the syndicated loan and perhaps key to understanding the arrangement is visibility, some would use the expression ego, on the part of the syndicate members is paramount. Particularly when the margins of the deal are close to cost there has to be other less tangible benefits.

The starring role of the book runner carries much kudos. The choice will depend on the reputation, resources and relationship with the borrower. You may also come across the phraseology 'co-leads.' This is the situation where the deal is brought to the market through more than one book runner.

The number two task is that of the facility agent; this is less prominent but by way of compensation the role provides long-term operational exposure to the borrower post-signing. Furthermore the agent can be in line for promotion to book runner on the next deal.

Further less prominent roles include public relations, preparing the information package and the documentation.

The bidding process

First to clear some confusion, a common question arising is that can the idea of a syndicate be consistent with any sort of open bid? For the majority of loans a number of banks will make separate bids, which are competitive. This will result in an unrestricted mandate, which consequently grants the winner the right to form an underwriting group and to distribute roles accordingly. This should not be confused with a multi-bank bid, which will be discussed in due course.

A borrower will advise the market, consisting of the banks which have a track record of a competence and capability within the loans sphere, of its intention to seek competitive bids. There are three methods. The most prominent consists of selective bidding; this is followed by open bidding which is comparatively rare. Finally there is multi-bank bidding.

If the borrower seeks selective bidding then there are two possible routes. They may seek bids from a small number of their relationship banks. During this process the borrower will probably receive unsolicited offers and will use these as a base for discussions with one of the contenders. Alternatively the lender may seek bids from banks specializing in a specific sector.

Multi-bank bidding is not particularly satisfactory for either party simply because it easily becomes unmanageable in terms of relative prominence and the allocation resulting in severe protraction of the deal.

Pricing the loan

Unfortunately for the scientists among us, the pricing, or the margin on the loan, cannot be reduced to standard formulae. This is because syndicated lending lies on the threshold between an art and a science. Pricing the deal involves a number of distinct parties including the syndication unit and the credit department. They will base their decision in part on the knowledge of the relationship manager whose job is to understand the business of the client in the context of how it can be effectively serviced from the bank's perspective. The manager will also know what constitutes an acceptable pricing arrangement to the borrower.

This syndication group will be intimately familiar with the market appetite for the credit. The market in this context is the potential participating banks, which will form either the rest of the syndicate or comprise active players in any secondary market. It is the job of the syndicate unit to also know what kind of structure and maturity would be acceptable. The credit department holds a wider perspective than the deal and is ultimately responsible for the decision to extend credit.

There are a number of distinct syndication strategies. The main differentiator is the yield and whether it will be appetizing for each member of the syndicate. Indeed central to understanding the loan syndication strategy is the trade-off between asset retention level, prominence of role within the syndicate and the yield. Generally the resulting structure is a compromise for each party. Even the winner of the bid will have to sacrifice income and asset base for the benefit of the deal as a whole.

It is important to realize that the yield is generally different for each syndicate member. Consequently when pricing a transaction it is incumbent upon the bidder to determine that it will be sufficiently attractive to be syndicated.

The key elements in the yield calculation depend on whether the loan is drawn or not. If the loan is drawn the key calculations involve the margin and front-end fees, if the facility is partially utilized then there is an extra-commitment fee. This will in general be lower than the margin and simply represents a charge for making funds available.

The yield calculation typically employed in the marketplace is the so-called straightline method. We give the example of a term loan of 10 years on a total of €500 million notional. After due consideration of the factors discussed above the deal was proposed at the margin of 50 bps per annum, upfront expenses, referred to as 'arrangement fees', of 40 bps[1] on the notional and €60 000, commitment fees of 20 bps per annum and agency fees of 0.5 bps per annum.

We calculate the all in yield, which represents the total cost from the perspective of the borrower. This represents a straightline yield on an annualized basis determined by dividing the flat yield by the average life of the loan.

To calculate the yield we need to factor some initial notions about how the borrower is likely to draw down the facility and pay it back; this will usually be part of the contractual process and consequently be quite accurate. In our example the borrower draws down in two tranches over the first 2 years; until the scheduled repayment time is reached in seventh year. The loan is amortized in equal amounts until it is payed back in the tenth year (Figure 2.3).

The yield will consist of four main components: the upfront costs, the agency fees, the commitment fees – usually treated distinctly from the other fees and the margin – which is the extra-component payed over the prevalent floating rate which reflects the credit worthiness of the borrower. This figure will be obtained from other similar loans, or to the spreads on the issuer's outstanding bonds observable in the

[1] See the next section on syndication strategy for a full breakdown.

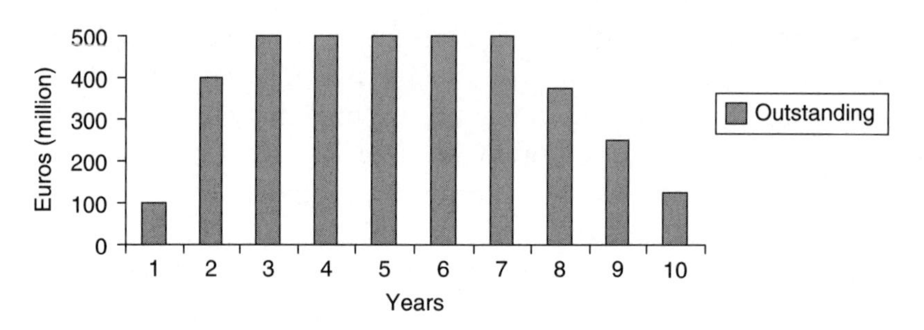

Figure 2.3 A 10-year term loan.

secondary market. If no loans or bonds exist then it will be close to the margin of other comparable borrowers.

Firstly we calculate the margin which is the amount of interest payable for each period (in this example annually, the convention on the loan is on an Act/365 basis):

$$\text{Annual interest} = 500\,\text{M} \times \frac{\text{number of days}}{365} \times 0.005.$$

This will only be the case when the loan is fully drawn, during the initial drawdown period it will be pro-rated accordingly.

Next stop, the commitment fees, these are calculated as an upfront cash amount. To do this we need to value a cash flow occurring in the future. Thus we use a discount factor, remembering to discount at the appropriate risky rate as the cash flow is not certain. The usual discount factor is that implied from the existing spreads on the issuer's debt; we discussed this issue in the previous paragraph. There are two cash flows, because it is drawn in two tranches, and the total upfront commitment fee will be the sum of them:

$$\begin{aligned}\text{Commitment fee} = {} & 400\,\text{M} \times \frac{365}{365} \times 0.002 \times \text{discount factor (1 year)} \\ & + 100\,\text{M} \times \frac{365}{365} \times 0.002 \times \text{discount factor (2 year)}.\end{aligned}$$

We have used the example of an AA borrower whose debt was yielding 5.3 per cent. Working through the above gives a fee of €940,566.

Finally we need to get the upfront agency fees; these again need to be discounted so we have 10 terms similar to that shown below, with the day count and discount factor set accordingly:

$$\text{Agency fee} = 500\,\text{M} \times 0.00005 \times \text{discount factor } (n \text{ year}).$$

Table 2.2 The fee structure.

Item	Fee
Agency fees	0.5 bps/annum
Arrangement fees	40 bps
Expenses	€0.06 million
Commitment fee	20 bps/annum
Margin	50 bps/annum

Summing up 10 years worth we have total upfront agency fees of €204 991.

The full Monty then is all the components summed:

$$\text{Upfront cost} = \text{agency fees} + \text{arrangement fees} \\ + \text{commitment fees} + \text{expenses}.$$

In monetary form:

$$\text{Upfront cost} = 0.205\,\text{M} + 2\,\text{M} + 0.941\,\text{M} + 0.06\,\text{M}.$$

This is divided by the average life of the loan to get a spread of 14.91 bps. The interest margin, quoted per annum, will often be added to this since it is meaningful to do so as the costs have been averaged on a yearly basis. Notice that arrangement fees (including participation and underwriting) are lumped together under front-end expenses (Table 2.2).

This would be the total cost to the borrower. A slightly different calculation is performed by each of the syndicate members. In particular this yield is only relevant to the borrower and not for other parties who would re-calculate dropping various elements. We discuss this in the next paragraph.

Syndication strategy

The bidder underwrites the full amount of the loan and if successful will form the syndicate, the credit committee acting on behalf of the bidder set the asset retention level. This might be no greater than €100 million using the above term loan as an example. This is important in determining the resulting strategy.

Upon receiving a mandate the bidder will arrange for the deal to be sub-underwritten by five other banks who further commit equal amounts of €60 million using the loan example from the previous section. Finally the deal enters 'general syndication', where the bidder will arrange for two other banks to commit €50 million.

The terminology describing each of these parties is overwhelmingly important. For our example we have one bidder, or arranger, five lead managers and two managers.

Upfront fees will include an underwriting and participation fee; we have used typical values of 10 and 25 bps, respectively, on the loan notional. These are payable to the relevant members of the syndicate depending on their status. For example, the two managers will not receive an underwriting fee. This syndication strategy typically generates 5 bps extra for the bidder, the so-called praecipium, as recompense for both organizing the deal and taking exposure to market risk. In this example, the total upfront fees paid by the borrower are 40 basis points which is equivalent to €2.0 million comprising the praecipium, underwriting and participation fees.

The yield has to be determined from each of the party's perspective. For example, the praecipium will be removed from the total fee and the remainder divided by the loan notional in order to determine the yield relevant to the arranger and lead managers. The flat yield is obviously different for each of the banks and is found in each case by dividing the total fees for each category by the amount of loan participation.

2.7 Pricing within a commercial bank

The pure commercial banks are in the business of making a larger number of smaller bilateral loans. These have a different organizational structure and a very different pricing mechanism – we briefly describe their methodology.

As you would anticipate the transfer mechanism is a strategic management tool acting as the main interface between the commercial and financial side of the operation. It has a number of functions highlighted below:

- An internal fund management and netting system.
- Costing internal funds.
- Reporting mechanism.

The bank can be thought of as a collective set of different distinct business units which have access to a common resource (i.e. the banks capital). The price of the loan is determined through a mechanism known as the funds transfer pricing (FTP) system (Figure 2.4).

Obviously the needs and resources will be generally unbalanced across business units and the FTP will net the differences and allocate funds when needed and purchase any surplus. This should be contrasted with

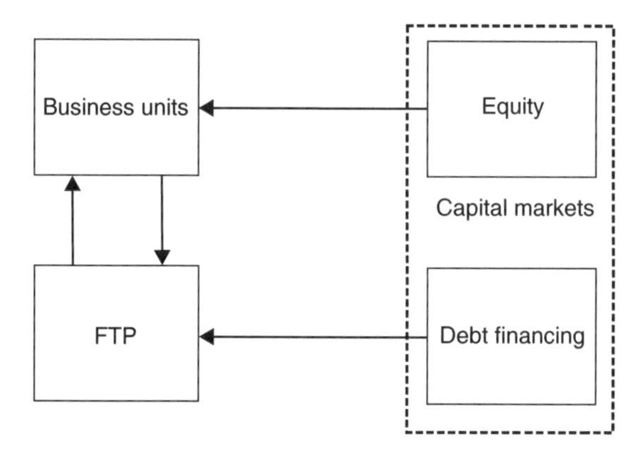

Figure 2.4 The FTP mechanism.

the treasury, which raises debt or invests excesses within the external marketplace. We can conceptually think of this arrangement as a central pool of funds where the pricing policy is only partially determined by the capital markets. The FTP actually sets the price with the weight towards commercial considerations.

The FTP system has two sources of funds: internal-business units and the external marketplace. Usually debt financing is arranged (equity is too expensive). The margin the bank adds to the internal-funding cost is known as the commercial margin. It is applicable to internal-business units and promoted through the FTP. This mechanism can be thought of as the 'internal market' accessed by the business units. There are differences between borrowing in the 'internal market' and the 'real market'. The transfer prices should be consistent with commercial policy.

Transfer prices then are subject to both. A correct price will ensure that funding constraints partly determine the transfer price. The main driver however, will be the commercial aspect of the company. The business might actually decide to subsidize the customer if that policy is in line with the core strategy. In normal market conditions however, business units extending loans at non-commercial spreads will discover over time a lack of internal funding. (Too high and there will be a lack of customers.)

The treasury will be responsible for minimizing the cost of funding. There can be some variation in how this policy is actually executed in practice. This is a consequence of the opportunity cost arising from a potential gain in a beneficial market movement. This would be neutralized by any systematic hedging policy. The treasury should normally operate as a cost centre but will be held responsible for any resulting saving in the cost of funds obtained through underhedging.

Table 2.3 The costs and charges.

Balance sheet		Rates (%)	
Assets	\$7000 M	Cost of equity	12
Liabilities	\$4000 M	Charge to customers	14
Equity	\$3000 M	Internal transfer price of resources	6
		Internal transfer price of funds	6
		Market funding rate	4

There are slight complications surrounding the fact that interest rates have a term structure. This means that a system based upon one transfer price equal to the average cost of funds would be inefficient because the funding will be higher for longer-dated commitments. The upshot is that transfer prices are differentiated according to maturity.

We demonstrate the build up of a commercial margin with an example; in general the overall or accounting margin applicable to the entire business is defined as

$$\text{Margin}_{\text{accounting}} = \text{Margin}_{\text{commercial}} + \text{Margin}_{\text{FTP}}.$$

Consider a commercial bank with the balance sheet displayed (Table 2.3).

The overall accounting margin will be

$$\$7000\,\text{M} \times 14\% - \$3000\,\text{M} \times 12\% - \$4000\,\text{M} \times 4\% = \$460\,\text{M}.$$

Stating that the assets return 14 per cent and the liabilities are composed of equities and debt with costs of 12 and 4 per cent respectively, we can also get to the accounting margin in terms of a sum of FTP and commercial margins. The commercial margin is

$$\$7000\,\text{M} \times (14 - 6\%) + \$3000\,\text{M} \times (6 - 12\%) = \$380\,\text{M}.$$

This margin is relevant to internal-business units which have access to the equity but do not have access to external financing. They can however access the FTP as a supplier and purchaser of funds. The FTP can be thought of as the adjustment to the commercial margin in order to equal the accounting margin.

Thus to balance the equation we add the FTP margin, which is the relevant calculation for the non-equity funding:

$$\$4000\,\text{M} \times (6 - 4\%) = \$80\,\text{M}.$$

Table 2.4 The build up of a transfer price.

Item	Charge (%)
Cost of debt	4
Cost of liquidity	1
Expected loss from credit risk	1
Transfer price	6

Conversely we tend to start out knowing the transfer price, built up from the factors displayed in Table 2.4 and furthermore an acceptable return on equity. How do we determine the customer rate?

Consider an example whereby the bank wishes to secure a 25 per cent return on equity, the accounting margin must be set at $750 million. This can also be written as the difference between the revenues and the cost of funds:

$$\$750\,\text{M} = \$7000\,\text{M} + \text{customer rate} - \$3000\,\text{M} \times 12\% - \$4000\,\text{M} \times 4\%.$$

This gives a customer rate of 18.1 per cent which translates into a margin of 12.1 per cent for the individual business units (=18.1 − 6 per cent).

2.8 Loan ratings

Standard and Poors have been rating loans since 1996 during that time there has been consistent growth in the number of facilities rated although it is still relatively small compared to the total size of the market (Table 2.5 illustrates the categories).

As we have discussed, the divide between the loan and bond markets is becoming narrower, resulting in greater transparency and competition. The loan market is steadily evolving from an inefficient, illiquid market controlled by a handful of banks acting on a buy and hold mentality to a more efficient liquid market. Ratings support these changes through the establishment of an independent benchmark of credit quality.

The rating process typically takes place over a 6-week period consisting of a top-down approach concentrating on a number of distinct areas. The first component comprises an assessment of the business risk within the sector that the borrower operates followed by a detailed evaluation of the company. These topics are common to the standard rating methodology and are also discussed in Section 1.17 on fixed income credit. It may be anticipated that the accorded rating on the loans will be that of the borrower, however this is not necessarily the case.

Table 2.5 Loan ratings (investment grade).

Short-term rating	Long-term rating
A−1+	AAA
	AA+
	AA
	AA−
A−1	A+
	A
A−2	A−
	BBB+
A−3	BBB
	BBB−

Bank loan ratings seek to determine the repayment possibility of a specific debt class. This analysis takes into account the specifics of the loan arrangement including the position of the facility within the capital structure and any existing collateral explicit within the covenants. This can imply somewhat counter intuitively that the loan rating may be higher than the corporate as a whole.

Collateral may include one or more assets. An estimate of their market value needs to be determined. Consequently it is important to assess the quality of the collateral and whether its value is likely to be maintained in the post-default scenario. The legal aspects of this process are systematic bringing into sharp focus the nature of the asset backing. This will include diligence on the collaterals jurisdiction together with the quality. For example, if the loan is collateralized against intangible assets then it will be very difficult to put any sort of value on this post-default. (Consequently this will be reflected in the rating given to the loan.)

Once this analysis is complete, ratios are determined to enable a comparison between the asset backing and coverage of the loan being rated to assess whether a protection margin exists. The subsequent step involves the priority of the loan payment within the capital structure. These priorities are as follows:

- Secured debt, will always carry the highest precedence.
- Secured bank debt vs. other secured debt. (The distinction here is that other secured debt may exist; debentures and mortgage debt are secured[2] on physical assets and get paid-off as a first priority.)

[2]There is always an exception in finance – some debentures are secured on a general pool of capital.

- Senior vs. subordinated debt (subordinated debt will provide an extra-cushion to the senior debt).

The proportion of debt within the capital structure that ranks below secured status is important in determining recovery rates. If the company defaults, the senior debt is accorded the highest priority and there may not be enough capital to compensate the subordinated junior debt holders.

The maturity of the facility is important. The agencies will view short horizons more favourably. The reason behind this is that the cumulative default risk will be lower for shorter maturities. Additionally some of the loan will probably have been returned resulting in a better asset to loan value coverage. These factors may produce potentially a single notch upwards in rating.

Surprisingly the extent of the covenant will not typically have a large impact on the loan rating. The covenant is simply a set of terms which govern the borrower's behaviour to assist in the repayment of the facility. In particular they include limitations on additional debt, actions on asset sales, maintenance of fixed-charge coverage and restrictions upon distribution of dividend.

2.9 Risk management

Commercial banks collect deposits and lend. All these transactions comprise 'the banking portfolio'. Their investment banking cousins and sometimes colleagues (in the case of large global banks), are also in the business of brokerage and trading. These transactions comprise the 'market portfolio'. This section is written from the perspective of the global bank which has large banking and market portfolios.

The major component of risk within the banking portfolio is interest-rate risk. This is because the asset base comprising loans and deposits usually have a different rate exposure causing interest-rate sensitivity and potentially liquidity risk. (There may also be embedded optionality.) This is a book about credit so we do not wish to dwell too long on these risks. But we must establish how credit risk is perceived and organized within the risk-management hierarchy. Figure 2.5 shows the risks inherent in both types of portfolio.

We now describe how the organizational structure of the bank reflects the risk activities.

Rate and liquidity risk within the banking portfolio is managed by the treasury. This concern addresses the issues of defining and devising hedging programmes for rate risk, liquidity and optionality. The

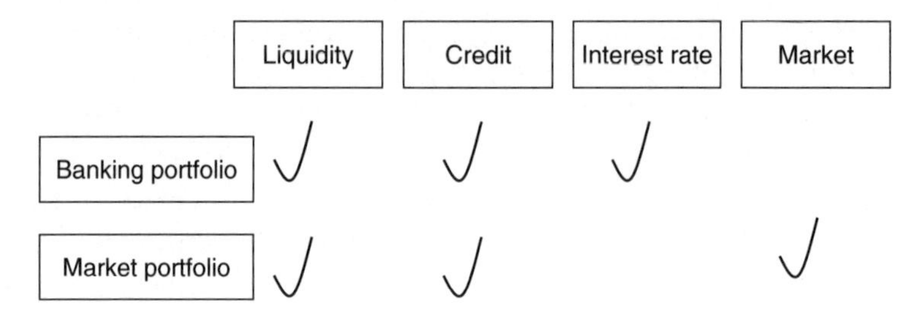

Figure 2.5 Origin of risks banking and market portfolios.

treasury does not typically manage credit or market risk on the trading book.

These are managed both centrally and in a more devolved manner. Decisions to extend credit are delegated to the syndicate desk and the subsequent credit exposure is managed by the loan portfolio group. Both of these functions are subject to some degree of supervision by the credit committee. We can see from Figure 2.5 that the various activities of the bank generate very different risks. The way to remember the distinction is that banking portfolio does not produce market risk and the market portfolio is not a source of interest-rate risk. Loan portfolio management is a central function. Most of the loans originated stay on the banking book, however if the bank has an appreciable investment banking operation a fraction will be transferred to the market portfolio where they will be managed at a more local level.

The rationale behind this arrangement is that the individual at the business level is committed to maintaining customer relationships together with the pressure of meeting commercial targets, there are incentives to take risk.

The committees are not affected by such concerns which makes it easier to judge what is an acceptable level of risk. The figure below shows a summary of risk management and supervision within a global bank (Figure 2.6).

Risk management is a central function which can be thought of as both a top-down and bottom-up process. At the top-level target earnings and risk limits are defined. These global goals are translated into signals to business units which line managers incorporate into customer transaction policy. The monitoring and reporting of risks however is a bottom-up activity starting with transactions and ending with consolidated statements.

Usually there are two specific organizational devices employed to execute the risk-management function. These are the transfer pricing systems between business units (central management devise the margin)

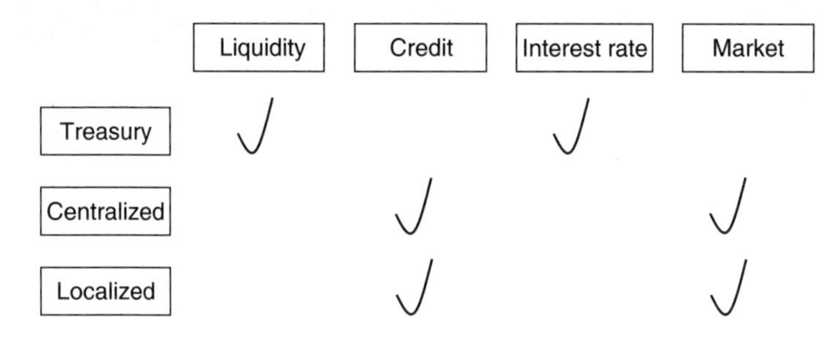

Figure 2.6 The management function.

and the capital allocation system which defines global risk in the context of the available capital.

2.10 Approaches to management

Goals of portfolio management

Banks are generally in the business of extending loans at margins that are at least neutral to their risk exposure. Implicit within the costing arrangement is the insurance premium for the obligor defaulting.

However this only captures the situation at origination. There will be an ongoing exposure which must be adequately managed. In particular if the credit worthiness of the loan beneficiary deteriorates then the banks suffer adversely.

This exposure is categorized according to expected and unexpected losses. Expected losses occur due to normal daily variations in the P&L caused by underlying market movements. The bank would generally hedge, carry these losses or use reserves. (This assumes the book is marked to market.)

Major international banks set aside economic capital to absorb unexpected losses. They typically have an internal risk-management structure both to quantify and respond to a gradual change of risk via economic capital. If this vital function is carried out on a less than timely basis there is a chance of a hit to the capital as a result of a sudden increase in loan loss provisioning.

The objective of the loan portfolio manager is to optimize the use of economic capital. Consequently the portfolio should generate an acceptable income relative to this capital base. Equivalently the risk-adjusted return should clear a hurdle ratio.

Modern portfolio theory is applied to the loan collection. One of the ramifications of this is that the capital that must be set aside is not simply proportional to the sum of the individual risks for each loan. This is because of diversification, which can either work for or against the loan manager depending upon the amount of correlation between the assets. Another way of describing this is the amount of concentration inherent within the portfolio. This can be large either because of exposure to a single name or possibly a sector. Consequently the job of the loan portfolio manager can be translated into one of concentration management.

The manager then requires a systematic way of capturing concentration in a loan portfolio context. One approach that is widely used is Risk Metrics™ Credit Metrics, which essentially determines the volatility of the portfolio by determining its likely future values.

Figure 2.7 shows the amount of economic capital required within a loan portfolio to maintain a category of rating. This is effectively a graph of the probability of the portfolio defaulting, which is very sensitive to the amount of 'concentration' or correlation within the portfolio.

This can be visualized with the help of Figure 2.8, which illustrates that the risk properties of the loan are quite distinct when held in a portfolio. In particular loan B diversifies the risk and thus lowers the concentration. This will obviously be dependent on the particular details of the portfolio.

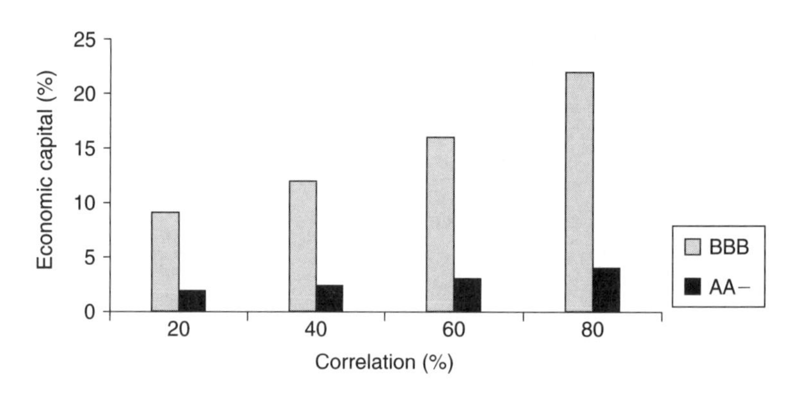

Figure 2.7 The economic capital required within loan portfolios. *Source:* Risk.

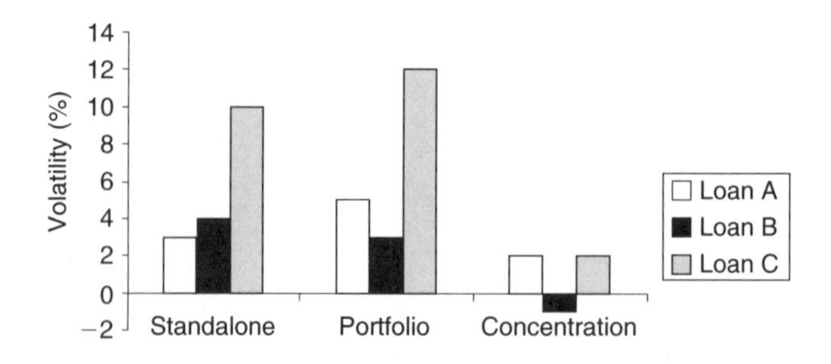

Figure 2.8 Concentration risk.

2.11 Economic vs. regulatory capital

Portfolio managers try to optimize the use of economic and not regulatory capital. What is the difference? First, we emphasize what they share; they both represent capital which the bank must hold to serve as a cushion against unexpected losses. Regulatory capital, however, is determined by the Basel accord according to a number of forfeits dependent upon outstanding balances and the category of counterparty. This definition produces an incorrect measure in the context of marked to market accounting; hence the need for economic risk.

These shortcomings can be categorized as the adoption of a measure for credit risk which does not distinguish between corporates. Further governments are assigned a very low credit risk somewhat arbitrarily. Finally the forfeits are identical for short- and long-term commitments, when obviously the latter carry higher risk. Most alarmingly the regulators measure portfolio risk as the simple addition of the individual risks which ignores diversification effects. This has the unfortunate effect of a diversified portfolio and a concentrated portfolio potentially having the same risk.

These concerns are being addressed within the new framework of Basel. We cover this in Section 2.16.

Due to these inefficiencies in measuring credit exposure any target performance based upon regulatory capital may not depend upon the true credit risk. Economic capital is intended to correct these distortions.

Ultimately any difference will be reflected in customer pricing; get this wrong and the bank could end up subsidizing the competition. Figure 2.9 shows how the use of regulatory capital will miss-price the loan.

The amount of economic capital is derived using the VAR methodology. There are a number of distinct steps involved in the derivation. These include:

- The shape of the loss distribution.
- A tolerance level.
- A horizon period.

It will be helpful to inspect the loss distribution of a loan portfolio depicted in Figure 2.10. The reader should note the distinct shape in comparison to a normal distribution. This is often interpreted as the distinction between credit and market risk. This can be misleading as market risk itself is really only approximated by the normal distribution. (The reason the normal distribution is so important in finance is

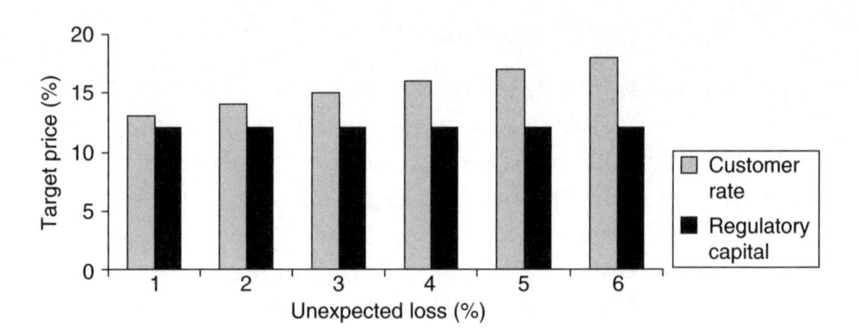

Figure 2.9 Target prices of credit risk.

that it is both a good approximation to reality and analytically tractable.)

We have highlighted in the chart the jargon beloved of the practitioner. Reading from left to right any loss on the portfolio between zero and the 'expected' loss is taken care-of through a combination of reserves, hedging and policies. As we pass the average loss, we move into 'unexpected territory', the implications for management are that losses in this region must be provisioned through capital.

We then encounter the next vertical line which depicts the limit of unexpected losses which is exactly the capital at risk (CAR). As we move further to the right the losses are no longer cushioned. Any loss that actually occurred would be referred to as 'exceptional losses'. They are not provisioned against because they are very rare and to do so would ultimately be uncompetitive because too much capital would have to be set aside.

From this picture it is implicit that we have separated out two vital ingredients necessary to establish risk management. The actual real world described by the distribution together with the human decision on the location of the vertical lines. The human involved employs seasoned judgement, gained through many years experience managing loan portfolios, no doubt.

If you are a neophyte there are a number of methodologies employed to establish the location of this line. One is a gimmick and depends on how risk averse the managers are. It is a gimmick because their hands are usually tied.

They are tied because of the restriction on the amount of available capital. We offer a little illustration. Suppose we use the gimmick and come up after much deliberation in committee meetings with a tolerance of two-and-a-half per cent on a loan portfolio with expected losses of 1.4 per cent per annum and a volatility of 6 per cent per annum then the maximum risk is given by:

$$1.4 + 1.96 \times 6 = 13.16.^{3}$$

However, the available capital is only 12 per cent of the nominal so:

$$1.4 + t \times 6 = 12 \Rightarrow t = 1.77.$$

This implies a tolerance level of about 3.8 per cent.

The main business driver of risk aversion is the *target rating*, mainly because of funding considerations, whereby the bank finances its business at libor plus a spread related to their credit rating.

Implicit in a rating is a default rate. Thus the tolerance level should be identical to the figure associated with the target rating. For example, if we assume that the target rating has a probability of default rate of 0.25 per cent, then under the assumptions of a normal distribution the multiple associated with this probability is close to three.

This multiple generates a requirement for capital of 18.26 per cent using the above figures for earning and volatilities. This is the economic capital required to achieve the desired rating. This is a somewhat extreme example, highlighting an unrealistic quantity of capital. The usual goal of management would be to ensure the portfolio has a loss volatility, at any time, consistent with the rating demand.

2.12 CAR

We gave some simple examples illustrating the build-up of CAR (Figure 2.10) from the confidence level. Moreover these were based on the unrealistic assumption of a normal distribution. With low confidence levels, indeed many banks will set out to achieve a 0.5 per cent tolerance level. The so-called 'tail risk' becomes of paramount concern. Unfortunately the shape of the so-called 'fat tail' in a loan portfolio makes the measure especially sensitive to the assumptions of the loss distribution. We describe modifications to the distribution in Section 2.3 on fundamental credit.

Choice of horizon

In general the probability of default grows with the increase of the horizon date. The so-called cumulative default rate can be obtained

[3] The assumed way of getting from the tolerance level to the monetary amount was none other than the normal distribution. (Consequently using 2.5% gives an inverse normal of 1.96%.)

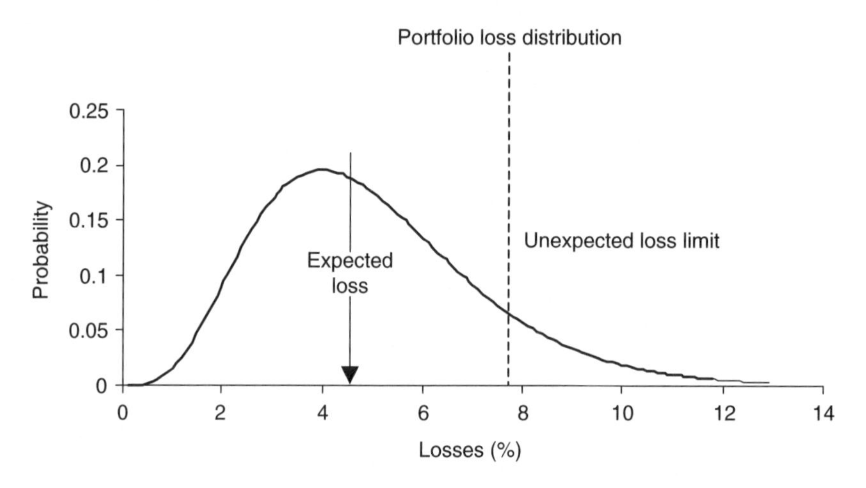

Figure 2.10 The definition of CAR.

from each of the yearly, variable default rates. Consequently the CAR for credit risk increases with increasing horizon length.

What horizon length should we deploy?

Within the loan market there are two possibilities of either using the residual maturity on existing facilities or the period of time required for raising capital, that is the existing capital only has to absorb losses until sufficient extra-funds are available. The assumptions here are worth questioning since in the event of loan provisioning it might not be possible to tap funds according to typical operations.

Build of hurdle rate given a capital at risk (i.e. risk-adjusted return)

We now move on to discuss risk-adjusted performance. Performance within the banking portfolio cannot adequately be captured using traditional accounting measures. This is simply because within the financial world there is no performance without a compensating risk exposure. Consequently only some risk-reward combination is meaningful.

The benefit of risk-adjusted performance is that it allows comparison of profitability across different loans.

The two main measurements of risk-adjusted profitability are the risk-adjusted return on capital (RAROC) and the shareholders value added (SVA).

Risk-adjusted ratios include return on risk-adjusted capital (RORAC) and RAROC which adjusts revenues for expected losses.

To obtain RAROC the expected loss should be deducted from earnings and the result divided by the capital necessary to absorb unexpected losses.

The definitions:

$$\text{RAROC} = \frac{\text{earnings} - \text{expected loss (EL)}}{\text{CR (or UL)}}.$$

The shareholders measure is

$$\text{SVA} = \text{earnings} - \text{hurdle rate} \times \text{CAR},$$

with examples in Table 2.6.

In Table 2.7 we set out the usual calculation for using the CAR to obtain the pricing of a loan. This is common within commercial banks

Table 2.6 Example of the RAROC and SVA calculation.

Item	Value
Loan portfolio valuation	$100 000 000
Expected default rate	1%
Volatility of default	5%
Hurdle rate	25%
CAR (=1.65*Vol. *exposure)	$8 250 000
Earnings	$3 000 000
−Expected loss =	$2 000 000
RAROC	24.2%
SVA	$937 500

Table 2.7 Customer rate given an RAROC.

Item	Value
Loan portfolio valuation	$100 000 000
CAR	$6 000 000
Expected loss	$2 000 000
RORAC	22%
Operating costs	2%
Cost of debt	10%
Risk premium, CAR × RORAC/loan portfolio valuation	1.32%
Price (expected loss + operating costs + cost of debt + risk premium)	15.32%

who wish to know how to maintain a rating; consequently the CAR is the value that drives the analysis.

2.13 Loan case studies

Introduction to the case studies

We provide two examples of portfolio loan management. To initiate the reader we take the simple case of two loans within the portfolio. The idea of this is to display the fundamental arguments without getting too bogged down in mathematical analysis. We then analyse a more realistic portfolio of 100 loans. Without further ado then, let us press onto the first example.

We have two assets in our portfolio both term loans, of nearly 4-year maturity,[4] comprising AA and BBB borrowers which for simplicity we assume to be in the same sector. Both loans are booked at par value and have a nominal of €100 million. We are interested in determining the capital that must be set aside as a cushion against unexpected loss over a 1-year period. We further assume mark to market-based accounting.

The two asset portfolio

The fundamental question is what are the possible values of the portfolio in 1-year time? We break this into steps. First we evaluate the rating at maturity and then the value in this state. The AA loan could end in one of the four possibilities, consisting of either gaining, losing or remaining at the same value. The loan could also default. For each possibility we also need to know the possibility that the BBB loan has either increased, remained the same value, decreased in value or defaulted. The possible states then are displayed in Figure 2.11.

So we have all the possible states of the portfolio. To quantify the analysis we unfortunately need more in the way of equations. In particular we need to know the probability that the portfolio will migrate into another state. One way we could achieve this is to say that we know the probabilities that the individual loans will increase, decrease, maintain or default from the transition probability matrix regularly published by the agencies. Table 2.8 shows the relevant entries for our components.

[4] We use the same maturity as the FRN used in the case study within the chapter on the credit risk of libor instruments for the reader's convenience.

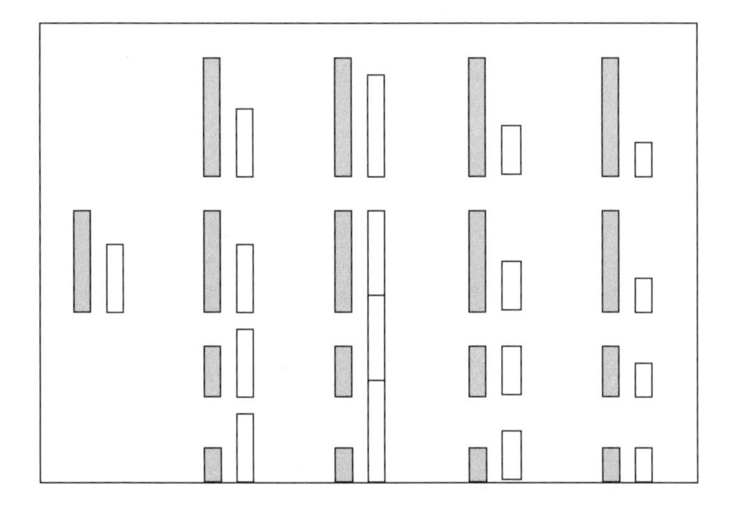

Figure 2.11 The possible states for a two loan portfolio.

Table 2.8 Migration rates.

Rating	Outcome (%)			
	Default	Value loss	Unchanged	Value gain
AA	0.01	11.66	87.76	0.57
BBB	0.37	NA*	95.24	4.39

Source: Standard and Poors, 2002.

* We have aggregate probabilities between investment grade and default partially for pedagogical purposes and further due to the lack of spread data on Euro denominated speculative grade credit.

Then the natural assumption is to say that the chance of the portfolio defaulting is simply the product of the individual probabilities, that is

$$\text{Probability of default} = \text{chance AA defaults} \times \text{chance BBB defaults.}$$

Unfortunately this is wrong. It is wrong because it ignores correlation, which is very important because without redress we tend to overestimate the chances of default and thus the amount of capital to be set aside. How then do we investigate correlation effects?

We employ a derivative of the Merton methodology which has widespread use among loan portfolio managers. An alternative would be to directly utilize default data or use secondary bond market spreads and imply the default rates. Either way proceed according to the discussion in Section 2.16. We offer a critique of these approaches and do not wish to re-peddle here.

The essence of the Merton type approach is to map the firm's asset value onto the rating. The motivation behind this is that the correlation

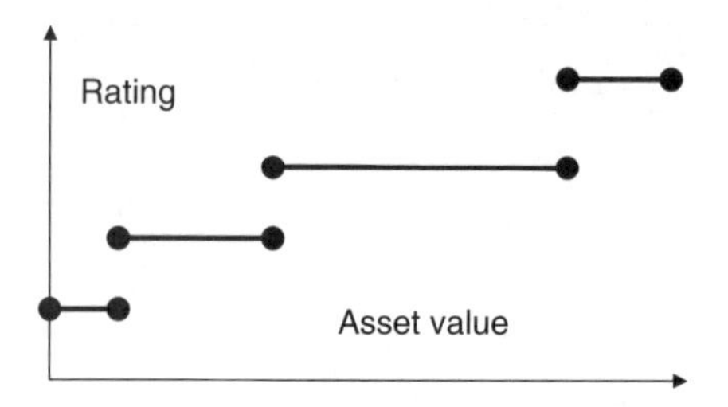

Figure 2.12 Mapping asset values to changes in state.

between equities is easily measured and further based on a liquid marketplace. Figure 2.12 shows how the mapping occurs.

We know the transition probability from the agencies. However we also know the distribution of asset returns – it is a normal distribution. Thus we just need to calibrate the distribution to the probabilities. We show the case of default below:

$$\text{Probability of default} = \text{cumulative normal}(\text{return}_{\text{default}}).$$

This will enable us to back out the equivalent threshold default return. You can use Excel to do this by calling

$$\text{return}_{\text{default}} = \text{NORMSINV (0.37\%)},$$

we also require this for the next step of isolating the loss of value probability:

$$\begin{aligned}\text{Probability of decrease} = {} & \text{cumulative normal}(\text{return}_{\text{decrease}}) \\ & - \text{cumulative normal}(\text{return}_{\text{default}}).\end{aligned}$$

Continuing on in this manner we end up with details as shown in Table 2.9.

For a one-dimensional normal distribution the returns scale by the volatility, consequently in order to get the actual return, we need to multiply by the volatility as displayed in the last column of Table 2.9. We are not through because we must do the same for the AA borrower – this is not just handle grinding because we need to introduce correlation. This is again conceptually simple – you are probably happy with the one-dimensional distribution. Just think of this in two dimensions, Figure 2.13 illustrates this.

The total area under the graph is one and correlation determines the exact 'shift' away from the uniform hump about the origin. This is mathematically easy to determine, simply by counting the area under the

Table 2.9 Returns from probabilities (mapping a distribution to a rating BBB borrower).

State	Probability from transition matrix (%)	Return (%)
Value gain	4.39	$>1.71\sigma$
Unchanged	95.24	1.71σ
Value loss	NA	NA
Default	0.37	$\leqslant -2.67\sigma$

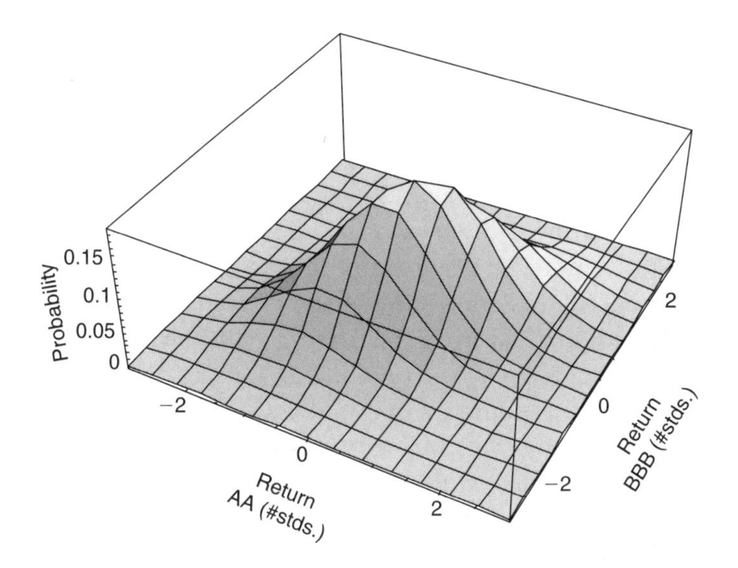

Figure 2.13 The joint-distribution probabilities.

graph between the relevant states labelled on the axis – mathematically this comes down to determining the definite integral below:

$$\begin{aligned}&\text{Probability both loans default}\\&= \int_{-\infty_1}^{\text{return}_{\text{default}_1}} \int_{-\infty_2}^{\text{return}_{\text{default}_2}} f(\text{return}_1,\ \text{return}_2,\ \text{covariance})\\&\qquad \times \text{return}_1 \times \text{return}_2\, d(\text{return}_1)\, d(\text{return}_2),\end{aligned}$$

where $f(\text{return}_1, \text{return}_2, \text{covariance})$ is the binormal density function. This can be evaluated from a standard mathematical library, such as Mathematica™ for example. The bounds are set according to the state for which we need to derive the transition probability. After evaluating all the states we end up with the joint default probability table (Table 2.10).

Table 2.10 Joint migration probabilities.

	BBB higher value	BBB maintained	BBB lower value	BBB defaults
AA higher value	0.07%	0.47%	NA	0.00%
AA maintained	4.17%	83.50%	NA	0.28%
AA lower value	0.22%	11.17%	NA	0.10%
AA defaults	0.00%	0.01%	NA	0.00%

Loan revaluation

We need to complete the analysis by valuing the loan for each of the states.

We can revalue using the spread from the simulated pricing curve for the appropriate rating. Drawn loans will be treated in the same manner as a floating-rate note, that is revaluing it in each future state by discounting the cash flows consisting of the loan margin at the appropriate discount rate implied from the pricing curve. We are also going to neglect the effect of any accrual on the loan for reasons of transparency and furthermore the standard methodology for evaluating risk is to take a 'snapshot' of market rates, either historical or projected, and see the effect on the portfolio while maintaining its maturity profile.

The loan commitment is a facility (which gives the obligor an option of borrowing up to the face amount). If the loan is not fully drawn it must be factored when attempting to revalue the loan. This characteristic introduces the need for further analysis because the borrower pays interest on the drawn amount and a fee which is different from the margin on the undrawn portion. Consequently when revaluing the loan in future states we have to know the amount currently drawn and the change due to the obligor's rating migration.

During an adverse credit environment the borrower will usually draw more and vice versa in a more conducive market. (You would also expect the covenants to have some bearing on the loan valuation. In particular if the interest spread is related to the obligor's performance then the effect would be to keep the loan near par and the only volatility remaining would be that due to a potential default.) In our examples we assume that such covenants are not in existence and consequently that the loan can be characterized as having an FRN like sensitivity to credit risk. If the practice is 'marking to market' we deploy the VAR approach outlined in Section 1.12 on fixed income credit but substituting the *credit sensitivity* from Section 5.3 on the credit risk of libor instruments, which we directly derived for the instrument.

Table 2.11 Changes in drawdown for the BBB obligation.

Horizon state	Current draw (%)	Change (%)	New draw (%)
AAA	20	−19.9	0.1
AA	20	−18.4	1.6
A	20	−15.4	4.6
BBB	20	0.0	20.0
BB	20	26.8	46.8
CCC	20	55.0	75.0
D	20	60.0	80.0

Table 2.12 Fee and utilization structure.

Rating	Fee	Utilization (%)
AAA	3	0.1
AA	4	1.6
A	6	4.6
BBB	9	20.0
BB	18	46.8
B	40	63.7
CCC	120	75.0

An estimate of changes of drawdown given possible rating changes is taken from Arsarnow and Marker. They provide both the amount of commitment at a given credit rating and further the utilization in the event of default. Given this information it is possible to revalue the drawn portions. As the borrower changes in rating we require the fee structure to revalue the undrawn portion in the new credit state. This is provided in Table 2.12. Table 2.11 illustrates the changes in the drawn portion of the loan for each of the states that the borrower may migrate to at the end of the period. In particular if the state is unchanged then the draw remains at 20 per cent. For the other states we need to determine the increment of the currently undrawn portion, that is 80 per cent that will be utilized. This is supplied from Table 2.12, where the last column reveals the utilization rate. Given this applies to the notional of a previously undrawn facility. We need to actually translate to a percentage on the currently undrawn portion of 80 per cent, the relevant percentage is $1 - 53.2/80 = 33.5$ on a BBB–BB transition. Subsequently multiply the undrawn percentage by this result to get the extra-utilization of 26.8 per cent.

We then go on to revalue the commitment for each of the year-end ratings.

Table 2.13 shows the final result for both changes in value due to changes in drawdown and the resulting differences in fee on the

Table 2.13 Revaluation for the BBB obligation.

State	Relative spread (bps)	Drawdown revaluation (€ in M)	Fee change (bps)	Fee change (€ in M)	Total change (€ in M)
AAA	−148	0.05	−6	0.06	0.11
AA	−132	0.74	−5	0.05	0.79
A	−95	1.53	−3	0.03	1.56
BBB	0	0	0	0	0
D	200*	(56.00)	111	(222.00)	(56.22)

* Default is at 200 bps to the BBB curve, assume fees are representative of the CCC grade.

Table 2.14 Portfolio revaluation.

	BBB higher value	BBB maintained	BBB lower value	BBB defaults
AA higher value*	1.53 M	0.02 M	NA	(56.21 M)
AA maintained	1.51 M	0	NA	(56.22 M)
AA lower value*	(2.34 M)	(3.85 M)	NA	(60.08 M)
AA defaults	(91.68 M)	(93.19 M)	NA	(149.41 M)

* We consider the higher and lower states to be a weighted combination of the rating states and consequently have used the marginal transition probabilities for the relevant outset rating.

remaining commitment. The relative spread is the difference in yield as determined from the relevant Bloomberg fair market curves as of 30 December 2002. The second column captures the impact of the revaluation on the new drawn amount (using a credit spread sensitivity of 0.035 on a €100 M notional). Finally we need to work out the fees on the new drawn and undrawn portion. We collect together the individual valuations and display these in the table. To determine the CAR on the portfolio we simply weight by the joint default probabilities.

We subsequently repeat the analysis for the AA and then collect the revaluation in each of the states in Table 2.14. To determine the expected value on the portfolio we simply weight the sum of the combined valuations in each final state by the joint probabilities of the portfolio ending in that state. This will also enable us to determine the standard deviation necessary for the CAR.

CAR for the portfolio

All we require having got the loan values and the probabilities of transitioning is to calculate the unexpected loss. This will be given by

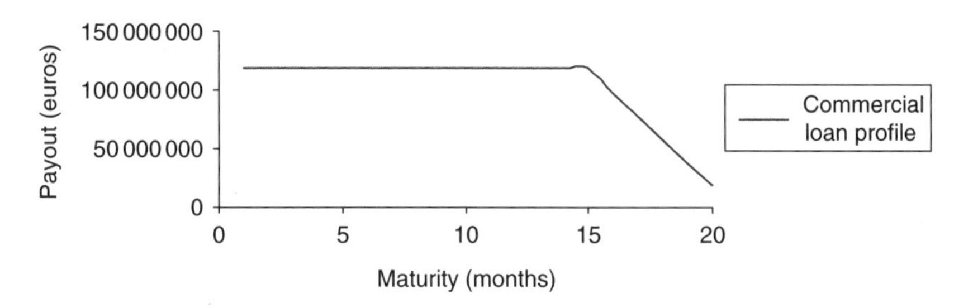

Figure 2.14 The profile of the 100 loan portfolio.

a scaling of the volatility, which is given by the standard formula:

$$\begin{aligned}\text{Unexpected loss} &= 1.65 \times \sigma \\ &= 1.65\sqrt{\sum_{\text{states}} \text{probability} \times (\text{return} - \text{average return})^2}.\end{aligned}$$

For a 95 per cent loss the CAR is determined as 3.11 per cent.

The 100 asset portfolio

Enough of the toy model. Let us analyse a proper commercial loan portfolio.

The profile of the loans is displayed above. The curve is comprised of the payouts consisting of both interest and redemption amounts, as the loans are medium to long dated, initially the bulk of the payments will be comprised of interest and then as we move towards maturity, redemption will become dominant. The majority of the loans were based on a floating-coupon structure; this means every year the obligor has to pay the relevant index rate – typically libor and a fixed margin which is dependent on the credit worthiness of the obligor (Figure 2.14).

There are approximately 100 loans under consideration with a nominal of 10 million. They were denominated in euros predominantly within the financial sector. This is the same example we have discussed in Section 4.9.

We require again the volatility of the losses. This was determined through a Monte Carlo simulation of the asset return. We assume that each loan is driven, as in the Merton type approach encountered in our two asset portfolio, by a purely firm-dependent factor but also a systematic component which represents the general economic environment in which the borrower operates. This is a type of beta model. We worked through these points in the example in Section 4.10. To apply this model to evaluate regulatory capital we determined the

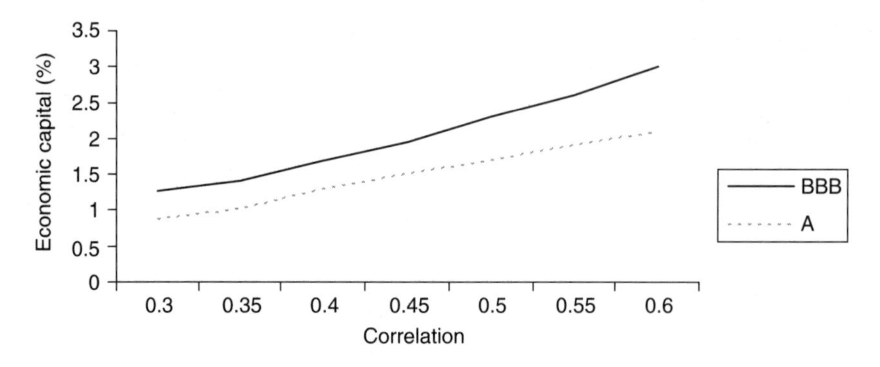

Figure 2.15 Economic capital and its dependence on correlation.

number of defaults per face value of the portfolio for a given level of correlation at the 1-year horizon. The economic capital is proportional to the average rating of the collateral within the overall portfolio. We took the default probabilities from the transition matrix in Table 1.19 on fixed-income credit, together with a global recovery rate of 50 per cent. The economic capital was determined to a 99 per cent confidence.

Figure 2.15 illustrates the outcome of various concentration scenarios vs. the quality of the loan portfolio. As you can see it is very sensitive to the level of correlation within the portfolio.

2.14 Concentration management

How to define and manage concentration

Having finally established how we determine the volatility of the portfolio we introduce how this calculation benefits managers in their decisions on whether to remove or extend existing positions.[5]

Figures 2.16 and 2.17 illustrate the quantification of concentration management. The benefit measure on the vertical axis is determined by calculating the volatility of the portfolio with and without the positions marked in black (hopefully they will not all be potential explosions, but portfolio managers as a breed tend to look at all loans this way until disarmed). If there is an appreciable difference the manager must contemplate selling the position. A possible cut-off point is represented by the horizontal line in the subsequent figure. Also displayed is a vertical line representing the threshold on individual position exposure.

[5]We have extensively analysed the process of loan origination, please consult the earlier section on pricing.

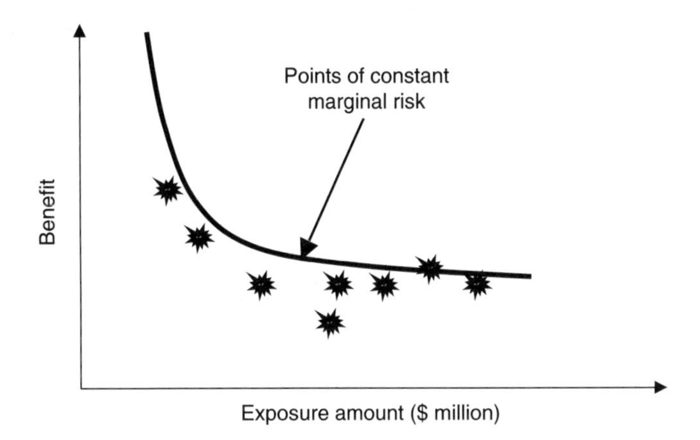

Figure 2.16 Definition of concentration.

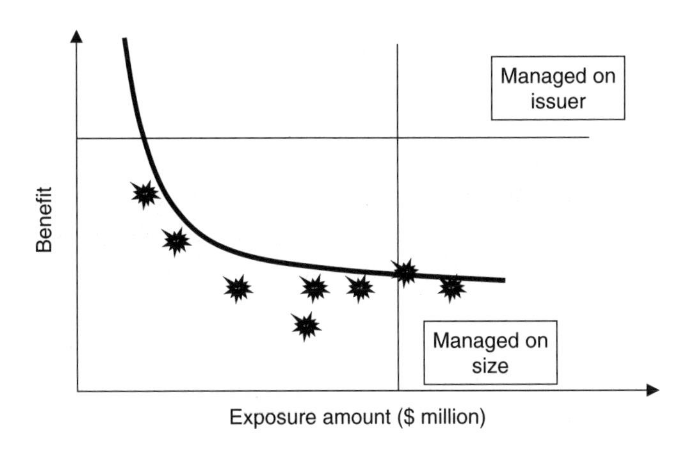

Figure 2.17 Ways of managing of concentration.

The product of the exposure, necessary to generate the same risk contribution, and diversification sensitivity is a good comparative measure; issues having the same credit risk will live on this line despite having very different notional amounts. This gives a third criteria, sell any loan appreciably above the parabola highlighted in black.

2.15 Hedging techniques

Securitization

A typical CLO consists of a senior/subordinated structure. Within this framework the precise details depend very much on the characteristics of the asset backing. Unfortunately no two securitizations have exactly the same profile. The methodology however, used in the formation of these assets and the subsequent evaluation by the rating agencies is generic.

The asset portfolio

The securitization we consider consists of a large number of commercial loans which prior to the deal were warehoused on the banks' balance sheet. The recent regulatory environment has changed in such a way as to prejudice the collection of low grade assets.[6] Our august bank thus wished to absolve the loans from the balance sheet.

The number of loans consisted of approximately 100 euro-denominated loans, with a nominal of €10 million. We refer you back to Section 4.9, where we have presented more detail for this example, including evaluating the formation of the assets and the subsequent stress testing applied by the agencies to evaluate their performance. Indeed these two steps should be considered interrelated since the analysis for the stress will help shape the profile of the securities.

Figure 2.18 shows the resulting securities. If you look at the profile, you will observe that the asset redemption and interest schedule match the pay-off profile of the underlying loans. (The situation is designed so the aggregate cashflow on the resulting securities in the indenture matches the incoming receivables.) The primary objective is to make the structure as efficient as possible. This will have been achieved when most of the incoming loan proceeds are distributed as fully as possible

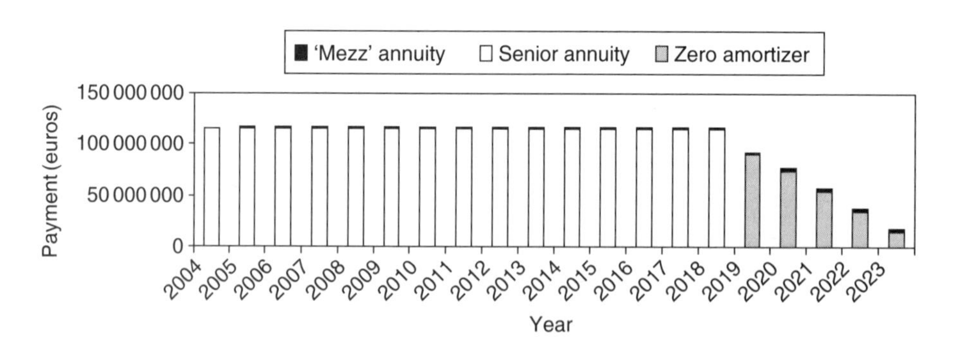

Figure 2.18 Asset pay-offs.

[6]This arrangement would probably not 'fly' due to reasons which are discussed in Section 4.9 on internal credit enhancement of Chapter 4. It is however, used in other non-banking activities, such as leasing or the government sector, for example. Whereby the sponsor wants to free up capital associated with the assets.

without the build up of an underlying cash pool. This will maximize the value of the overall structure. However, there should be an element of 'over matching' otherwise we are exposed to the contingency of inadequate receivables to service the market instruments if one or more borrowers should default. A possible solution is to build up the 'reserve' pool, and then any shortfall is accessed from this 'reserve'. This is 'internal enhancement'. It may be more effective to out source the arrangement, these solutions are discussed in Section 4.9.

In Section 4.11 we drill down into the 'profile' and consider the assets that comprise the offering in light of the investor base. A knowledge of this community is vital to selling the instruments and is an integral component of their design.

Credit default swap

The basic structure in the marketplace is very much like an insurance arrangement.

In Figure 2.19 the bank hedges a loan through buying protection, this is payed for by a regular premium. This will hedge both spread and default risk. In theory a default swap can be written on any name and on any part of the capital structure. In practice, however the contracts are written on bonds rather than loans and concentrated in the $10–$20 million range with 5-year maturities the most common.

Other credit derivatives

The CDS is the main building block for hedging the credit risk on a loan. Within a portfolio context the next major category is the synthetic balance-sheet CLO. This is an arrangement where the credit risk on a banks' loan portfolio is transferred, but not the legal ownership. These have been commonplace in order to reduce the regulatory capital charged to a bank. This activity should not be confused with the more recent tranched portfolio default swaps (TPDs) which are structured by banks on specific parts of the loan portfolio in order to exploit an arbitrage opportunity.

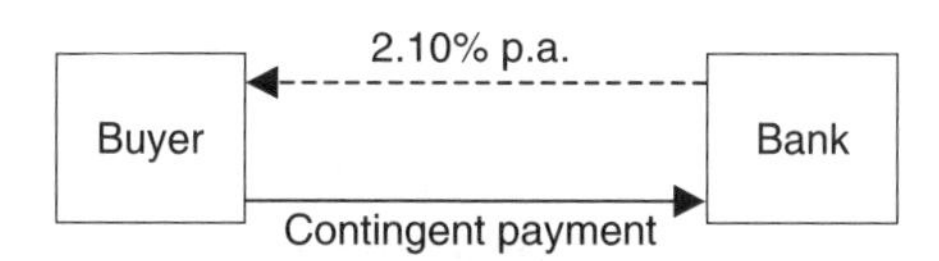

Figure 2.19 The simplest element of credit management.

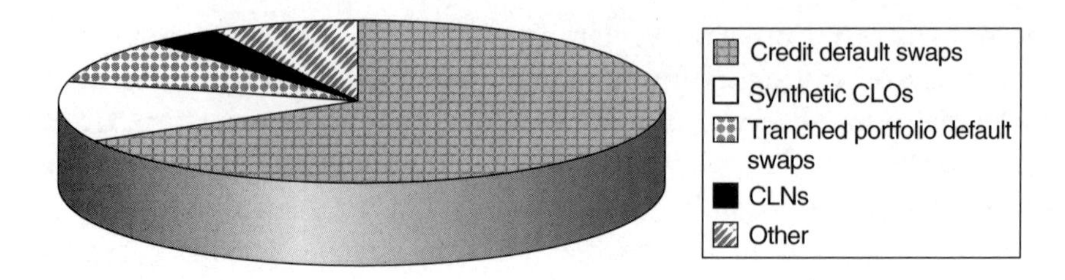

Figure 2.20 The most common credit derivatives. *Source:* Risk (2002).

In Figure 2.20 we illustrate the aggregated portfolio notional outstandings, the other categories are explained in more detail in Chapter 3.

2.16 Central themes

Expected loss

The average loss expected either on an individual loan or a portfolio is given by the equation,

$$\text{EL} = \text{exposure} \times \text{EDF} \times \text{loss severity},$$

for a single loan. The exposure is the amount of the loan, EDF is the expected default frequency and the loss severity is the amount recoverable in the event of a default.

Unexpected loss

The terminology is not helpful, how can we quantify an aspect that is unexpected? The simplest possible situation, and the most amenable to analysis is determined by

$$\text{UL} = \text{exposure} \times \text{LS} \times \sqrt{\text{EDF} \times (1 - \text{EDF})},$$

where EDF is the expected default frequency and LS is the loss severity. The formula is derived from a binomial assumption on the distribution of credit loss. Thus the obligor either defaults or it does not.

Within a portfolio context we are able to sum the expected losses, but unfortunately the unexpected component is more complicated. The reason for this can be illustrated by a simple example of a bank making a loan to two corporations based in a skiing resort, one manufactures skiing equipment, the other provides bicycle hire. (Which of course all tourists embark upon in the absence of snow.) The season

Table 2.15 Potential lending opportunities.

	Ski equipment manufacturer (%)	Bicycle hire (%)
Snow	10	−10
No snow	−15	20

lasts for 6 months which is the loan duration. Table 2.15 displays the outcomes of the loan portfolio.

The question now arises as to how the loan manager utilizes this information to originate a portfolio. First we assume the loan manager does not have to worry about building or maintaining relationships, thus the decision can be made totally on the basis of the tabulated data. The alternatives are that the manager loans out to the bicycle hire. If it does not snow he enjoys a 20 per cent return, if it does snow then he loses 10 per cent of the loan. The case for a loan to the ski equipment manufacturer is 10 per cent and a loss of −15 per cent respectively. Instead of 6 months we may consider the effects of a fully committed term loan facility, in which case the average return on the ski equipment is 5 per cent loss per annum and a 10 per cent gain on the bicycle hire. So we always lend to the bicycle hire? Clearly we anticipate it is more likely to snow but can we go one step further and create a situation where by a suitable loan weighting we break even independent of metrological conditions?

There is indeed such a solution, if the loan manager lends 4/7 of his capital to the ski equipment manufacturer and the remainder to the bicycle hire then he will be indifferent.

Now to tie this back to the discussion on unexpected losses, our measure will be the degree to which losses are spread around the unexpected. This means the worst case will not just be the sum of the individual worst cases. For example, if I had 50 per cent in either loan the worst case is never 50 per cent of −15 per cent plus 50 per cent of −10 per cent because these are the cases for snow and no snow, rather we only add real world situations. Translated, this means that loans do not all perform badly in unison rather they perform in a mixed manner. Mathematically it means a correction to the sum as displayed in the formula below:

$$\mathrm{EL\%} = \sum_{j=1}^{N} \sum_{i=1}^{N} w_i \times \mathrm{EDF}_j \times \mathrm{LS}_j,$$

$$\mathrm{UL\%} = \sqrt{\sum_{i=1}^{N} w_i^2 \times \sigma_i^2 + \sum_{j=1}^{N} \sum_{i=1}^{N} w_i \times w_j \times \sigma_i \times \sigma_j \times \mathrm{correlation}(i, j)},$$

where $\sigma_i = \text{LS}\sqrt{\text{EDF} \times (1 - \text{EDF})}$. This expression also makes some swinging assumptions on the nature of default. It assumes a fixed-loss severity, that is a binomial distribution of loss based on a fixed default, neglecting higher-order types of default.

Here w_i is the weight of the loan for asset i, σ_i is the volatility of the loan and correlation (i, j) is the correlation between loan i and loan j. We can see the unexpected loss is determined by the sum of the individual unexpected losses and the 'correction' due to their co-movement. For a very large portfolio the individual or idiosyncratic component will tend to be zero leaving the co-movement.

The default frequency

A fairly innocuous question may be 'ok I have the formulae for the unexpected loss; this involves the default frequency for the obligor, where do I find these?'. Unfortunately there is no clear-cut answer. Instead there are alternatives, with a consensus. There are three routes for determining defaults: use observed histories, the marketplace or possibly a third-party model. However, it is important to realize that the majority of third-party models do not provide default frequencies of individual names as output. Before disparaging the providers we must be sympathetic that the problem they address is one of many assets in a portfolio as opposed to a standalone loan. This is a fundamentally different business with individual risk being comparatively unimportant among the risk hierarchy. They further take the view that a good portfolio model should take the individual default probability as input, in the same spirit that standard risk-management software requires individual asset volatility. Let us then examine the alternatives (Table 2.16).

Looking at a counterparty's history is unlikely to provide us with any meaningful information because it is unlikely to determine the future EDF. So we resort to a standard methodology that sacrifices name specific information.

This method is to directly observe default rates among issuers who have similar characteristics such as domicile, sector and creditworthiness. This is the approach taken by the rating agencies and it is commonly adopted among users due to the widespread acceptance of their ratings supported by extensive data. The proviso is, and there is always a qualification in this game, if the issue is not large enough to be assigned a rating then the approach cannot be used.

To determine name specific default frequency we can consider other possibilities. Chief among them is to observe the price of the names

Table 2.16 Portfolio model approaches.

Type	Feature
Structural	Posits that the driver of default probabilities is an 'indirect' process. For example, the equity market is deemed a very relevant source of information on the creditworthiness of the obligor (provided it has public liquid stock). Becoming increasingly mainstream; KMV and Credit Metrics are representative.
Direct default data	Based on models used in the insurance industry, assumption is that default rates are continuous random variables, changing on a daily basis, as distinct from relatively static ratings.
Conditional default	Similar foundation to the 'direct default data' approach. The key difference is the further assumption that the default rates are conditional on a common driver. For example, the state of the global economy.
Spread based	Implies default information from the price of traded securities within the fixed-income/structured credit markets. Both the secondary bond market and the credit derivatives markets are valuable sources of the market perception of default probability.

traded debt. The discrepancy in price between a comparable government security is deemed to represent the likelihood of the issuer defaulting. A more subtle approach is to extract the default frequency from the firm's liability structure. This is the standpoint of KMV corporation which consider firms equity as a call option on its assets.

Regulatory capital

Basel is a city on the border between Switzerland and France, of all the Swiss cities it is perhaps one of the most unloved, perhaps this has connotations with its distinct industrial flavour as a consequence of its location on the Rhine. Or just may be it is tied up with the home of the Bank for International Settlements (BIS); a regulatory authority housed within a characteristic brown high-rise building. The 36 stories of the building in common with the regulatory environment could be said to be an acquired taste.

Regulatory treatment of loan portfolios is currently in a state of flux, nonetheless the existing treatment of capital is well known. It is appropriate to examine this prior to moving onto Basel II.

Financial institutions have a range of regulations and controls, a primary one is the level of capital that a bank holds to provide a cushion for the activities the banking engages on. These terms were set by the BIS, within the EC Solvency Ratio and Capital Adequacy Directive (1992).

Under the requirements all cash and off balance-sheet instruments in the bank's portfolio will be assigned a risk weighting, based on their perceived credit risk, which determines the level of capital set against them. This is known as BIS1 or the Basel Capital Ratios.

The methodology is as follows, each counterparty is banded into different risk categories 0, 20, 50 and 100 per cent – this percentage represents a default probability, it determines but is not the capital however. To get this we multiply the risk weight by the exposure and subsequently by the '8 per cent' factor, which rather confusingly is not always 8 per cent, but counterpart specific.

The details of the categories are as follows:

- OECD sovereigns receive a 0 per cent risk weight.
- OECD banks receive a 20 per cent risk weight. Then a 1.6 per cent charge on the notional.
- Undrawn loans receive a 50 per cent risk weight. If the funds are drawn, the bank would assign 100 per cent. These both attract an 8 per cent charge on the notional.
- For corporate debt and non-OECD sovereigns assign a 100 per cent risk weight, then an 8 per cent charge on the notional.

Basel II

The reason for this section is that the first Basel accord is approximate. So the issues addressed in this section will be an assessment of the shortcomings and further what is being done to correct it.

The Basel Accord of 1998 can be viewed as the mechanism of assigning capital against an individual obligation. The actual details of this were described in the previous section but in essence each asset is assigned a weight represented by a percentage, which is based upon their perceived credit risk. This weight is multiplied by the notional value of the exposure. If we just had one asset we would further multiply this number by 8 per cent, for example, then the final figure would represent the capital we must assign to guard against capital loss.

However the ultimate goal is to get the capital assigned against an entire portfolio, so we need to go from an asset to a portfolio. At this stage the temptation proved too great and the rule is enshrined in Basel I, 'add the individual weighted exposures'. So for practical purposes we do risk weight times notional outstanding then add this for each assets. We then multiply this figure by 8 per cent (as appropriate).

Hopefully by the stage you do not need your author's guidance on where, to be politically correct, the amendments should lie.

First, the risk weightings themselves are inconsistent; second, risk in a portfolio context as any good, or even bad, MBA student will inform you is not the sum of the individual exposures; third, what happens with maturity where presumably longer-dated loans have correspondingly larger credit risk?

Answers to these questions can either be considered to be a tweak or full-scale road works. The tweak was christened the standard approach and is a refinement on the risk bucketing approach that modifies the crude risk weights of the 1988 Capital Accord.

The standard approach stipulates risk weightings for bands as determined by the rating agencies. The weightings are shown in Table 2.17.

Now for the revolutionary piece, banks should base their capital assignment using an internal model. This is called the internal ratings-based approach. This approach is further split down into the foundation and advanced option. To provide an incentive for the bank the capital assigned using either of the IRB approaches is lower than the standard.

Assuming you wish to use the advanced model driven approach, the first question to arise will probably be what are the components of such a model? How do I get it to work? How can I insure that the model is recognized by the Committee on Banking Supervision?

Let us think of the elements of credit risk as the big three. The first of these is exposure, the second is the probability of default and then given a default what is my expected loss. Under the foundation approach we can use the Basel model for default probability estimates, and then apply our own exposures and collection amounts in the event of a loss.

The advanced approach enables the bank to use their own approach to model all three. All the regulatory authorities provide for us is the formula that transforms default probability and loss given default into the actual risk weights. It is quite a complicated formula and we now explore its foundation.

Table 2.17 Proposed Basel II standardized risk weights.

Obligor	AAA to AA−	A+ to A−	BBB+ to BBB−	BB+ to B−	Below B−	Unrated
Sovereigns	0%	20%	50%	100%	150%	100%
Banks 1*	20%	50%	100%	100%	150%	100%
Banks 2*	20%	50%	50%	100%	150%	50%
Corporates	20%	50%	100%	150%	150%	100%

* 1: based on risk weighting of sovereign in which the bank is incorporated, 2: based on assessment of a non-incorporated bank.

It is useful to know the composition of the formula because this will at least give you a deeper understanding of the nature of credit. The formula consists of three parts: an overall factor, a function which represents the systematic credit risk in the portfolio and an adjustment for loan maturity.

Technical detail of the models underlying the IRB

The model is an equation transforming estimates of default probabilities and loss, given a default into weightings upon which capital is assigned.

What is the origin of the equation? Well, as you might anticipate there are a plethora of approaches (we have covered their assumptions in Table 2.16). Within this section we take the opportunity to demonstrate how the various approaches are reconciled.

The approaches taken by the industry models are somewhat different. (JP Morgan and KMV base their estimates of default on methodology developed from standard option pricing theory, whereas McKinsey uses an econometric model. Finally Credit Suisse follows an actuarial approach.) Have some sympathy for our poor regulator. Rather unsurprisingly prior to Basel II the conclusion was drawn that portfolio modelling could not be applied to determine capital requirements of credit portfolios.

What then has changed? To cut a long story short a number of technical papers have demonstrated that in the case of one systematic risk factor the models are equivalent. The essence of this is that a simple formula exists that translates losses within a portfolio into a reserve requirement. Basel effectively calibrated the details.

What calibration has Basel performed? Recall the model's task is to provide the amount of tail risk present in a portfolio. Translated into English this means that the losses on a portfolio will be some shape or distribution. We are interested in the losses that occur causing a loss greater than the average. These will appear in a probability vs. loss diagram towards the far right. So we can think of it as the tail of that probability distribution.

So the first objective for Basel was to decide how much of the tail was relevant for extreme risk. They have set 50 basis points as the loss-level confidence. Once this assumption is used the risk weighting for capital is the following:

$$\text{Probability of tail} = N\left(\frac{\alpha + \sqrt{\text{correlation}} \times Z}{\sqrt{1 - \text{correlation}}}\right).$$

What is the origin of this equation? If our claim is that the various credit default modelling programmes are equivalent then we ought to be able to deduce this formula from the Credit Metrics framework. As we know from Section 6.2 we have a choice of probability measures including the so-called unconditional default probability which represents the chance that the issue will default over the next year (or user defined horizon) given no further information.

However for a realistic treatment we have to introduce the effects of the external environment that the company operates within. Hence the origin of the term conditional default probability which represents the chance that the issue will default over the horizon given relevant background information. The essence of this is that if growth or production is relatively bad then we would expect a higher chance of default.

We could treat a portfolio of obligors as a set of individual companies that may default independently, pair wise or higher order, then directly model these events on how they depend upon the external environment. The indirect approach is to treat each company using information about the capital structure.

Credit metrics produces default probabilities indirectly. The chance of a default is governed by the likelihood that the assets of the company fall below its debt .The probability of this can be implied from the volatility of the share price. This price is assumed to be log normally distributed and so it returns constitute a mapping from the return to default or non-default.

Correlation can be introduced between two companies, between a company and the external environment through a standard process, given by the formula below:

$$\begin{aligned}\text{Obligor return} &= \sqrt{\text{correlation}} \times \text{environment return} \\ &\quad + \sqrt{1 - \text{correlation}} \times \text{specific return.}\end{aligned}$$

The specific return is assumed to be the normal distribution beloved of the equity world. Now given the regulators, assume a fully diversified credit portfolio, we would not expect any variance due to the individual company within a so-called tail. (With reference to Section 6.1 we are now entering the realms of a single default probability which is applied to all of the loans.)

This means that the systematic loss distribution is just given by the sum over the individual obligors. We can write this as an equation below:

$$\sum_{\text{Loan}_i}^{\text{Loans}} \text{Expected loss } (\text{loan}_i) \times \text{probability of default (systematic factor)},$$

where expected loss is the loss given default. From the equation above in order to get the distribution of the extreme left we just need the distribution of the systematic factor towards the extreme left. Consequently the contribution of one of the loans to the total portfolio tail risk is often called the systematic risk contribution, given by the formula below:

$$\text{Systematic tail risk contribution} = \text{expected loss} \times \text{default of tail } (X_{99.5\%}).$$

Now the variable $X_{99.5\%}$ is just given by the standard inverse normal to 50 bps of confidence = 2.58. So the only question remains is to determine alpha, which is the probability that given an economic environment, the subsequent threshold return through which the company would be in default. The formula above implies this when the return is less than $(\alpha + \sqrt{\text{correlation}} \times 2.58)/\sqrt{1 - \text{correlation}}$, where α is the inverse normal of the default probability of the exposure under consideration.

Before we substitute the choice of values into the formula, then we arrive at the following:

$$\text{Systematic risk} = \text{exposure} \times N\left(\frac{\alpha + 2.58 \times \sqrt{\text{correlation}}}{\sqrt{1 - \text{correlation}}}\right).$$

(Where we assume the exposure is the loss given default.)

The committee chooses a correlation of 20 per cent and further we remove the total exposure because the object is to find a risk weight which is a percentage, consequently the formula becomes

$$\text{Systematic risk} = \text{scaling factor} \times N(1.12 \times \alpha + 1.29).$$

Using

$$\frac{1}{\sqrt{1 - \text{correlation}}} = 1.12$$

and

$$\frac{2.58 \times \sqrt{\text{correlation}}}{\sqrt{1 - \text{correlation}}} = 1.29$$

The scaling factor is specified by Basel II as 976.5, there is also an additional adjustment to address loans with a non-3-year maturity.

The scaling factor can be understood in terms of Basel I; recalling under the old scheme we would do the following:

$$\text{Systematic risk} = \frac{100}{0.08} \times 50\% = 625.$$

Consequently in order to reconcile between the two measures a figure of 976.5 was settled upon. The primary reason for the remaining difference is because of an extra-factor due to the so-called 'granularity adjustment'. This recognizes that most portfolios will not be fully diversified. This area is still under review at the time of writing. In conclusion the salient features of the model have been addressed, and given a default probability and an exposure the capital to be set aside will be given by,

$$\begin{aligned}\text{Systematic risk constribution} &= 976.5 \times \text{exposure} \\ &\quad \times N(1.12 \times N^{-1}(p) + 1.29).\end{aligned}$$

This applies to a very well diversified portfolio with an average default probability of p and a 3-year maturity. The default probability could be obtained through the banks own estimates.

References

Gupton, Finger and Bhatia, Credit Metrics™ – Technical Document, *Risk Metrics Group.*

Finger, Sticks and Stones, *Risk Metrics Group.*

Koyluoglu and Hickman, Reconcilable Differences, *Risk*, October 1998.

Phelan and Alexander, Different Strokes, *Risk*, October 1999.

Wilde, IRB Approach Explained, *Risk*, May 2001.

Asarnow and Marker, Historical Performance of the US Corporate Loan Market: 1998–1993, *The Journal of Commercial Lending*, Vol. 10, No. 2.

Rhodes *et al.*, Syndicated Lending, *Euromoney Publications.*

3

Credit derivatives

What are credit derivatives?

3.1 Introduction

Until quite recently undesirable credit exposure was one of the few remaining business risks for which no tailored risk-management product existed.

For example we consider the situation of the loan portfolio manager who originates business with the best intentions to make a profit. But what happens if he anticipates that one of the assets in his portfolio, that is a loan will no longer perform according to his original expectations?

The avenues open to him will consist of either selling the loan or possibly a portfolio management exercise consisting of diversifying the names. He may now also contemplate the wares of the credit derivative marketplace.

Other examples of commercial activities with systematic credit risk include insurance companies having commitments to provide financing involving low-grade credits; while everyone is familiar with the need for fund managers to enhance their yield through the active seeking of credit exposure.

These entities commonly employ more familiar derivatives to hedge exposure to variables they do not want to actively manage, usually either interest rates or foreign exchange rates. But whatever strategy is devised a credit element can sometimes remain. Traditionally derivative users have mitigated these risks by purchasing insurance, guarantees, or letters of credit. Often under a collateralized arrangement.

However these strategies are very inefficient simply because there is no separation of credit risk from the other components to which the asset is exposed.

For example if we consider a corporate bond, then it is apparent that we are exposed to a number of quite distinct risks. These include the interest rate risk, which may be hedged according to the duration measure, however convexity risk will remain. The bond may furthermore have a call attached.

Fixed income derivatives introduced the ability to manage the interest rate exposure as distinct from the other risks intrinsic to the asset.

The credit element within the bond can be broken down into two distinct components consisting of the default risk of the issuer, but further the chance of the bond losing value because of the widening in spreads between the issuer and the government funding rate.

Credit derivatives have now conferred the ability to manage credit exposure separately from the other characteristics of the bond. This is both true for default and credit spread risk.

Simply credit derivatives are bilateral arrangements whereby the credit risks are separated from the ownership of the financial asset and distributed to a party comfortable with the exposure. An important aspect of this process is a resulting efficiency gain because of the process of market completion due to the separation of credit risk from other risks. Credit derivatives allow the resulting credit exposure to be transferred even when the underlying asset is illiquid.

Credit derivatives are changing the way banks originate, manage and account for credit risk. But fundamentally their definition captures the properties of many instruments that have been hitherto available, including guarantees and letters of credit.

The marketplace for these flexible assets has grown hugely and continues to grow. Figure 3.1 displays the almost exponential growth associated with this market.

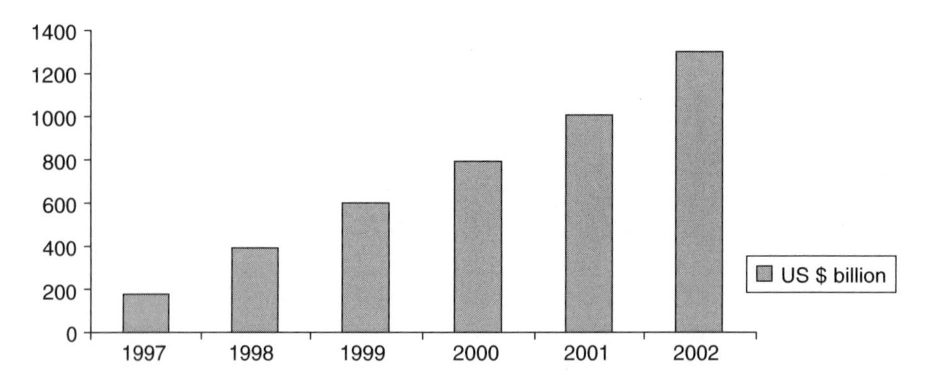

Figure 3.1 Credit derivative volumes 1997–2002. *Source:* Credit Trade.

3.2 Why use credit derivatives?

The significance of this new group of products is the precision by which they can isolate certain aspects of credit risk. There are several distinct characteristics which combine to make their success. We examine these in turn.

Confidentiality

The reference entity whose credit risk is being transferred need not be aware of the transaction; this enables banks and corporate treasurers to manage their credit risks without impacting important relationships. This also means that the terms of the credit derivative transaction can be customized to meet the needs of the counterparties rather than the underlying borrower. It is also to be believed that they introduce transparency and rigorous pricing into the marketplace. Consequently it can be argued that they form objective credit pricing benchmarks.

Shorting credit

Credit derivatives allow the user to go short credit. This is a major development because it has been hitherto impossible to sell the underlying in most types of credit exposure. For example we have already discussed the situation of the loan where underlying business relationships prejudice any attempt of the loan manipulation. Even in the bond markets it is practically very difficult to short the underlying because the bond is usually borrowed under a restrictive REPO arrangement.

The credit derivative market creates the economics of a short position. This is often called a 'synthetic short' and allows the user to reverse the asymmetric nature of credit exposure, whereby the user can lose a large amount in return for earning a small premium. Now with the advent of shorting you pay a small premium for the possibility of a large gain upon credit deterioration. One of the secondary aspects of this development is the possibility of a whole range of arbitrage opportunities involving credit.

Off balance sheet nature

Credit derivatives in common with most derivative structures are termed 'off balance sheet' which means the notional amount of the deal does not appear on either the asset or debit side of the ledger.

The appeal of this arrangement will depend on the cost of the balance sheet which is dependent on how the institution is funded. The more costly the item on the balance sheet the greater the appeal for an off balance sheet arrangement. For example it makes little sense for a bank with a speculative grade rating to loan money to an institution with a higher rating simply because the margin is disadvantageous. Even lending money to a poorer credit may not be attractive given the regulatory capital that needs to be set aside as a cushion.

However by taking exposure to loans using a credit derivative the bank can avoid both the financing and administrative costs of direct ownership. The degree of leverage achieved will depend on the amount of upfront collateral required by the counterparty.

Convention in the market

The typical arrangements in the marketplace can cause some confusion.

The buyer of protection is a seller of credit exposure and the seller of protection is a buyer of credit risk.

Thus if we consider a corporate bond where the owner requires protection, then he would be a seller of credit exposure since he would be immune to any deterioration in the issuer, by virtue of being long the underlying.

Definition of a credit derivative

A bilateral financial contract in which the buyer pays a premium in return for a contingent payment in the advent of a credit event.

3.3 Definition of a credit event

Credit derivatives are negotiated transactions and because of this the market development has been hindered by the absence of standard documentation containing strictly defined legal terminology. This problem has been addressed by the International Swaps and Derivative Association (ISDA) which issued a standardized Long Form Confirmation in 1998 and more recently (July 1999) new definitions encompassed within the Short Form Confirmation. We list below the ISDA specified credit events.

The user of a credit derivative must be aware that the instrument does not always provide protection against either market related 'events' that lead to a spread widening (and consequent losses for bondholders) or to rating downgrades.

Table 3.1 ISDA credit derivatives definitions source.

1999 ISDA credit derivatives definitions:

- *Failure to pay:* shortfall relative to that required (typically $1 million); allowance is made for administrative error. A grace period may be extended
- *Bankruptcy:* corporate is unable to pay its debts
- *Repudiation/moratorium:* the reference entity challenges, or rejects, their obligations. This provision applies only to sovereign entities
- *Restructuring:* modification of the debt obligations of the reference entity
- *Obligation acceleration/default:* payment on an obligation has been made earlier than necessary due to default, or similar condition (the aggregate amount of obligations must exceed $10 million).

Source: ISDA.

A credit event is most commonly defined as the occurrence of one or more of the following:

- Failure to pay
- Bankruptcy (for non-sovereign borrowers)
- Repudiation/moratorium
- Restructuring
- Obligation acceleration/default.

The first two and restructuring apply to corporates, while all, except bankruptcy, are applicable to emerging markets and governments. For an explanation of the terms please refer to Table 3.1.

ISDA Credit derivative policy

ISDA credit derivative definitions are shown in Table 3.1.

3.4 Credit default swap

The basic structure in the marketplace, very much like an insurance arrangement (Figure 3.2).

The buyer of protection, in return for a periodic fee, receives a contingent payment dependent upon any credit event undergone by the name upon which the swap was based. These arrangements are typically used by banks wishing to protect themselves against any adverse movements within their lending portfolios. Typically the sellers of so-called 'protection' will include leveraged funds. Typically there may not be a liquid 'cash' asset on which they wish to gain exposure. The premium received will be characteristic of such a proxy asset.

A credit default swap is a contract comprising the exchange of a fee for a one-off payment in the event of a credit default. There are no limits on either the size or maturity of a credit default swap (CDS) contract.

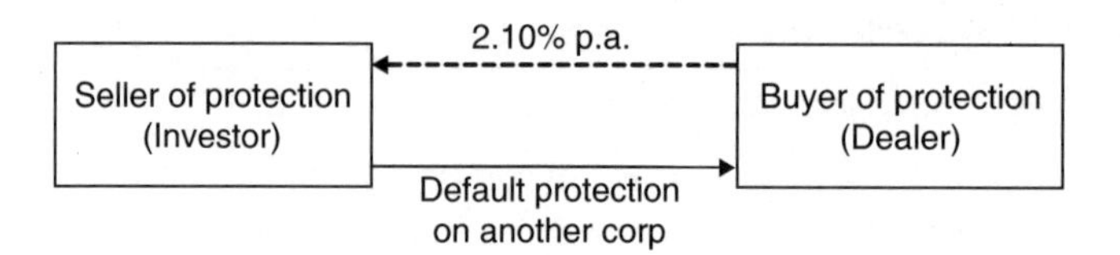

Figure 3.2 Mechanics of a CDS.

In general, however, deals are typically struck on a notional of between $10 and $20 million and with a maturity range of between 1 and 10 years. Five year maturities tend to be the most common. This instrument together with the total return swap, which we will encounter later, hedges both default and 'spread' risk. The premium payable is a function of the perceived credit worthiness of the reference and as such can be hedged prior to maturity.

Sometimes the arrangement is referred to as an 'upfront default swap'. This would be the case for distressed credits where the fee is paid upfront. The premium is usually paid over time, however, similar to the more conventional interest rate swap. The premium is typically payable quarterly on an Act/360 basis.

If a 'credit event' occurs then the seller of protection, in the case of cash settlement, gives the buyer of protection a terminating payment and the contract lapses. The precise details of this credit event are covered in the documentation. The terminating payment will be the difference between par and the recovery value of the asset. We have described cash settlement, it is increasingly the situation that physical settlement is adopted whereby the buyer delivers the defaulted asset and receives par from the seller of protection.

The premium that the seller receives is close to the compensation over and above the risk free rate that an investor would receive on a bond issued by the same credit. It is standard to take libor as the reference for risk free borrowing. The investor would receive an interest rate spread relative to the risk free rate to compensate them for bearing this extra credit risk. Replication arguments discussed in Section 3.11 demonstrate that the asset swap margin of a *par bond* is similar to the credit default swap premia.

Protection can be commonly purchased on a bond or loan, but also on the counterparty credit exposure within a standard interest rate derivative. The protection can be linked up to an individual name or a basket of credits.

Table 3.2 shows some typical features associated with a default swap contract, the terms will be available in the so-called 'term sheet' which sets out the details of the trade to provide transparency.

Table 3.2 The term sheet of a default swap.

Detail	Example
Default protection buyer	European bank
Default protection seller	Insurance company
Reference obligation	ABC Corporate 7% June 2010
Currency	Euro
Buyer pays	100 bps on a quarterly Act/360 basis
Final maturity	5 years
Trade date	Today
Effective date	Trade date + one calender day
Seller pays upon credit event	Physical delivery of asset for par
Credit event	See Table 3.1
Documentation	Standard ISDA agreement
Notional	$100 million

3.5 Total return swap

TRORs represent an off balance sheet transaction, they are becoming less common in the market.

The arrangement on this instrument is rather similar to a hire arrangement. Whereby the lessee receives the benefits without paying the upfront price of the asset she is enjoying. This analogy can be taken further. The consumer will be expected to pay any costs because of damage to the equipment.

Returning to the financial world while this analogy is still clear in our memory, the asset is some type of financial security usually a bond. The lessee is usually called an investor because she enjoys all the cash flow benefits from the security without actually owning the security. She would be said to receive the TROR. However the dark side of this arrangement is that she should make good any decline in price. This makes clear the advantage to the leaser, or TROR payer. Who would have the underlying asset on their balance sheet. They are now protected against both adverse movements of the market and adverse credit developments.

The total return payer passes the total return of the security to the receiver. The payment is often based on a floating rate reference such as libor and the asset can either be a bond, loan, equity receivables or even a payment linked to an index.

The total return payer holds the reference asset on its balance sheet for the duration of the transaction and it will have created a short position in both the credit risk and market risk of the asset by virtue of selling the 'TROR' and so the net position is neutral.

Figure 3.3 shows the payments associated with this instrument.

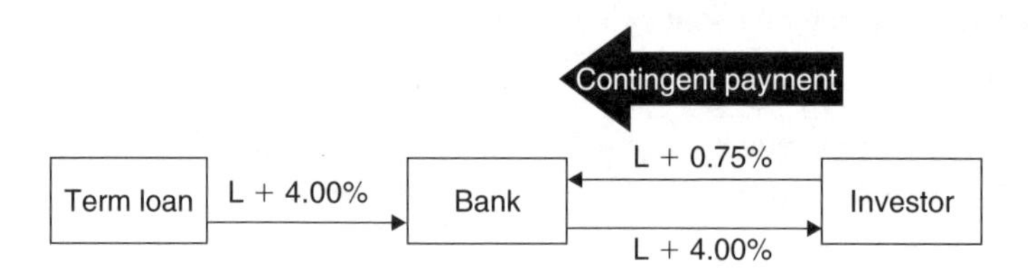

Figure 3.3 TROR payments.

Table 3.3 The term sheet of a TROR.

Detail	Example
Total return payer	European bank
Total return receiver	Investment manager
Issuers	Company A
Interest payable	L + 30 bps
Final maturity	10 years
Trade date	Today
Payer pays	All cash flows on the reference FRN
Receiver pays	Premium based on a spread to libor
Termination payment	Notional × (100% − market value/100)*
Termination trigger	Publicly available information of a credit event
Calculating agent	Total return payer
Documentation	Standard ISDA agreement
Notional	$100 million

*If positive, the receiver will make this payment; if negative, the receiver will be in receipt.

TROR term sheet

Table 3.3 shows the typical features associated with a TROR, this is the so-called 'term sheet' which lays out the details of the trade for reasons of transparency.

Settlement

There are three ways of settling the TROR instrument:

- If a credit event occurs on the reference asset then a contingency payment is made equal to the difference between the original price and the recovery value. The difficulty here is the possibility of not being able to price. In which case the documentation must allow for the substitution of the price on a reference asset of comparable credit quality.

- Other methods include the protection buyer having to make a physical delivery of the obligation in return for payment of the face amount. The contract usually allows any one of a basket of obligations to be delivered. These are said to be ranked 'Pari-passu' because they have the same value on liquidation as a consequence of having an equal claim on the assets of the entity.
- More rarely the counterparties can fix the contingent payments in advance – this is known as binary settlement.

The total return receiver has a synthetic long asset. The term synthetic is employed because the investor is receiving the proceeds from the security just as if he owned it. At the maturity date of the security the receiver gets the difference in market value of the asset if positive, and pays if this is negative. In the event of a default prior to the maturity date of the TROR, then the agreement terminates and the receiver compensates the payer.

The total return receiver is said to make the payer 'whole' for the credit and market risk of the instrument. Either the investor can pay the difference between the original price of the instrument and the current market price or he can take delivery of the defaulted reference asset and pay the buyer of protection the original price as compensation. Once either of these arrangements has occurred then the TROR terminates.

TRORs are often compared with a REPO arrangement, the reader should be wary of adopting this analogy. In a REPO arrangement one party agrees to sell securities in exchange for cash and repurchase the securities at a pre-specified price in the future. Obviously the seller has to pay interest on the cash for the duration of the agreement, the so-called REPO rate. Contrast this with a TROR where the receiver is not obligated to purchase the assets. Further there is no pre-arranged price for the reference asset at the maturity of the transaction.

The primary use of TRORs is that of financing positions. Indeed for most arrangements the net cash flow from the receiver's perspective, subtracting the floating payments from the received income is positive. This is a marvellous arrangement. The investor enters an agreement and receives a positive payment. Table 3.4 shows the return on the deal for various types of investors.

There are other benefits which we list below:

- The maturity of the synthetic asset can be tailored.
- Higher returns on capital because of their off balance sheet nature.
- Reduction of administrative costs.
- Exposure to a desired asset class, such as a loan, which otherwise would be denied.

Table 3.4 The economic returns for a TROR.

	Leveraged fund	Institution
Asset yield	10.5%	10.5%
Funding cost	9%	
Collateral	5%	
Leverage	10	1
Leverage return	15% (product of leverage with the return net of funding)	10.5%

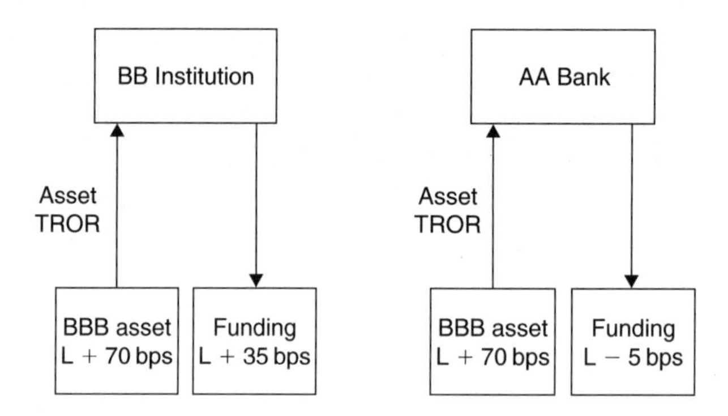

Figure 3.4 A TROR funding application.

Benefits to the payer:

- Investors unable to short securities can hedge a long position through paying the TROR.
- Long-term investors who feel the assets may underperform in the short term may enter into a TROR that has a shorter maturity than the asset.
- Benefits in some accounting regimes – losses can be deferred without risking further loss. Again the maturity of the TROR is less than the asset.

Funding opportunities

The sequence of Figures 3.4–3.6 illustrate how two parties can have comparative advantages by entering into a TROR swap. Either could directly buy the asset, but this would not be particularly attractive to the BB bank because of its high-financing cost. The AA bank on the other hand has an asset with a large credit risk. By entering the swap the BB has a better spread on the asset and the AA has a stronger credit on its balance sheet. In Figure 3.4 we illustrate the deal from each perspective.

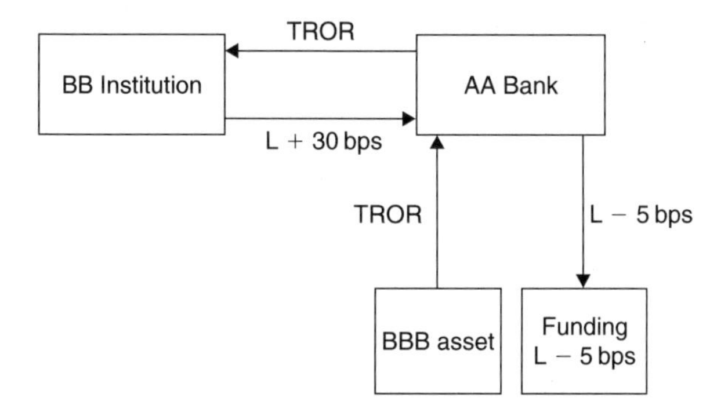

Figure 3.5 The bank enters a TROR.

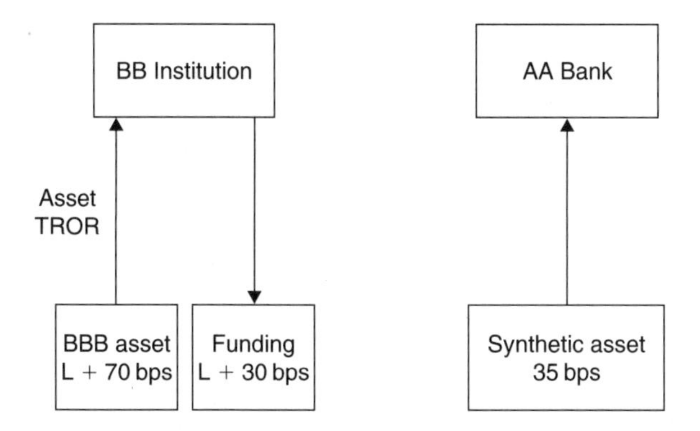

Figure 3.6 The net financing arrangement within the TROR.

Figure 3.5 shows the TROR transacted between the bank and the institution. This arrangement is financially the same as being 'long' the asset in the individual cases. However a significant advantage is now conferred, providing the asset and the BB institution have a low default correlation.

Finally Figure 3.6 illustrates the 'synthetic' asset for each counterparty. The institution has an unfunded asset as in Figure 3.4, but the periodic financing is five basis points cheaper. While the bank has a high-quality credit on its books; with a higher rating than the original asset.

3.6 Securitization overview

In this section we wish to introduce an important application of credit derivatives within the context of securitization, we are furthermore going to use the investment management business as an example. In order to achieve this some background is required on securitization in general.

The phrase CDO is a generic expression applied to any securitization backed by a pool of debt, usually bonds and/or loans. There are two main categories, the cash flow and the arbitrage.[1] The distinction is made on the basis of collateral backing and motivation. CDO issuance constitutes a major activity within continental Europe, indeed comparable to other varieties of ABS. The term arbitrage arises because a vehicle is established in order to benefit from the funding gap which may temporarily exist between the assets, typically high-yield bonds and the liabilities, typically investment grade bonds. This has to be positive for the viability of the vehicle.

The cash flow CDO is employed by banks to remove assets from their balance sheet. The backing consists of loans no longer profitable because of regulatory reasons. The arbitrage CDO is issued by a portfolio manager purchasing backing in the secondary market. The resulting structure is typically sold to institutional investors. There are many advantages to the manager including the ability to grow assets under management.

Both CDOs have similar structures consisting of asset backing, the creation of a bankruptcy remote vehicle (SPV) and the structuring of the liabilities appealing to the net end investor. When the backing is mainly bonds the CDO is referred to as a CBO, with loans the term CLO is used. These arrangements are addressed in Section 7 within the chapter on securitization. We also give examples of the synthetic CLO, where credit derivatives are employed by banks wishing to seek regulatory relief. In this section we wish to focus on the use of credit derivatives within the investment management community.

An important development in the market has been the inception of the investment grade CDO. This represents a new type of mandate for the investment manager. The phraseology is misleading because the collateral is a combination of assets including investment grade bonds or loans. The benefits are considerable, and in common with the traditional arbitrage variety include the opportunity to grow assets and consequently the fee base but further to leverage the existing expertise. There are three alternatives: traditional 'cash flow' CDO's using investment grade bonds as the collateral; a fully synthetic market value CDO which instead of having a tangible instrument backing the indenture rely on the cash flows from credit derivatives and finally a market value hybrid consists of a combination of credit derivatives and cash bonds

[1] The arbitrage CDO is further divided into the *cash flow* and *market value* categories. The basis of distinction is that cash flows are used to pay principal in the former while receipts from sales on the collateral provide the principal repayments in the latter. This implies that the manager can freely trade the backing in the market.

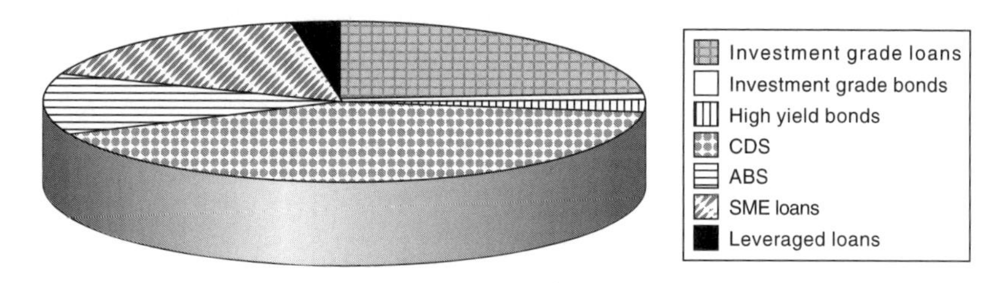

Figure 3.7 Backing for European CDO in 2002. *Source:* Dresdner Kleinwort Wasserstein.

to supply the backing. Having swallowed these details the reasoning for the mushrooming of styles will be now be elaborated upon.

The advantages of the traditional arbitrage CDO must be balanced with the obvious shortcoming represented by the somewhat fleeting nature of the arbitrage and yet another piece of phraseology coined the 'ramp up period'. This sounds intimidating and it refers to the period when the physical assets that will be contained in the vehicle are collected. Due to these constraints managers often plump for the synthetic deal type, in particular they do not suffer from any 'ramp up' exposures because assets do not have to be physically assembled. Furthermore the arbitrage is easier to maintain, they do however require familiarity with the credit derivatives marketplace. Also the risks may be more than pure default risk.

The majority of investment grade deals have an average credit quality of around A to BBB− for collateral consisting of corporate bonds. We discussed above, because of the difficulty of capturing arbitrage for any extended period, additional asset classes must be included. Figure 3.7 shows a typical breakdown by asset category.

The choice of collateral is not straightforward and will generally be made with due consideration to at least three major factors including the amount of diversity the asset class can introduce, its liquidity and possibly the outlook for the sector. Diversity is key to the performance of the resulting securities that are issued; otherwise a seemingly isolated credit event could cause premature repayment, or worse, if the portfolio is inadequately constructed. It is part of the task of the rating agencies to assess and quantify this aspect of the deal. Liquidity is also very important given the short-term nature of the arbitrage. It is necessary to have the ability to exit at all times. We can examine each of the asset categories in these contexts; *high yield* is a much smaller marketplace in Europe, issuance is quite small and furthermore it also suffers from being quite concentrated towards the telecom sector. This places strong reservations on the appropriateness. *Leveraged loans* on

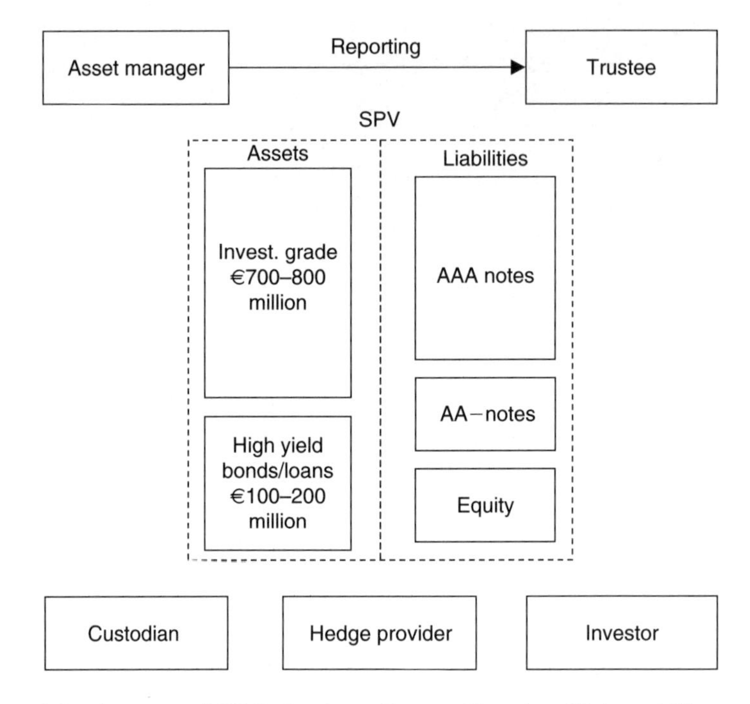

Figure 3.8 A managed CDO structure. *Source:* Dresdner Kleinwort Wasserstein.

the other hand are much more diverse and enjoy a better spread for a comparative rating. They are usually difficult to source and reinvestment into an equivalent asset could pose a challenge. *Asset-backed* securities also offer good diversity but suffer from a lack of a developed secondary market within Europe. *Emerging market* paper is quite broad in terms of credit quality but has restricted European denominated issuance. Unfortunately this sector suffers from a contagion factor. Bank capital is a distinct source, enjoying a yield pick up relative to senior bank debt but is less liquid usually denominated in small trading sizes of less than 10 million Euros.

A typical managed CDO structure

Instead of taking a standard approach and drawing lots of arrows we attempt to explain the operation of the CDO illustrated in Figure 3.8 by discussion. Firstly the 'asset manager' will contract with the equity provider (or the 'investor') in the above diagram. Usually this is arranged through the investment banking community who also undertake the hedging arrangement, that is the 'hedge provider'. At an opportune moment in the market the manager starts collecting assets initiating the 'ramp up period', the risk of this period is held by the 'investor' and

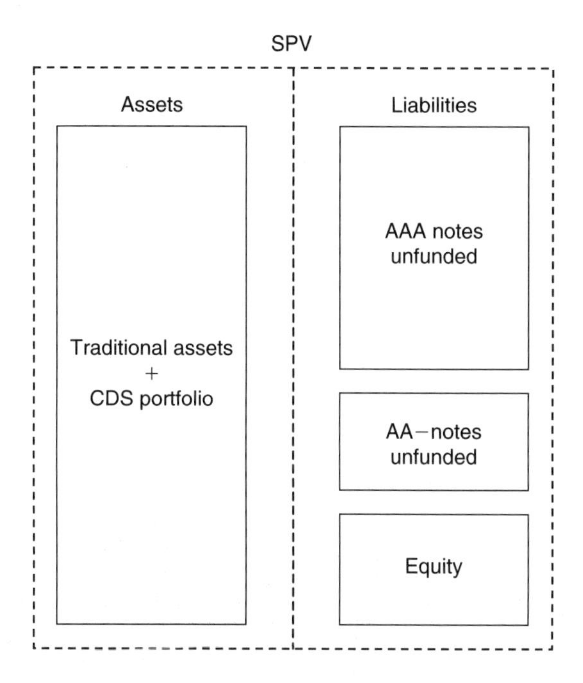

Figure 3.9 A synthetic CDO.

is purchased with a bridge loan from the arranger. After the assets are collected, they are transferred into the 'company' which is a separate legal entity and held by the custody bank. Securities are then issued into the marketplace and the equity is issued. The certificates are held by the Trustee, who deals with the administrative aspects of the company. At this point the loan is paid off to the bank from the proceeds. Finally because the assets are usually fixed coupon and represent a potential currency exposure, there will be an interest rate (and possibly forex) hedge between the vehicle and the 'hedge provider'.

The synthetic CDO

We can introduce a synthetic deal into the context of this discussion. The basic organizational arrangement remains the same but the structure of the company or trust alters, we can examine this in Figure 3.9.

Effectively the 'physical' collateral has been replaced by a set of credit derivatives, usually default swaps on the underlying credits. The stream of protection premia flows into the partially funded indenture. This means that the investor does not have to supply capital. There are a distinct number of advantages to this arrangement including the comparative rapidity of the time to market and the ease which the positions

Table 3.5 The characteristics of the collateral.

Characteristic	Value
Pool size	€1 000 000 000
Number of assets	100
Number of obligors	100
Moody's diversity score	47
Average pool rating	A–
Average life of pool	6 years
Average pool spread	181 bps
Largest single obligor	1%
Largest industry concentration	12% Utilities
	10% Telecoms
	9% Construction

can be traded. Consequently there is a movement towards managed synthetic CDOs, although at present most are static. The example displayed in Figure 3.9 is more relevant to the types of structure involving the fund management community. It is increasingly common for banks to take out protection on each of the individual tranches and manage the risk accordingly.

Collateral quality

Examining the collateral is one of the critical ingredients to the success of a managed CDO. We begin by presenting the characteristics of a typical pool.

The measure that will require a little elaboration is the concept of the diversity score which is widely used within the industry, so it is worth the effort and is discussed in detail in Section 6.7.

Consider the portfolio, in Table 3.5, and assume for one moment that the one hundred assets are independent and consequently have correlation of zero, what would be the default characteristics of the portfolio? It turns out to have an expected loss of the default probability multiplied by the recovery rate and loss distributed binomially around this average. Increasing the correlation both 'skews' and creates more losses in the 'tail'. In the extreme case where all the assets are 100 per cent correlated, the portfolio either defaults or it does not. Thus the distribution is composed of two spikes. In Figure 3.10 we illustrate the effect this has on each tranche consisting of a junior taking the first 10 per cent of the losses, a mezzanine the next 10 per cent and a senior receiving the final 80 per cent.

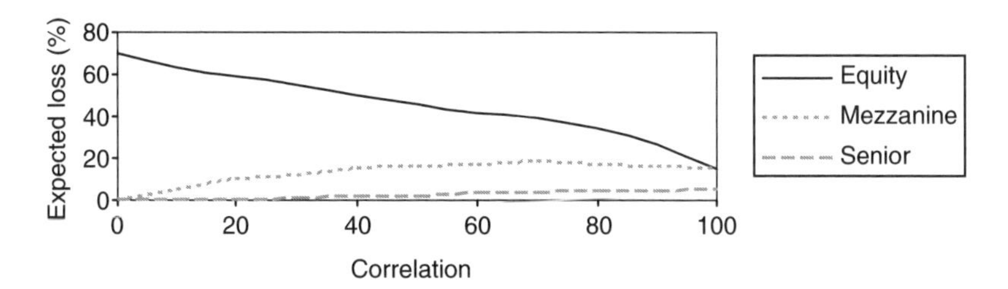

Figure 3.10 Tranche loss as a function of default correlation. *Source:* Lehman Brothers.

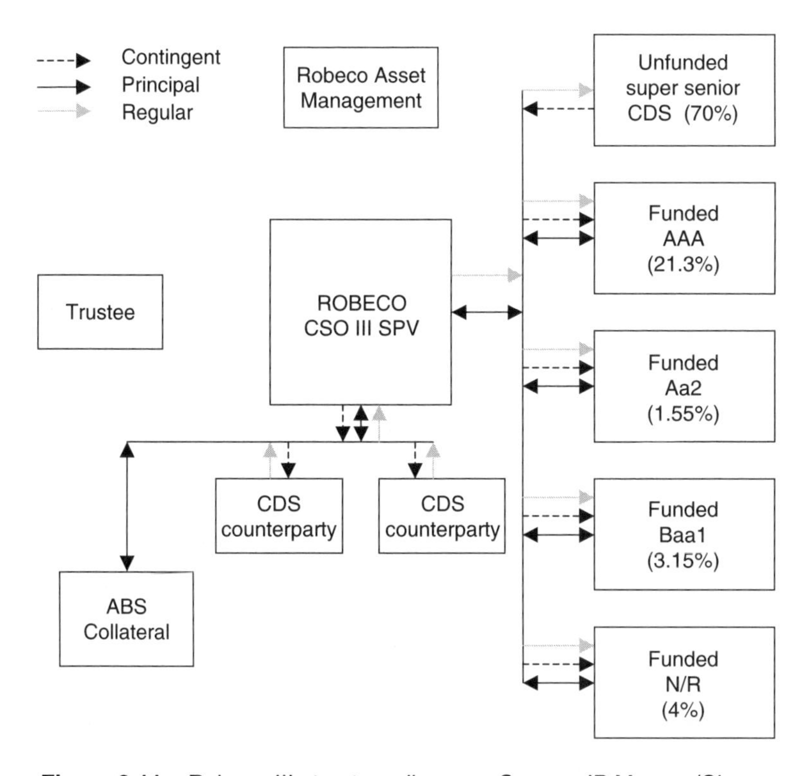

Figure 3.11 Robeco III structure diagram. *Source:* JP Morgan/Chase.

When no correlation is present, the losses are entirely contained within the equity tranche, which can be very high depending on the size of the equity tranche and the credit quality of the portfolio. In our example with backing having default probability of 14 per cent and recovery value of 50 per cent corresponds to an expected loss of 7 per cent, thus in the case of zero correlation up to 70 per cent of the equity would be lost. At the other extreme of all assets fully correlated, the portfolio behaves as just one asset. However the senior debt is differentiated by having a claim on the recovery value. If this is high then it implies the

Table 3.6 Note tranche summary.

Class	Amount	Per cent	Rating	Type	Coupon
Class A	213	21.30%	AAA	Floating	3 million euribor + 55 bps
Class B	15.5	1.55%	Aa2	Floating	3 million euribor + 85 bps
Class C	31.5	3.15%	Ba1	Floating	3 million euribor + 275 bps
Subordinated	40	4.00%	NR	Variable	
Class P	7.5		Ba1	Variable	

Source: JP Morgan/Chase.

expected loss is very low as a fraction of its notional. In our example the maximum loss is restricted to 30 per cent of the senior tranche and a correspondingly lower fraction of the face value.

The mezzanine portion is more difficult to evaluate, and a model of default is required. We give an example of such a structural-based model in Section 4.9.

In Figure 3.11 we display a managed synthetic CDO. This is representative of a 'third generation' CDO in the sense of mixing both cash and synthetic assets. In this particular example the backing partially consisted of asset-backed securities serving as collateral on the senior notes. Additionally there is an interest guarantee arrangement taken out through a third party. The additional 'assets' consist of the premia from credit default swaps. The underlying references are freely traded by the manager. The other noteworthy point is that the resulting liabilities consist of funded notes, listed in Table 3.6. The unfunded portion is referred to as a 'super senior CDS' consisting of a credit default swap.

3.7 Dynamic credit swaps

One of the difficulties of managing credit risk within the traditional interest rate derivative world is that the exposure to the counterparty itself varies. This increases the potential volatility of the transaction from a credit perspective considerably, which is determined in a dual manner. Firstly, the deal is valued on a mark to market basis, then the total future replacement cost is established. These aspects depend purely on the existing and forward values of market variables and their volatilities. To this must be added an assessment of the credit migration of the counterparty. We deal with the standard methodologies in more detail within the chapter on the credit risk of libor instruments. But just to emphasize the potential exposure and credit evolution could be correlated, such a transaction is known within the marketplace as a 'wrong way swap'.

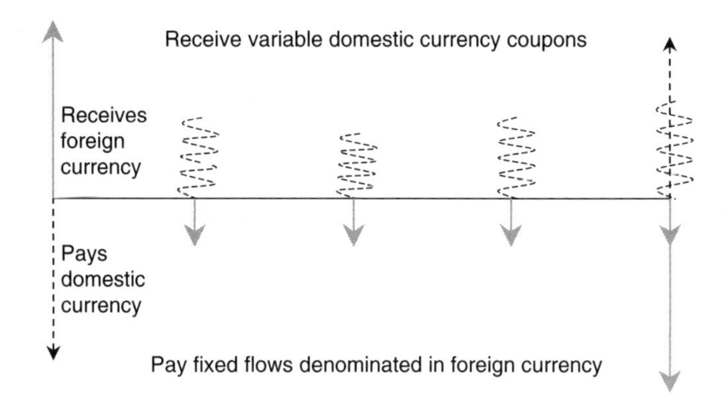

Figure 3.12 The currency swap.

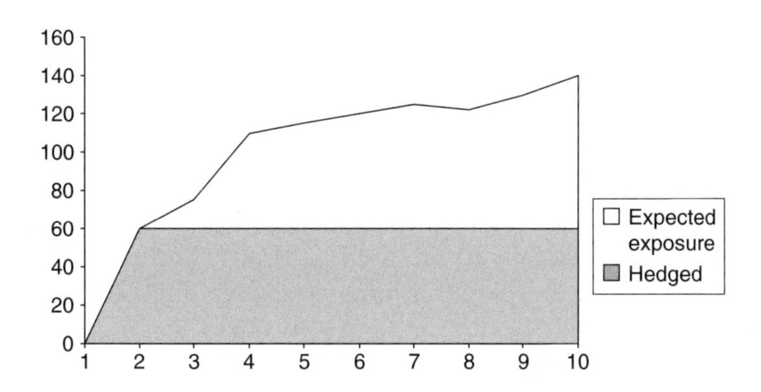

Figure 3.13 Counterparty credit exposure on a currency swap $ million.

Ideally the credit protection must be variable. For example if you transact a currency swap, then the cash flows are shown in Figure 3.12.

The currency swap consists of an exchange of payments. Usually one is a fixed amount and the other is a floating quantity but the payments are denominated in different currencies. There is usually an exchange of principals.

The current exposure to the counter party is just the present value of the deal; this is determined by pricing the two legs using the relevant time value of money structure for each of the currencies, then converting the foreign value into the domestic currency using the prevailing exchange rate.

However taking the present value of the swap is not sufficient to evaluate counterparty risk because we also have to address the potential value of the swap in the future. This analysis is called determining the replacement cost for the instrument, because if the counter party defaults then you have to replace the swap.

Within Figure 3.13, we show the projected exposure of the deal 10 years into the future. At the deal outset the value was zero, however as time evolved the foreign currency weakened and interest rates dropped. Consequently the counter party exposure has increased considerably. It is possible to take out a dynamic credit swap whereby the notional protection is linked to the marked to market value of the reference swap. A protection buyer only pays a fixed fee agreed at the outset, a more cost effective solution might be to take out protection on a certain amount of this anticipated exposure. This is illustrated in the diagram above where the losses are hedged at 60 million.

3.8 Credit options

Credit options are either put or call options on the price of a bond, floating-rate note, loan or asset swap. The first question that may occur to you is the nature of an asset swap?

We mentioned it in Section 1.8 purely as an arrangement used by a borrower to convert from fixed to a floating liability. However let us understand it in terms of the motivations of the so-called 'asset swap' investor; who seeks exposure to a credit, because they are bullish on the name. The way to exploit this opportunity would be to purchase one of the financial assets of the company, in this case a bond. However if the company only has fixed rate debt outstanding upon purchasing the bond the investor will have both credit and interest rate exposure. He may wish to hedge the rate risk, this can be achieved through an asset swap. The bond is purchased and the fixed coupons are passed to the counterparty, who in turn pays the investor a floating amount.

Figure 3.14 shows the resulting cash flows.

The net result is that the investor still has the credit exposure he requires, but is not too exposed to any interest rate risk.

The end result of the asset swap from the investors perspective is shown in Figure 3.15 (*note*: there is an extra margin which the counterparty pays, as usually the bond and libor have a different credit standing, the investor for bearing the full credit risk if the bond defaults). The obligation entails maintaining the fixed and redemption payments to the counterparty, hence the compensating payment.

In the case of a credit put option the option buyer has the right but not the obligation to sell to the option seller the reference asset at a pre-specified price. The converse is true for a call. Settlement may be on a cash or physical basis.

We illustrate an option exercisable into an FRN (Figure 3.16). (The asset swap goes through in the same manner, but upon exercise the holder receives the floating payment plus the spread.)

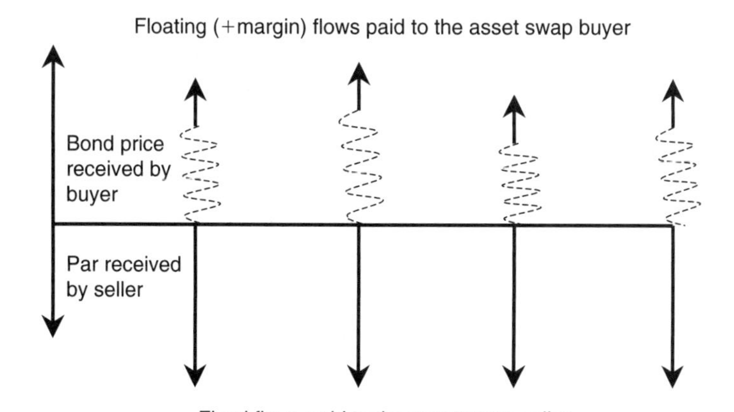

Figure 3.14 The cash flows of an asset swap.

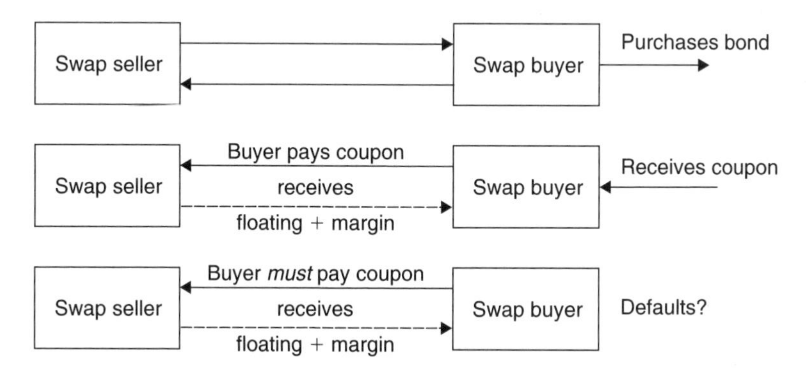

Figure 3.15 The net cash flows of an asset swap.

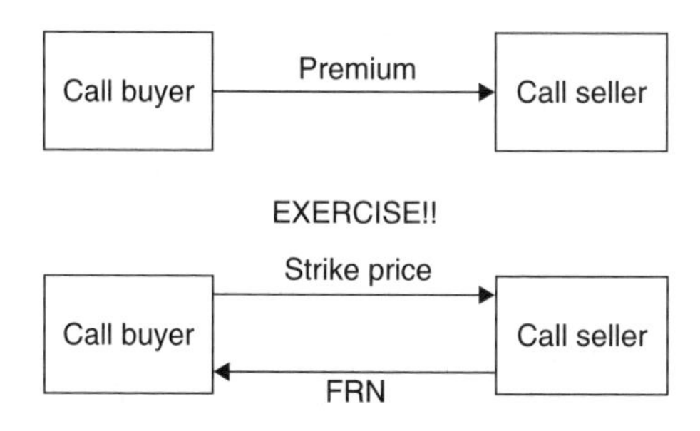

Figure 3.16 The credit call option.

Here the call buyer pays a premium for the right to buy the FRN at a specified reference price. The buyer in the event of exercise receives floating libor plus a pre-determined spread, which is the strike spread.

The option premium in common with other options depends on the volatility of this underlying spread.

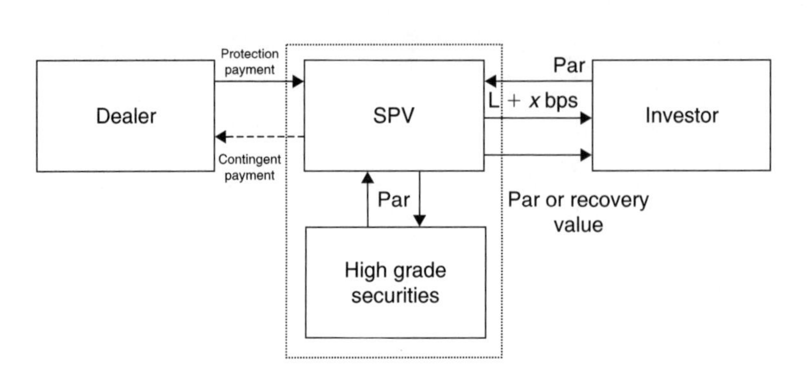

Figure 3.17 Note issued by SPV.

Credit options have strong appeal to institutional investors as a source of yield enhancement, generating exposure to a credit where the bond is unavailable – the investor is short a credit collecting income in return for the risk of losing an asset in the future (in the case of a call).

Other users of credit options are banks and dealers who seek to hedge their marked to market exposure to variations in credit spreads. As these institutions run leveraged balance sheets the off balance sheet nature of the position created by a credit option is attractive.

3.9 Credit linked note

Credit linked notes (or CLNs) allow exposure to a credit in funded form. It seems to the investor like a conventional credit bond. But behind the façade is a subtle piece of financial engineering. They are commonly packaged within the debt issued by an SPV (Figure 3.17). The vehicle enters into a default swap arrangement with a counterparty buying protection. This resulting premium is passed on to the investor who consequently has an enhanced yield relative to the risk free rate. The SPV uses the funding to secure collateral. In the event of a credit event the collateral is used to make the compensating payment to the protection buyer. The investor bears the credit risk on both the reference entity and the collateral.

3.10 First to default

These types of credit derivatives have increased in popularity mainly due to the fact that the investor can leverage their credit exposure,

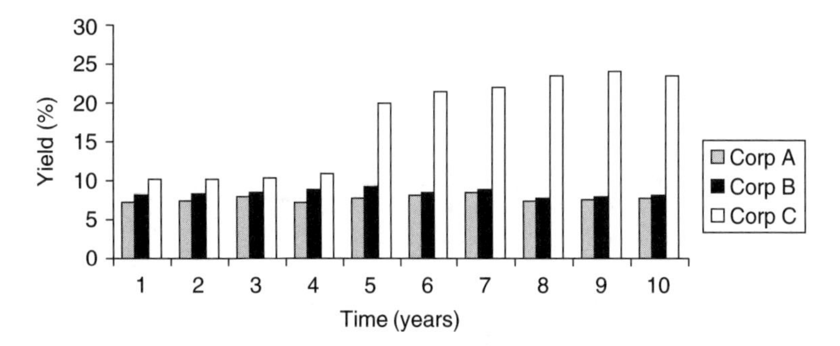

Figure 3.18 The yields on three companies (% vs. Time).

without increasing their downside beyond the first name that defaults. Further the premium received will usually be much higher than selling protection on just one name. A very recent development has been the supply of index swaps, which pay the return received on a standard index in return for a floating periodic payment. These are obviously popular enabling an unfunded exposure to a wide variety of, potentially, diverse credits.

A first to default note will consist of exposure to a number of credits with the size being the notional at stake. After the first credit event the note terminates and the investor must pay the protection seller either a compensating one-of-payment (cash settlement). Or receive the 'damaged basket' and make good the difference between this and par.

In Figure 3.18 the note is written on the three corporates whose yields are depicted in the figure. We can see that Corp C defaults which would trigger settlement.

The note will either be cash settled or physically settled in which case the owner of protection will deliver the damaged asset in return for par. This is often the case for first to default notes issued by an SPV. The amount for cash settlement is the difference between par and the final price of the reference obligation.

The yield that the investor receives on a first to default spread note will be somewhere between the spread of the worst individual credit and the sum of the spreads on all. This will be close to the sum of spreads if the correlation is low and vice versa for high correlation. The reason for this is that in the case of no correlation the portfolio will have the properties of a sum of individuals while if they are all correlated they effectively behave as the worst asset. Figure 3.19 shows the first to default spread curve and how it depends on correlation. The first to default spread is equal to the worst in the case where the correlation is equal to 100 per cent.

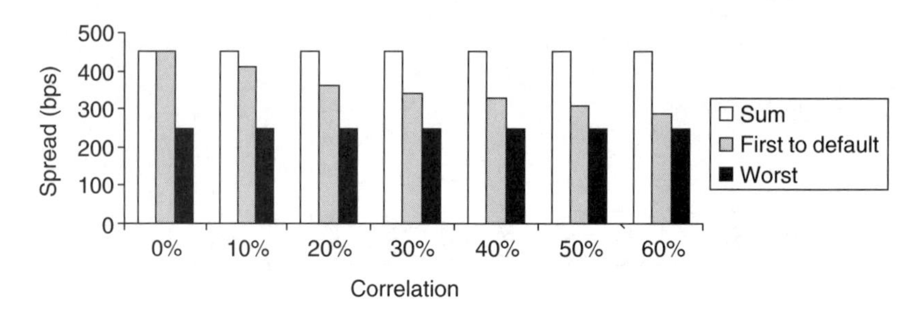

Figure 3.19 The first to default note bps against correlation.

The premium payable on a first to default is primarily dependent on:

1. The number of names in the basket
2. The spread of the names
3. The degree of correlation between the names
4. The recovery rates.

The joint probability of default cannot be given through a closed form expression. Instead we must rely on numerical procedures. A number of dealers use the Copula methodology described in Section 6.6. This considers each of the assets to have a marginal distribution, which are joined together to produce the overall portfolio distribution, the higher moments of this resultant distribution will generate the joint default probability and thus enable a premium to be set.

3.11 The default swap basis

The credit derivatives market has created a number of relative value opportunities. Diverging slightly from our credit theme, relative value is a term traditionally employed to describe strategies predominantly within the fixed income marketplace which are not directional in nature. For example if you buy a bond out right you are taking a view on yields. You either make or loose money depending on the direction that the yield changes. To exploit a relative value opportunity however, you would short a bond and from the proceeds buy another bond so you are neutral with regard to the direction of the market (usually only duration is hedged). The hope is to gain from a change in shape from the existing yield curve.

The default swap basis is the spread between a bond and the premium demanded by the market for credit protection on the bond. We would expect a strong relationship between these two spreads but often this

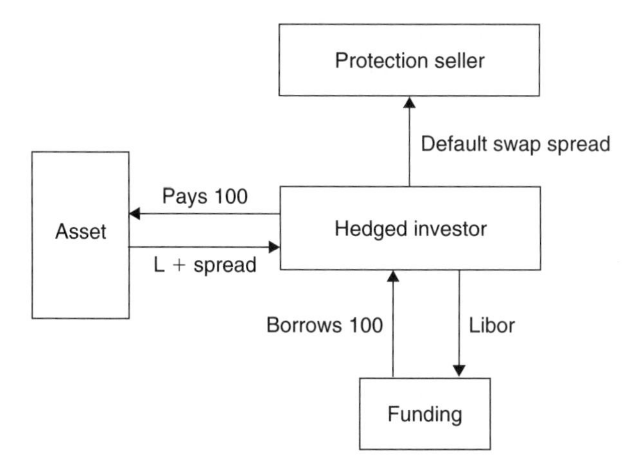

Figure 3.20 The risk free basis trade. *Source:* Lehman.

can breakdown, the relative value default swap trade seeks to exploit these opportunities. There are two ways of exploiting this difference the first is the long basis trade in which the investor buys the assets and simultaneously buys protection. The converse is a short basis trade in which the investor sells the asset and simultaneously sells protection.

Long basis trade

There are a number of ways of going along the basis for a particular credit, the choice to a certain extent will depend on the types of instruments the borrower has issued into the market. We begin with an analysis of a basis trade which is carried out by purchasing a par FRN and protection. This will illustrate the relationship between the spread on the floater and the default protection premium. From Figure 3.20 we can see that the default spread is equal to the asset swap spread when the asset is at par.

Buying protection

If an investor wishes to be immunized against the default of the issuer there are a number of assumptions which must be considered prior to constructing the hedge. It is not a simple case of sourcing protection, but rather the details depend on the nature of the underlying asset. We consider the case of a common example; an asset swap on a vanilla bond. (The motivation and arrangement of this have been discussed in some depth within Section 3.8.)

Table 3.7 The payoff for a hedger of protection.

An asset swapped bond with credit protection				
Component	Bond	Swap	Funding	CDS
Entry	– Price	– (100 – Price)	100	0
Immediate	Recovery	100 – Price	– 100	100 – recovery
Default later	Recovery	M to M	– 100	100 – recovery

Asset swap

Our investor purchases the bond through an asset swap. But is concerned about the credit in the short term, and thus takes out protection on the bond. The rather frustrating aspect of the hedge is that it is only partial. We can elaborate with regard to Table 3.7, which features a bond with a notional of €100.

We can see from the Table 3.7 that the initial hedge of taking out protection on the nominal value of the bond subsequently asset swapped leaves some unedifying consequences. The entry price, assuming the purchaser funds at libor, is flat. Further the carry on the trade, assuming the asset swap margin is fairly valued and equal to the default swap premium, is close to zero.

If the bond was to default immediately the investor would be in the unfortunate position of not being fully hedged if the bond was trading away from par, which could be due to a change in the prevailing interest rate relative to the inception. Thus the effectiveness of the hedge depends on the underlying interest rate environment, together with the perceived credit risk of the issuer supplying the bond.

To be a little bit more specific we will work through some numbers. The bond on asset swap unfortunately involves some mental gymnastics. (However it represents the most common arrangement of hedging rate risk inherent in a bond.)

The carry on the structure will be

$$\begin{aligned}&\text{Bond} + \text{asset swap} + \text{default swap} + \text{funding}\\&\quad = \text{coupon} + \text{libor} + \text{margin} - \text{coupon} - \text{premium} - \text{libor},\end{aligned}$$

which nets out to be

$$\text{margin} - \text{premium}.$$

What about the profit assuming immediate default? That depends on where the bond is trading relative to par. If the bond is above par then we lose money because the protection only gets us back 100 – recovery. But we gain on the carry. The converse is true when the bond is trading below par.

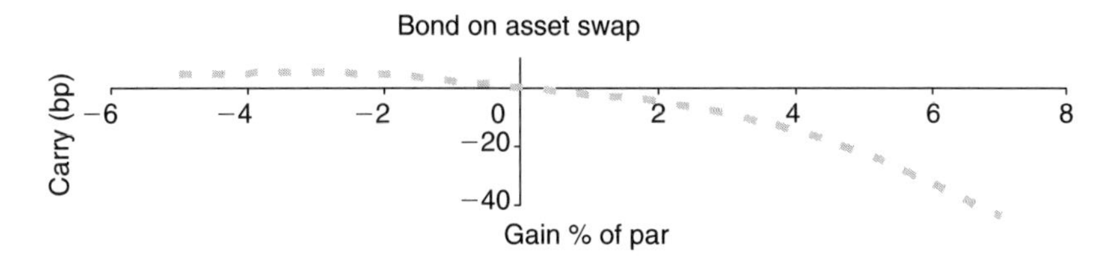

Figure 3.21 The gain on a face value hedge 5 year 6% bullet bond.
Source: Lehman.

Table 3.8 The inputs required to determine the hedging payoff.

Characteristic	Source
Hazard rate	Simulated
Risk free rate	Prevailing libor
Recovery rate	Assumption

We reproduce the graph (Figure 3.21) which illustrates these characteristics.

These results can be obtained by examining any bullet bond with a fixed coupon on asset swap and the model described in Table 3.8.

To determine the gain we need to calculate the price of the bond this is given by the formula:

$$\begin{aligned}\text{Bond price} = {} & \text{coupon} \times \sum_{\text{coupon}}^{\text{all coupons}} \text{survival probability}_{\text{coupon}} \times DF_{\text{coupon}} \\ & + 100 \times \text{survival probability}_{\text{maturity}} \times DF_{\text{maturity}} + (rec.) \times 100 \\ & \times \sum_{\text{coupon}}^{\text{all coupons}} \text{marginal probability}_{\text{coupon}} \times DF_{\text{coupon}},\end{aligned}$$

where DF_t is the discount factor at time t and *rec.* is the recovery value in the event of default. The survival probability is normally implied from the default swap market, and we refer the reader to Section 3.14 where there is a worked example of this 'bootstrap' methodology. However in the example displayed in Figure 3.21, the survival probability was taken as the standard function of a uniform hazard rate.

$$\text{Survival probability}(t) = \exp(-\lambda t).$$

Having determined the bond price, the carry is the difference between the asset swap margin and the default spread (which is just an expression involving the survival probability, the recovery rate (which has to be assumed) and the risk free rate.) The asset swap margin can be determined through the standard formula:

$$\text{Margin} = \frac{\sum_{\text{coupon}}^{\text{all coupons}} \text{coupon} \times DF_{\text{coupon}} + 100 \times DF_{\text{maturity}} - \text{bond price}}{\sum_{\text{coupon}}^{\text{all coupons}} DF_{\text{coupon}}}.$$

Finally the chart is obtained by simulating over different values of the hazard rate.

To circumvent the above we could always consider buying differing amounts of protection. In particular we would like to hedge the initial investment. This means buying more or less protection depending on the price of the bond. The amount of protection we should buy is given by the formulae below:

$$\text{Hedge ratio} = \frac{\text{bond price} - \text{recovery}}{100 - \text{recovery}}.$$

This is determined by equating the loss on the bond with the gain on the default swap bearing in mind that the latter instrument is par based. The shortcoming with this approach is that it is only good if the actual recovery matched the estimated, otherwise there will be a loss or gain of

$$(1 - \text{actual recovery}) \times \left(\frac{\text{bond price} - \text{expected}}{100 - \text{expected}}\right) - (\text{bond price} - \text{actual}).$$

To guard against this investors will occasionally take out what is termed a 'zero recovery' hedge. This assumes nothing is recovered when the bond defaults, as such her capital is safe because an amount of protection is purchased equal to the price of the bond. However it over hedges and leaves her unable to benefit from any opportunistic situations.

3.12 Pricing

We introduce the influences on pricing within the credit derivative marketplace.

The most important insight when trying to understand what the premium payable for protection should be (which is the terminology for

Table 3.9 Jointly supported ratings 1997.

	AAA	AA+	AA	AA−
AAA	AAA	AAA	AAA	AAA
AA+	AAA	AAA	AAA	AAA
AA	AAA	AAA	AAA	AAA
AA−	AAA	AAA	AAA	AA+

Source: S&P.

'the price of the derivative') is to think what this should depend on. Most of us will have an intuition based on our lending, however small, experience. The major driver would be the probability of default of the underlying credit. Furthermore the counterparty's credit would also enter the fray, because they have to be in position to pay in the event of default. Hence the importance of the joint default ratings is displayed in Table 3.9. The upshot is that even a low-rated issue and counterparty have a joint higher rating.

We can use the example of the credit derivative struck between the bank and an institution displayed in Figure 3.2 to explore how this table is utilized. The bank has an asset on which they enjoy protection. The only occasion upon which they would never be compensated is if the asset defaults at the same moment as the counterparty. The chances of this happening are very much lower, and so the relevant credit risk is found by taking the rating of the asset from the *row* and seeing where it intersects with the rating of the seller found in the relevant *column*. The rating of the asset is the appropriate grid entry from Table 3.9.

It is all very well to talk in terms of ratings but how can we quantify this? The answer to this unfortunately is not straightforward and we enter the realms of some gentle statistics. Consider the case of the bank which buys credit protection from another bank on an underlying loan.

If the underlying reference defaults then the bank is still protected via the other bank. If the Bank providing that protection defaults, then it is more nuisance value, since the originating bank can always purchase protection from another source. As previously mentioned of most concern would be the scenario where the other bank defaults and then the underlying reference defaults. This is the so-called conditional probability of default.

Although the bank worries about this contingency the actual likelihood of it occurring is considerably lower than the default risk of either the obligor or the other bank. The upshot of this is that a bank can reduce the amount of capital it sets against the original loan. Indeed the bank no longer has exposure just to this original deal but also to the counterparty of the derivative. The probability of default on this combined exposure is generally much lower than the individual probability of default. The probability is called a 'joint default'.

The joint probability of default is given by the equation below:

$$P_J = P_o \times P_c + \rho_{o,c}\sqrt{P_o(1 - P_o) \times P_c(1 - P_c)}.$$

where P_J is the joint probability of default; ρ is the correlation between the obligor and the counterparty; P_o is the probability of default by the obligor; P_c is the probability of default by the counterparty.

The reader may be disappointed to learn that there is no commonly accepted methodology of systematically pricing credit derivatives. This unfortunate state of affairs exists because of the underlying nature of a credit default and the difficulty of replicating a claim synthetically.

Given the behavior of credit, that is characterized by an occasional large loss, it is very difficult to construct a replicating portfolio and hence an arbitrage pricing schema. Another source of difficulty is the lack of 'calibration' information. To remain positive it can be argued that most of the ingredients of a good pricing model have been recognized and we reproduce these as follows:

- Probability of default of the underlying credit.
- Loss given a default of the underlying credit, that is projected recovery rate.
- Probability of default of the counterparty.
- Correlation between the underlying and the counterparty.
- Maturity of the deal.

The most fundamental uncertainty surrounds default, and then given a default, the amount of capital that can be returned. A good derivative pricing model should predict the premium given the inputs of say, a default probability of 1 per cent, and that the loss given default is 50 per cent. There are now a number of accepted models and we provide an example of a common approach encountered within the market in Section 3.14.

A number of secondary considerations come into play when pricing CDSs including liquidity, regulatory capital requirements together with market sentiment.

3.13 Source of pricing

The questions arise as to where these mysterious default probabilities can be determined. One obvious source is historical information, but

Table 3.10 Marginal default rates.

	Year 1(%)	Year 2(%)	Year 3(%)	Year 4(%)
Pool A	4.3	4.2	5.6	7
Pool B	2.2	2.1	1.8	1.5
Pool C	7	7.2	7.3	7.5

there are a number of shortcomings with this approach. The first is the relevance of history to the future; the second concerns the actual set of historical data.

We familiarize the reader with both the various terminologies and the data which will confront them in the market. Table 3.10 is representative of the type of default data available for homogenous pools as they vary across time. The marginal rates are simply the probability of a sample company defaulting in that year – it varies across time; be very careful on how you combine these across different periods, to generate a resulting figure known as the cumulative default probability. For example if the annual default probability is 1 per cent then the cumulative default over 2 years is not 2 per cent, but slightly less because it must have survived in the first year to default in the second (it will be 99% × 1% + 1%).

The most comprehensive default analysis was performed on US corporate bonds. The reader should be aware prior to an examination of the literature that there are two common definitions of default employed; the first is the ratio of names that default divided by those remaining.

The second is to take the ratio of the nominal of debt defaulting against the nominal value outstanding. You will encounter the terms marginal defaults and cumulative; the marginal default is simply the default relevant to any 1-year and the cumulative is the sum of the marginals. As stated, care is required in interpreting these results. Just adding marginals in this way will produce a figure which will tend to overstate the default probability on any one issuer, because the actual default probability is conditional upon the issuer surviving up to the period of interest. Strictly they should only be applied if starting with the same notional on each period.

There are two basic methodologies based around these distinctions, Altman and Kishore determine the default probability on a pool of relatively homogeneous corporate debt, broken down by rating category. Moody's, Carty and Lieberman determine the issuer default on a pool enlarged to encompass convertible and foreign bonds.

The details of this analysis can be seen in the excellent text by Altman.

Table 3.11 The default swap premia for various names.

Default swap premium for protection on various credits				
Credit	6 months	1 year	2 year	3 year
EDF	100	100	100	100
DT Lufthansa	100	100	100	100

Source: Bloomberg LP.

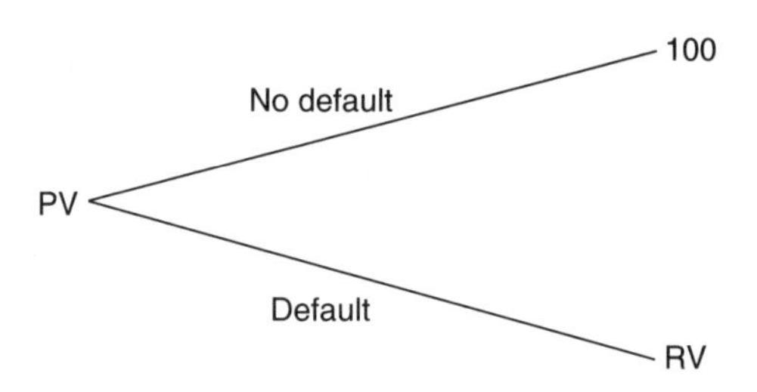

Figure 3.22 The default process.

Another major source of default information is the capital markets themselves. Indeed some would argue that this is the only viable route to establish a derivatives price. Table 3.11 illustrates that each company has a unique default premium driven in part by its rating and further by the sector. This spread depends on the maturity of the issue.

Yet market spread data is a classic example of the joint observation problem; credit spreads imply loss severity given a default but this can only be determined if you make an assumption about what this simultaneously states about recovery.

When all is said and done, most institutions price risk directly from the market price of traded securities. Roughly translated this means that the security issued by the credit will trade at a different price to a similar government security. The difference in price represents an implied default on the part of the borrower. Within the fixed income market, practitioners do not tend to discuss prices but rather yields. This means the implied default is translated into a spread.

In Figure 3.22 we explore these points quantitatively using a zero coupon bond, the price will be given by

$$PV = \frac{1}{(1 + r_{\text{risk free}})}\left[(1 - P^{\text{d}})100 + P^{\text{d}}RV\right]$$

but also the bond can be priced by discounting using the yield spread, which can typically be observed in the secondary bond market, this represents the excess over the risk free rate that compensates the investor for bearing the credit risk:

$$PV = \frac{100}{(1 + r_{\text{riskfree}})(1 + r_{\text{spread}})},$$

$$P^{\text{D}} \approx \frac{r_{\text{spread}}}{(1 - RV/100)}.$$

For example, if the recovery value is 88 and the spread is 50 bps then

$$P^{\text{D}} \approx \frac{0.005}{1 - 0.88} = 4.2\%.$$

The other major input required for derivative pricing is the default correlation. There are a number of choices relevant to its derivation. Direct default data can be used, and then the following formula to establish the correlation is used:

$$\text{Correlation} = \frac{\begin{bmatrix}\text{joint default probality} \\ - (\text{company}_1 \text{ average} \times \text{company}_2 \text{ average})\end{bmatrix}}{\sqrt{\text{company}_1 \text{ variance} \times \text{company}_2 \text{ variance}}}.$$

This can be written after replacing the variance (this can be found in Section 6.1):

$$\text{Correlation} = \frac{P_{1,2} - P_1 \times P_2}{\sqrt{P_1(1 - P_1) \times P_2(1 - P_2)}}.$$

Assuming we have the individual default probabilities implied from the derivative market, the remaining quantity is the joint default probability which is very difficult to obtain. Most practitioners rely on a Merton like approach, because this is based on a very liquid marketplace (the equity, typically). Then we use

$$\text{Correlation} = \frac{\begin{bmatrix}BN(\text{threshold}_1,\ \text{threshold}_2) \\ - N(\text{threshold}_1) \times N(\text{threshold}_2)\end{bmatrix}}{\sqrt{\begin{matrix}N(\text{threshold}_1) \times [1 - N(\text{threshold}_1)] \\ \times N(\text{threshold}_2) \times [1 - N(\text{threshold}_2)]\end{matrix}}},$$

where N is the cumulative normal distribution; BN is the cumulative bivariate normal. The threshold value is the return on the equity below which the company would default.

3.14 Pricing examples

We illustrate in this section how the default swap market can be used to derive the default probability for the corresponding maturity periods. In order to achieve this we need to separate out the default swap into its constituent legs and then value these independently. For the swap to be fairly priced these legs will be equal in value, that is

$$\text{Present value(premium leg)} = \text{present value(protection leg)}.$$

The premium leg will depend on the value of a stream of payments, very similar to discounting a series of cash flows in traditional fixed income analysis. However the proviso is that the cash flow will only arise if the underlying credit has not undergone an event. We must allow for this contingency, the value of the premium leg is thus

$$\begin{aligned}\text{Premium(maturity)} \times \sum_{\text{payment}=1}^{\text{final payment}} & \text{discount factor(value date, payment date)} \\ & \times SP\text{(value date,payment date)} \\ & \times DCF\text{(payment} - 1\text{, payment)},\end{aligned}$$

where SP and DCF are the survival probability and day count fraction respectively. This expression neglects the premium that will have accrued if default occurs between a premium date (typically this is quarterly). The value of the protection leg is given by

$$(1 - \text{recovery}) \times \int_{\text{value date}}^{\text{maturity}} SP(\text{time})\, DF(\text{time})\, \lambda(\text{time})\, d(\text{time}),$$

where λ(time) is the probability of default in a very small passage of time d(time). This is a very tricky customer to evaluate, and it is standard to decompose the protection period into a set of discrete times where the integrand is evaluated, replacing the product of SP and DF with the difference in survival probabilities for neighboring periods, and the final result is the sum. If we sample S times per year then the equation above can be written as

$$\begin{aligned}(1 - \text{recovery}) \times \sum_{\text{counter}=1}^{S\times\text{maturity}} & DF(\text{value date, time(counter)}) \times \\ & [SP(\text{time(counter}-1)) - SP(\text{time(counter)})].\end{aligned}$$

```
hazard 6M        0.0166
premium leg      =spread_6M/10000/(1-recovery)*(0.25*EXP(-libor*0.25)*EXP(-hazard_6M*0.25)+0.25*EXP(-libor*0.5)*EXP(-hazard_6M*0.5))
protection leg   =EXP(-1/12*libor)*(EXP(-hazard_6M*0/12)-EXP(-hazard_6M*1/12))
                 =EXP(-2/12*libor)*(EXP(-hazard_6M*1/12)-EXP(-hazard_6M*2/12))
                 =EXP(-3/12*libor)*(EXP(-hazard_6M*2/12)-EXP(-hazard_6M*3/12))
                 =EXP(-4/12*libor)*(EXP(-hazard_6M*3/12)-EXP(-hazard_6M*4/12))
                 =EXP(-5/12*libor)*(EXP(-hazard_6M*4/12)-EXP(-hazard_6M*5/12))
                 =EXP(-6/12*libor)*(EXP(-hazard_6M*5/12)-EXP(-hazard_6M*6/12))
```

Figure 3.23 An extract from Excel illustrating the 'bootstrap' steps.

Lets us now demonstrate the use of these equations in determining the default probabilities. First we require the 6 month default rate. We equate the premium leg to the protection leg, there will be two premium payments and we sample monthly in order to evaluate the integral. We further substitute the following expression for the $SP = \exp(-\lambda \text{time})$. This gives

$$\frac{P(6\,\text{M})}{(1-R)} \sum_{n=3,6} DCF(t_{n-3}, t_n) \times DF(t_v, t_n) \times \exp(-\lambda_{6\text{m}} \times t_n)$$
$$= \sum_{\text{counter}=1}^{6} DF(t_v, t_{\text{counter}}) \times [\exp(-\lambda_{6\text{m}} \times t_{\text{counter}-1}) - \exp(-\lambda_{6\text{m}} \times t_{\text{counter}})].$$

An approximation that has been made is that the 3 month rate is equal to the 6 month rate, and at all intervening sampling points. The subscript ν indicates valuation date. In Figure 3.23 we have illustrated the steps required to determine the 6 month hazard rate; consisting of firstly setting out the premium leg, there will be two payments conditional on the obligor surviving. (We have assumed a parallel libor curve and a day count fraction of 0.25.) Secondly lay out the protection legs, monthly sampling results in six terms. The payout is dependent on the obligor defaulting during the relevant period. Also note that the actual payout has been divided into the premium leg. We used 'goal seek' to determine the hazard rate which makes the two legs equal. This process continues for the 1 year rate, using the derived 6 month rate as an input.

Table 3.12 shows the resulting term structure of default spreads using the data on the obligor EDF specified in Table 3.11. This can be used to price any debt issued by EDF. We give an example of an annuity, having a rate A and a non-zero recovery rate R (Table 3.13).

We value each of the payments by assuming that the issue could either default. In which case we receive the recovery rate, or we receive

Table 3.12 Cumulative default probabilities.

	Default probabilities from the 'bootstrap' process			
Maturity	Risk free (%)	Hazard rate (%)	Survival probability (%)	Default probability (%)
6 months	2.6	1.66	99.17	0.83
1 year	2.6	1.66	97.54	1.63
2 year	2.6	1.66	95.93	1.61
3 year	2.6	1.66	94.36	1.58

Table 3.13 Three year annuity.

	Cumulative default probability			
	Risk free *DF*	Annuity payment	Defaulted payment	Total *PV*
6 months	0.9871		*R**0.0083	*R**0.00819
1 year	0.9743	*A**0.9754	*R**0.0163	*A**0.9504 + *R**0.0159
2 year	0.9493	*A**0.9593	*R**0.0161	*A**0.9107 + *R**0.0152
3 year	0.9250	*A**0.9436	*R**0.0158	*A**0.8728 + *R**0.0146
Total				2.734**A* + 0.0539**R*

the annuity payment. We then discount these potential payments by the discount factor implied by the risk free rate.

3.15 Regulatory environment

Regulatory capital

Financial institutions have a range of regulations and controls, a primary one is the level of capital that a bank holds to provide a cushion for the activities the banking engages on. This should not be confused with the use of reserves which also guard against losses. Capital is set aside to cushion against 'unexpected', or very rare, losses. Of course there is the crucial element of how 'unexpected' is defined – it could be determined through a combination of assessing historical losses and informed selection. Setting aside too much capital would be inefficient.

The decision is taken out of the managers hands and replaced by the work of a banking supervisor. Such then, is the remit of the Bank for International Settlements (BIS), who set out the terms within the EC Solvency Ratio and Capital Adequacy Directive (1992).

The banking activities are divided for purposes of regulatory treatment into a *banking portfolio* and a *trading portfolio.* The distinction is one of holding period, the former relate mainly to loans held by the bank for extended periods. The trading book consists of more liquid bonds and assets held for shorter periods because of either market making or brokerage activities. The trading book is furthermore required to be marked-to-market.

We begin by discussing the banking book. Under the requirements all cash and off balance sheet instruments in the bank's portfolio will be assigned a risk weighting, based on their perceived credit risk, which determines the level of capital set against them. This is known as BIS1 or the Basel Capital Ratios.

The methodology is as follows, each asset is banded into different risk categories, these grades are loosely connected with the probability of the issuer defaulting on their obligation. This percentage is multiplied by a further percentage, the so-called '8 per cent rule'. To determine the capital set aside we multiply this percentage by the notional outstanding.

The details of the risk weights are as follows:

- Sovereign debt for member countries of the OECD will receive a 0 per cent risk weight (this means the bank does not need to reserve any capital against these assets).
- The senior debt for OECD banks receives a 20 per cent risk weight. Then a 1.6 per cent charge on the notional.
- Loans are treated according to whether they are either drawn or not. If the loan is not committed then a 50 per cent risk weight is employed. If the revolver funds then the bank would assign 100 per cent. Then a 8 per cent charge on the notional.
- For corporate debt and non-OECD sovereigns, assign a 100 per cent risk weight. Then a 8 per cent charge on the notional.

For example if we consider a bond issued by an OECD bank, with a maturity of 6 years and a notional of €25 000 000 then the appropriate risk weight is 20 per cent, multiplying this by the notional gives us the risk adjusted balance of $5 000 000. We then multiply by the risk asset ration of 1.6 per cent to arrive at the *risk capital amount of €80 000.*

These weights are a first attempt to create 'a one fits all' system of rating. As such there are major shortcomings, in particular some rather strange consequences have arisen. These include the case of Turkey – which is an OECD member and thus incurs a 0 per cent risk weight. Their debt however trades at a very large spread to the risk free rate. Another unforeseen consequence is the removal of high-grade corporate loans from balance sheets because they all carry the same charge.

Regulatory treatment of credit derivatives is currently in a state of flux and a revised framework is due. One of the difficulties is they came into being after the 1998 accord. With this as a qualification we move onto consider the case of credit derivatives within the banking book according to the 1998 rules.

It should be borne in mind that the regulatory requirements provided by the Basel Committee are used as the minimum standard adopted by local regulators. Furthermore because credit derivatives were not covered in the original accord there is some flexibility in the precise treatment. However all local regimes share the treatment of a short protection credit derivative as a long artificial position in the reference asset, in which case the Basel weights reviewed above apply.

A buyer of protection constructing a hedge on a cash position (i.e. an owner of the underlying asset) is usually granted capital relief provided it can be demonstrated that the credit risk has been transferred to the protection seller. In practice this means that the capital allocation is determined from the category of the counterparty selling protection. For example if the reference is a corporate (requiring 100 per cent of the nominal) and the hedge is purchased through an OECD member bank, then the charge falls to 20 per cent of the nominal adjusted by the risk ratio of 1.6 per cent from 8 per cent.

There is a major shortcoming inherent, which is the relevant probability of default is not the OECD bank but rather the joint default probability. Further, there is no regulatory gain in buying protection from a corporate enjoying a better rating than the bank.

On the positive side the amount attracting a charge is lower than the notional and equal to the difference between the notional and the recovery value. There is also a difference in treatment for an asset partially hedged in terms of the protection having a shorter maturity than the asset leading to a forward exposure. Typically two different weights are employed. We refer the reader to section two within the chapter on the credit risk of libor products where maturity 'adjustments' are discussed in detail.

Regulatory capital example

We introduce one of the applications of TRORS to exploit regulatory inefficiencies. The regulatory environment has a great effect on the effective return earned by an off balance sheet item. In Table 3.14 we illustrate the situation of a bank entering a TROR with different counterparties. On the one hand the regulators require 100 per cent risk weighting whereas on the other the risk weighting is only 20 per cent.

The asset income in each situation is identical to 60 bps. This should mean the banks indifference to the counterparty, but because of the

Table 3.14 The return on an asset based on risk capital.

	Risk-weighted asset	
	100%	20%
Category risk weight	100%	20%
X capital requirement	8%	8%
Notional	100 000 000	100 000 000
Net income 60 bps	600 000	600 000
Capital	8 000 000	1 600 000
Return on capital	7.5%	37.5%

inefficiencies in the way these counterparties are treated from a regulatory perspective means the capital assignment differs and hence the return.

3.16 Terminology

As a guide to the reader we produce some definitions on the phraseology encountered within the market. These are discussed below.

Obligation

The term obligation referred to in the ISDA documentation relates to different categories of asset. There are six possibilities; bond, bond or loan, loan, borrowed funds, payment and reference obligations only. Furthermore there are further legal characteristics of these obligations. These can be specified as 'not domestic' either issuance, law or currency. 'Specified currencies' implying the default have to occur on obligations issued into those specified. 'not contingent', that is there are no contingencies such as options on the obligation. 'Pari-passu' is defined to be at least as senior as the reference obligation. Finally 'listed' refers to whether the obligation must be traded on a recognized exchange.

Reference asset

Required to determine the seniority of the debt that is covered and the recovery value if the derivative is cash settled.

Materiality

This arises because the reference asset has financial characteristics distinct from credit, allowances must be made and will be documented under the materiality clause. Operationally this requires another asset simply because the reference asset can change adversely in value due to changes in the general level of interest rates which have nothing to do with a credit event. The reference asset will obviously be a very strong credit.

Substitution

If the reference asset is materially reduced then the calculation will be based upon a substitute issue. The reduction can be due to a number of contingencies including illiquidity and debt buy backs.

Basis risk

Basis risk is a term employed more generally within the derivatives market. It refers to the risk undertaken because the hedge is a poor proxy for the asset we are seeking to protect. We illustrate by taking an extreme example. If I had a portfolio consisting of the FT-SE 100 shares, I could hedge this by selling a share of Vodafone in the correct proportion. It would not be a very good hedge because the index is composed of shares additional to Vodafone.

Returning to the credit derivative world the assets on which I am seeking protection is often poorly correlated with the reference asset potentially, because of materiality or substitution.

You should also be aware that the documentation changes considerably depending on whether protection is provided on either a sovereign or corporate name. For example both the term sheet (of which examples are presented for each derivative type) and the details of the ISDA obligation and deliverable categories and characteristics vary.

There are moves towards an international framework but many of the details including the number of items on the list above is under debate, in particular the inclusion of acceleration and moratorium are under review. Furthermore there are a number of grey areas surrounding the precise nature of an event. Major discussions concern the definition of restructuring and the determination of the reference asset. A specific example is provided by the case of Rank Xerox extending the maturity on its debt in June 2002. Protection sellers argued that this was not a restructuring caused by deterioration in creditworthiness. Furthermore the demerger of National Power begged questions as to the location of the reference entity and obligation post-merger.

Legal technicalities aside there remains the pure quantitative aspects of what constituents a fair value for the protection premium and finally the value of the contingent payment?

Following further discussion with market participants ISDA has scheduled a new release of documentation for implementation in May 2003. This was partially in response to the controversy that had developed surrounding the interpretation of restructuring and demerging.

2003 Update

Specifically the renegotiation of bilateral loans may no longer trigger a credit event. A new clause is inserted stating that a credit event can be defined as a restructuring only if the obligation is held by more than three non-affiliated holders.

Under the new methodology if one of the demerged entities inherits three quarters or more of the original debt then it becomes the successor in the contract. If the new entities have between a quarter and three quarters then the CDs protection is split. If the demerged entities have less than one quarter and the parent still exists then there is no change in the contract. If the parent ceases to exist then the entity taking possession of the larger fraction is the subject of the new contract.

Definition of bankruptcy as a credit event

A bankruptcy can only have occurred if the default occurs on the reference entity itself. For all other credit events the default can occur on any obligation.

Four types of restructuring clause

These clauses, applicable to corporates, came into effect because of so-called 'soft default'. This is different from 'hard default' comprising bankruptcy and failure to pay. Following a 'hard' event, all the entities debt will be similarly affected. However subsequent to a 'soft' event, there are considerable valuation differences. This had opened up a cheapest to deliver opportunity for the seller:

- *No restructuring* eliminates the seller incurring losses due to deterioration in the reference obligation not due to default.
- *Full:* The buyer can deliver bonds of any maturity after debt restructuring.
- *Modified and modified restructuring:* The buyer is restricted to the types of bonds that can be delivered in terms of maturity.

Definition of deliverable obligations

These are now defined to suit the needs of the counterparties:

- The direct obligation of the reference entity.
- The obligations of a subsidiary (to qualify the subsidiary must have more than 50 per cent owned by the reference entity).
- Obligations of third parties guaranteed by the reference entity.

References

Altman and Kishore, Defaults and Returns on High Yield Bonds, *New York University Salomon Centre*, 1997.

Carty and Lieberman, Corporate Bond Defaults and Default Rates, *Moody's Special Report*, 1996.

Caouette, Altman and Narayanan, Managing Credit Risk: The Next Great Financial Challenge, *Wiley*.

Leander, Robeco's Synthetic Age, *Risk*, March 2002.

Masters *et al.*, The JP Morgan Guide to Credit Derivatives, *Risk Metrics Group.*

O'Kane, Credit Derivatives Explained, *Lehman Brothers.*

O'Kane and McAdie, Trading the Default Swap Basis, *Risk*, October 2001.

O'Kane and Turnbull, Valuation of Credit Default Swaps, *Lehman Brothers.*

Tavakoli, Credit Derivatives: Guide to Instruments and Applications, *Wiley.*

4

Securitization

Credit within the context of securitization

4.1 Asset-backed securities

Market review

We introduce the main structures within the marketplace and its historical development.

The US in common with many types of financial development has led the way with securitization. What began as an opportunity to provide house purchase financing has mushroomed into many different ways of originating and distributing capital. Indeed the key concept behind securitization is the separation of the ownership from the origination. Generally this leads to a more effective marketplace. The growth of securitization proceeds apace. What began as a local development has rapidly spread to become global. The size of the current marketplace in terms of issuance can be comparable to that of the major government bond markets.

The term securitization encompasses a number of different types of structure. These include asset-backed securities (ABSs), mortgage-backed securities (MBSs), collateralized debt obligations (CDOs), collateralized bond obligations (CBOs) and collateralized loan obligations (CLOs). At this introductory stage we will emphasize what is generic and examine some of the nuances at a later stage.

Each acronym reflects an arrangement whereby a pool of financial assets can be transferred onto the balance sheet of a legal entity created specifically for the purpose. The question naturally arises as to why anyone should be sufficiently motivated to go to the lengths of establishing a new company just to transfer a collection of receivables?

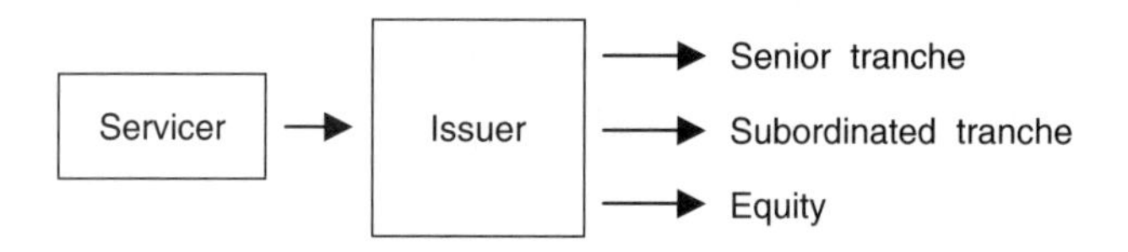

Figure 4.1 The mechanism of a typical securitization.

The arrangement is advantageous to a number of independent parties including the investor and original owner of the assets.

The main advantage to the parent company is that the balance sheet is 'freed up', because it is the recipient of the proceeds from the sale of the assets to the newly created entity.[1]

The investor on the other hand is able to invest in an asset which matches his yield and maturity requirements. Indeed one of the major considerations when structuring a securitization is the requirement to create securities with characteristics which match the investor profile.

Figure 4.1 shows a simplified arrangement typical of most securitizations. The servicer represents the pools of assets and sometimes is responsible for the administrative aspects to their operation. (This latter function is critical to the valuation of the asset pool.) Moving from left to right, we then have the issuer which represents the distinct legal entity and finally the resulting issues which will be issued and possibly trade actively in the secondary debt capital markets.

Figure 4.2 reveals in a little more detail the main parties involved in a securitization deal. The extra players are the trustees who administer the issuance vehicle; referred to as the special purpose vehicle (SPV) which may be a corporation or trust, on behalf of the investors ensuring the resulting obligations in terms of interest and principal payments are met. A key characteristic of the SPV is the 'bankruptcy remoteness'; this is achieved in part by the economic removal of the assets from the servicer.

The SPV is a separate legal entity which, in the case of a 'true sale', purchases the assets from the selling party and subsequently issues market securities. As mentioned, not all securitizations physically transfer the collateral. Some are just mediating the economic risk, in which case the economic risk is transferred. It is important to appreciate that the same parent organization may hold both the original assets and originate the SPV. Indeed this is the route banks explore when they wish to free capital from their balance sheet as a consequence of lending to risky borrowers.

---

[1] This is the case for a 'true sale' where the physical assets are transferred. Increasingly, just the risk is transferred.

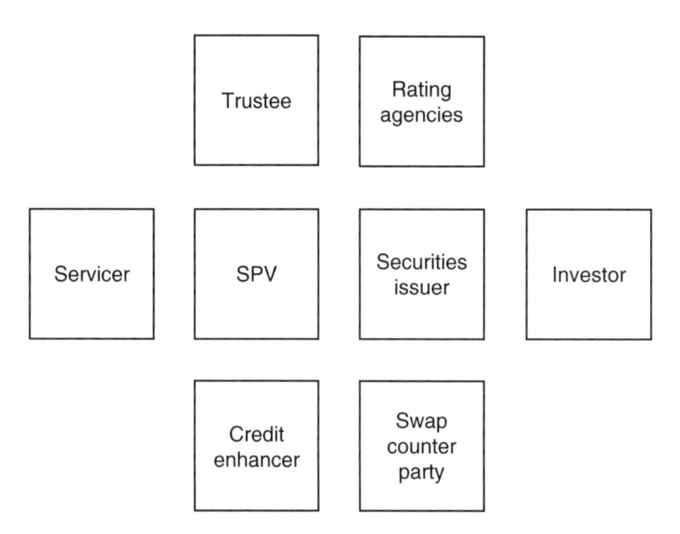

Figure 4.2 The parties involved.

The credit enhancement provider will guarantee payments in the event of a default, for certain classes of investors, in return for a fee. (Note that this function is not always a third party, we will evaluate this critical facility in a separate section on credit enhancement.) The role of credit enhancer is often fulfilled by a third party.

Remaining players include the hedge counterparties. They exist to eliminate potential interest-rate risk countenanced by the investor. The assets backing the securitization are often tied to a variable level of interest, this will often be the case encountered within the loan market. If the resulting securities are offering a fixed-interest rate because of investor demand, then there resides interest rate risk in the structure which must be hedged. The interest rate swap (IRS) is a common application. Figure 4.3 depicts this arrangement where the party, which could be the SPV receives floating, in return for a fixed payment. Here the fixed is paid semi-annually and the floating is received on a quarterly basis.

Finally we draw your attention to the rating agencies, whose role in stressing the overall issuance structure and subsequently providing a rating to each issue is key to investor activity.

Major types of securitization

We now consider each of the major types of asset-backed securitization. We refer you to Figure 4.4, which illustrates the relative importance of the different categories within the US market. This is dominated by the MBS. For this reason a large component of this chapter will address this

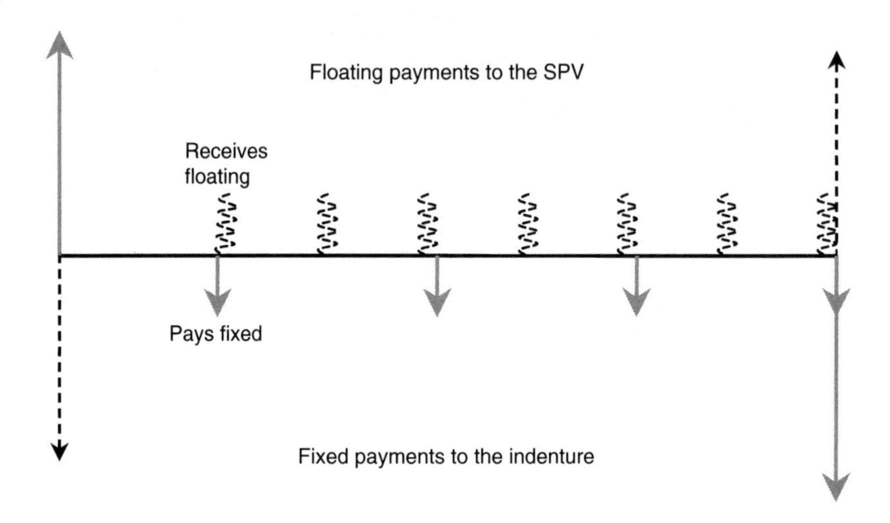

Figure 4.3 The cash flows of an interest rate swap.

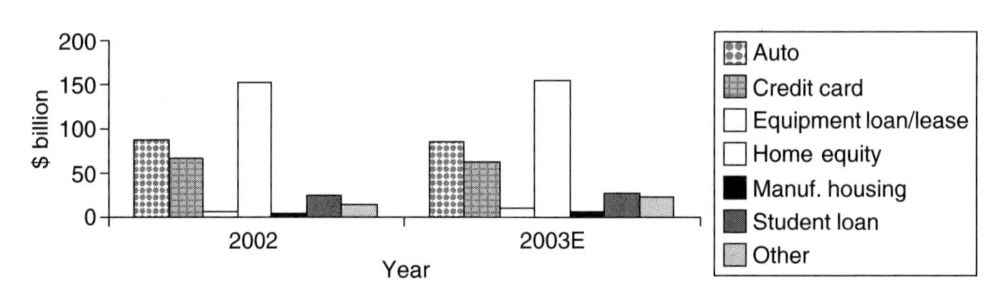

Figure 4.4 Relative importance of different asset type by supply (May 2003). *Source:* Barclays Capital.

marketplace. We also look at the remaining types under the example of the auto loan market for the reason that they are relatively homogenous and stable. These activities are likely to serve as a template for the continued development of the European market.

4.2 Mortgage-backed securities

Most of you have familiarity with the mortgage arrangement. A loan is provided which is backed with the underlying property of the subsequent purchase. Mortgages can be either fixed or floating rate. In the US mortgages are generally amortizing. This means that the monthly payment is composed both of interest and principal redemption. Within the UK, possibly more heterogeneous than either the US or Europe as a whole, there is a wide variety of possibilities including

Table 4.1 Issuance of MBSs ($ billion).

	2003*	2002	2001	2000	1999
FHLMC	198	531	379	159	226
FNMA	410	727	524	213	299
GNMA1	51	111	109	59	108
GNMA2	19	63	67	46	46

Source: Bloomberg LP. *Until April 2003.

interest only, typically with an endowment policy, or straight repayment mortgages, also common are capped and fixed rate.

The capital markets, obviously, are not interested in individual debt obligations. However if all of these obligations are pooled together then the characteristics of the collection are often attractive. Such then is the motive behind MBSs. In the US certain MBSs enjoy government sponsorship; in which case the credit rating will be AAA. There are three agencies which are either owned by, or have government association. These are the Government National Mortgage Association (GNMA), the Federal Home Loan Mortgage Corporation (FHLMC) and the Federal National Mortgage Association (FNMA). The overwhelming majority of mortgages will be financed by these agencies. Do not think however that the consumer goes directly to the agency. They lend to intermediaries. Table 4.1 illustrates the development of this phenomenon.

MBSs are issued both as ‘pass through’ and ‘pay through’ securities, often referred to as CMOs. The latter formed by pooling ‘pass throughs’, and redistributing the principal and interest according to a pre-set formula.

‘Pass throughs’ represent an undiluted claim on the asset base. Cash received by the vehicle (no distinction is made between interest and principal) is passed directly on to the underlying securities. These all have a single class structure, that is no holder has rights to the cash flow that are senior or subordinated to the other holders (Figure 4.5).

There are a number of varieties of pass through which can be categorized as ‘straight pass through’ whereby interest and principal is paid directly to investors as it is received in the pool. ‘Partially modified pass through’, where some payments may be delayed but ultimately covered by the guarantee[2] and then the ‘modified pass through’ whereby all payments are made regardless of whether there is money in the pool. There is also a type of pass through which categorizes the investors into two groups the ‘callable’ and the ‘call class’. The latter receive nothing but hold the right to call the security at a certain price and date in the future.

[2]The guarantee must supply the extra funds.

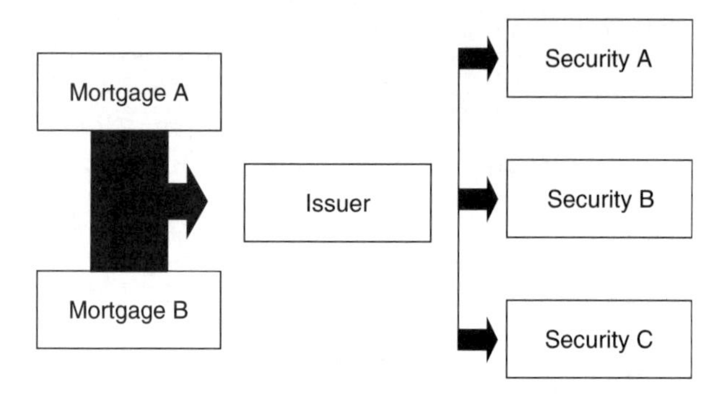

Figure 4.5 The CMO arrangement.

CMOs were created to obviate the problem of pre-payment. In the US almost every borrower can refinance their mortgage without incurring penalties. This causes considerable problems for the investor because the maturity of their security is not known. CMOs address this issue by separating out the interest and principal payments such that some tranches entirely bear the pre-payment risk.

'Pay through' securities are the manifestation of the CMO, representing aggregations of pass through securities. They represent differentiated interests on the underlying assets. Cash received by the vehicle is distributed according to the class of the security. Thus senior debt has a preferential claim. We now discuss the common tranche types.

Tranche types

Sequential pay

These are organized into a sequence for the repayment of principal. This principal is received and distributed according to the class letter. But if the principal is redeemed more quickly than expected the maturity of the class will decrease. Conversely if pre-payment grows more slowly, then the average life is expanded. Thus, the pre-payment is vital in determining the maturity of the security and hence its market value.

Planned amortization

The PAC is set up to pay principal at a pre-determined rate when prepayments occur within a specified range. This provides protection against both early and delayed amortization. This is arranged by subordinating principal payments to other tranches. Because of the greater certainty of maturity investors will accept a lower yield.

Targeted amortization

The TAC gives investors protection against early pre-payment. This is done by ascribing a constant rate of principal payment to the class. If pre-payments occur more rapidly than expected the excess is diverted to the other tranches.

Support class

Designed to alleviate pre-payment on other categories. Investors agree to subordinate their principal repayments to other holders in exchange for a higher return.

Floating-rate tranches

These pay floating rates of interest usually expressed as a spread to a common interest rate.

The call class

Investors in this category receive no interest or principal until the other classes have been paid. They potentially have the longest life of all the tranches. Scheduled interest payments that are missed are added to the principal amount until cash becomes available following the retirement of other classes. This is a benefit because when interest payments begin they will be based upon a larger principal.

IO and PO mortgage-backed securities

Subsequent securities can be stripped into their component interest and principal payments. The US expression of stripping refers to the fact they trade independently and in the manner of a zero coupon bond which has appeal to certain types of investors.

Figure 4.4 shows the relative importance of mortgage activity within the US and Figure 4.8 displays the relative importance within the European marketplace.

4.3 Auto- and loan-backed securities

These constitute an important section of the market and you will be pleased to learn one of the simpler. The subsequent securities can be structured into both single asset and multi-class structures.

Auto-backed securities are set against underlying loans which are provided to purchasers of vehicles. These assets behave in a fairly uniform manner. This is because pre-payments are much less sensitive to changes in interest rates than in the mortgage world. The loans are

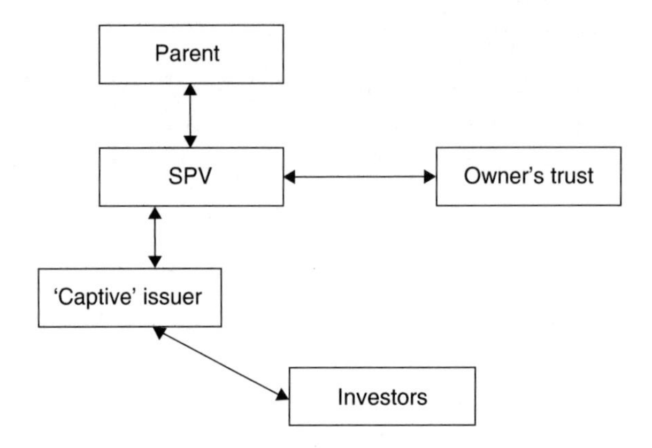

Figure 4.6 Auto-backed securitization.

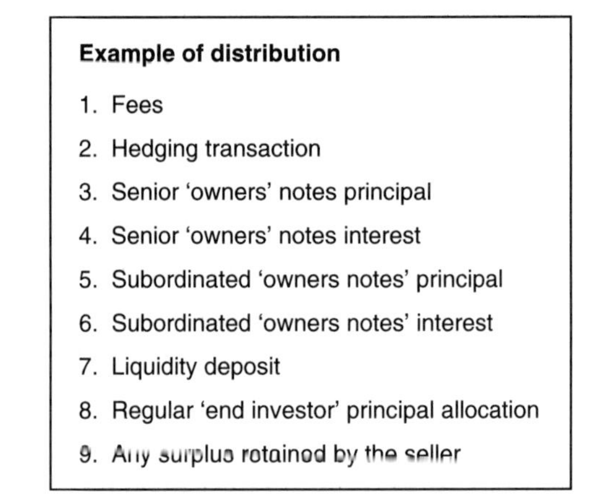

Example of distribution

1. Fees
2. Hedging transaction
3. Senior 'owners' notes principal
4. Senior 'owners' notes interest
5. Subordinated 'owners notes' principal
6. Subordinated 'owners notes' interest
7. Liquidity deposit
8. Regular 'end investor' principal allocation
9. Any surplus retained by the seller

Figure 4.7 The priority of payment within an auto-backed arrangement.

amortized according to a schedule and repaid, usually over a 6 year period. They are collateralized against the vehicle purchased and so consequently offer strong backing.

Figure 4.6 illustrates the common arrangement within the vehicle financing operation. The parent company usually sets up two independent trusts. It physically transfers the receivables into the first trusts (or SPV). The SPV preferentially transfers some of these receivables into the 'owners' trust. Which issues securities with a correspondingly lower yield because of the priority accorded to payments. The SPV is financed usually by a subsidiary of the parent company who issue investor securities for the net end investor (the so-called 'captive' issuer).

The resulting securities have payments prioritized according to Figure 4.7.

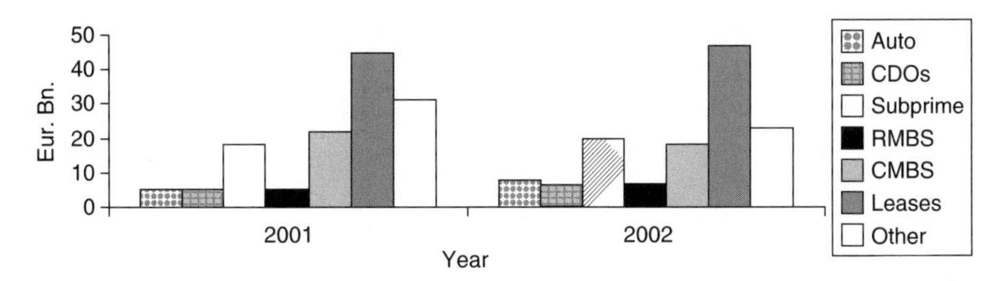

Figure 4.8 The types of ABSs within the European market (€ billion).
Source: Dr. KW.

European summary

The European market has not developed to the extent of the US. However the categorization and relative importance is similar. Figure 4.8 illustrates the volumes and should be compared with Figure 4.4.

4.4 Collateral analysis

We discuss the collateral structure of an MBS and in particular how it influences the security type. The conventions in the US are the level payment fixed-rate mortgage, whereby the monthly payment of interest is specified. The characteristics are such that the mortgage has a fixed-term maturity and a fixed-interest rate hence the name 'level pay'.

The monthly payment on a conventional fixed rate of mortgage is given by

$$I = M\frac{r(1+r)^n}{(1+r)^n - 1},$$

where M is the original mortgage amount; I is the total monthly payment; r is the monthly rate; n is the term of the mortgage in months.

The level of interest payment and principal can be determined from

$$p = M\frac{r(1+r)^{t-1}}{(1+r)^n - 1},$$

where p is the monthly principal amount; t is the month, starting from 1 and

$$i = M\frac{r((1+r)^n - (1+r)^{t-1})}{(1+r)^n - 1},$$

where i is the monthly interest payment made at time t.
Of course

$$I = i + p.$$

Another type of mortgage common in the US market is the adjustable rate mortgage (ARM). This is simply a loan in which the interest payable is variable and dependent upon an external reference. The reference is typically called prime, or another common index such as cost of fund index (COFI). Generally borrowers prefer to fix their mortgage costs rather than countenance a rise in interest rates and face higher debt servicing costs.

You may also encounter the graduate repayment mortgage which is aimed at the more financially challenged borrower. The initial interest rate, for up to 5 years, for example is set at a discount to a conventional mortgage – of course in the future the payments are higher.

Mortgages are long dated, typically 20–30 years. There is usually no restriction on the amount of principal that can be returned to the lender, prior to the ending date. This represents a considerable risk to the fund provider which can be understood as follows. The loan has an existing market value, which is dependent on the general level of interest rates relative to the rate at which the loan was made. Thus if the loan was originally made at 8 per cent and the current interest rate is 6 per cent then it has a higher value. In the phraseology of the market it would be deemed to be at a premium to par. The converse would be a discount. Par refers to the fact that most loans are originated at the prevailing market rate.

If the borrower returns the loan, the lender no longer has a valuable asset. But rather a cash amount which can only be invested at prevailing interest rates. This loss of value to the lender is termed repayment risk.

There are two main reasons why the borrower may pay off the loan early. Either they move and pay off the debt with the proceeds of the house sale, or if interest rates have decreased, then taking out a new mortgage arrangement, called remortgaging, is an attractive proposition. The proceeds from the new mortgage will pay off the original.

There are other reasons which are comparatively less important; these include the borrower defaulting on the debt, or a natural disaster when the property is destroyed.

The ramifications for securitization are considerable. An end investor who is purchasing an asset in which the underlying cash flows are backed, or collateralized, by housing loans will be alarmed if the repayment level is high, because the assets will lose value. It is the

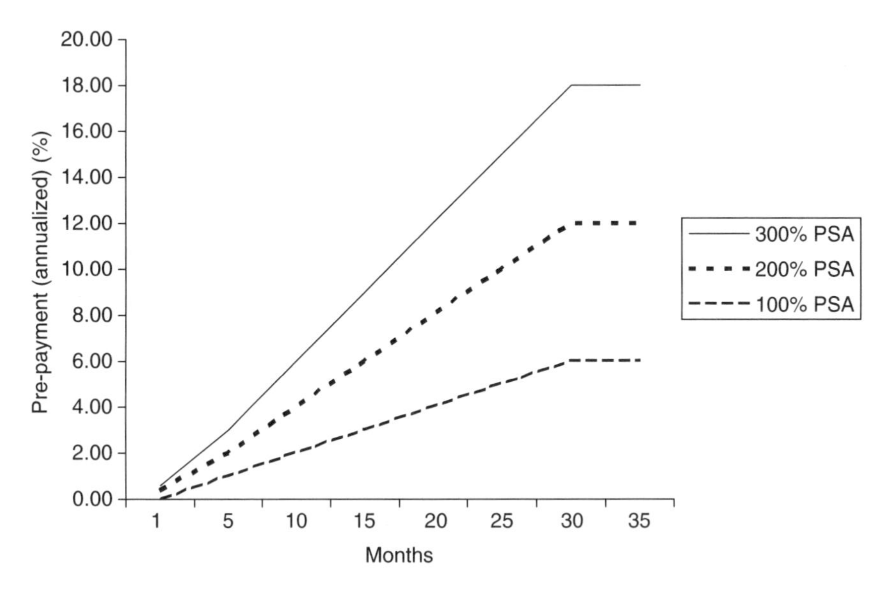

Figure 4.9 The PSA approach.

province of the structurer in harness with the agencies to address pre-payment so the structure can support variations from the average rate of pre-payment.

The question as to what the average should be based upon is not quite as clear cut as perhaps the various parties in a securitization would wish. However a standard approach is to assume a pre-payment rate that varies uniformly over the lifetime of the loan. Such a model is referred to, rather perversely, as having a constant pre-payment rate.

The standard is set in the US by the Public Securities Association (PSA), which has developed a scale based upon assumed repayment rates. It is actually calibrated against a monthly mortality rate. This is defined as the percentage of a pools outstanding principal which is pre-paid in any month.

The repayment within the 'standard' varies over the lifetime of the loan; this is quite a natural assumption. A pool is deemed to be 100 per cent PSA if it redeems at 0.2[3] per cent in its first month, rising by 0.2 percentage points in each subsequent month until it reaches 6 per cent at 30 months. Pre-payment for other scenarios is then measured relative to these benchmarks. For example a 75 per cent PSA has 4.5 per cent pre-paid by month 30. Figure 4.9 illustrates other scenarios.

The level of pre-payment has a major impact on the cash flows received by the security holder. The graphs below illustrate the various cases of

[3] Annualized. The actual monthly prepayment is this rate divided by 12.

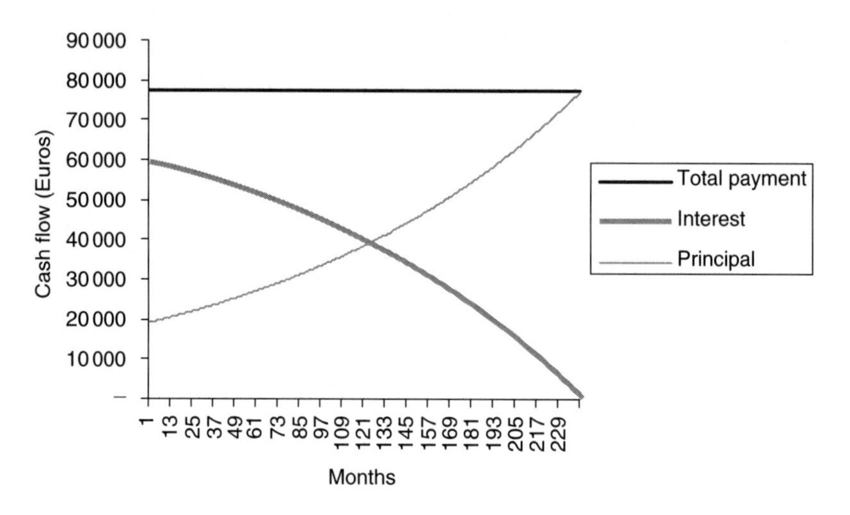

Figure 4.10 Structure of payments without pre-payment.

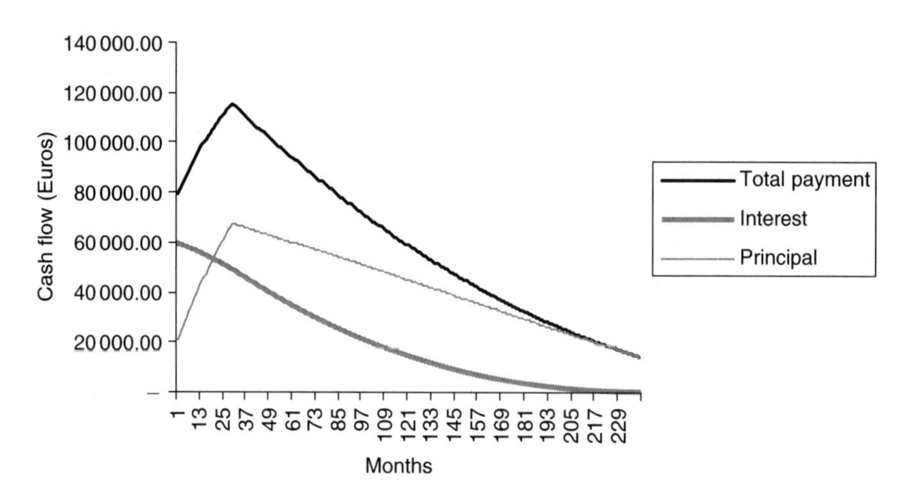

Figure 4.11 Structure of payments with 100% PSA.

mortgage cash flows with and without pre-payment. When there is no pre-payment the monthly amount is constant although the composition between interest and principal varies over time. Initially the payment has more interest but eventually the majority is principal. When the pre-payment level is non-zero the underlying cash flow is modified as follows:

$$cf = \text{interest} + \text{principal} + \text{pre-payment},$$

where cf is the cash flow received by the pool backing the MBSs and the amount of pre-payment is calculated from the PSA figures:

$$\text{Pre-payment} = \text{CPR} \times (\text{amount outstanding} - \text{principal payment}),$$

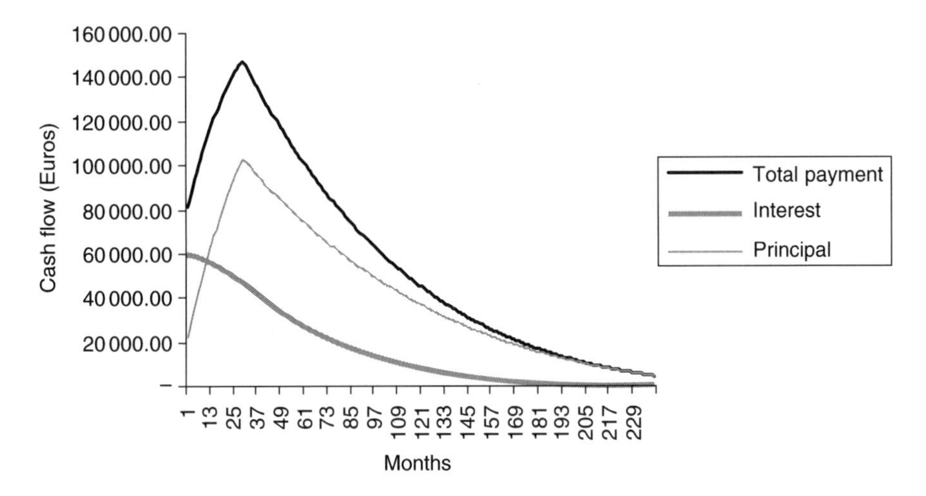

Figure 4.12 Structure of payments with 200% PSA.

where CPR is the constant pre-payment rate, obtained from the graph. Principal payment can be determined from the standard formula, at the beginning of the section, with the nominal adjusted for pre-payment.

Figures 4.10–4.12 demonstrate how the profile changes as the pre-payment level goes between the standard assumption and a scenario with twice as much pre-payment.

4.5 Analysis of securities

We discuss how the collateral structure influences the risk of the associated securities.

Once an estimate of the cash flow has been obtained we are in position to evaluate the mortgage-backed bonds. This is necessary because the investor will obviously wish to make a comparison with other securities such as corporate bonds to determine their relative attraction. One of the main factors in determining the behaviour of a bond is its maturity. The problem with a mortgage-backed bond is that because some pre-payment will occur the actual maturity date is subject to some uncertainty. Thus the convention in the marketprice is to use an estimated value for the maturity, the so-called average life. This can be determined from the formulae below:

$$\text{Average life} = \frac{1}{12} \times \sum_{t=1}^{N} \frac{t \times \text{principal}(t)}{\text{total principal}},$$

where the individual principal payments received at different months, t, are summed up to give the total principal received. We want an amount expressed in years hence the need to divide by 12.

Duration is also an important measure. This is used within the bond market to determine the risk of a particular issue due to changes in the interest rate environment. As we previously discussed a bond with a high coupon will be more valuable than a lower coupon of the same maturity and issuer. But bonds with the same coupon having differing maturities will be accorded different values. This is because the longer dated issues will pay out more which must be balanced by the delay in receiving the principal. These factors are vitally dependent upon the current level of interest rates. In summary duration is the single measure which pulls the picture together. This metric is a quantification of the change in price of the bond due to changes in interest rates. To determine it we need the projected cash flows together with a bond price, once we have these ingredients we can calculate a yield from the formulae below:

$$P = \sum_{t=1}^{N} \frac{C(t)}{(1 + y/12)^t},$$

where P is the price of the bond, yielding y and $C(t)$ is the coupon received on the bond at time t.

For example, Table 4.2 illustrates the effect on yield for various levels of repayment.

Then, duration is obtained from

$$D = \frac{1}{12 \times P \times (1 + y/12)} \sum_{i=1}^{N} \frac{t \times C(t)}{(1 + y/12)^t}.$$

You will also come across the techniques of option adjusted spread valuation for mortgage-backed bonds. Although the phraseology is rather intimidating; the idea, however, is quite simple. The price of a bond,

Table 4.2 Illustrating bond performance as a result of pre-payment.

	Pre-payment effect on yield
Premium	Decreases
Par	Decreases
Discount	Increases

as every man in the street knows, is inversely related to its yield. Now with an MBS, there exists the possibility of pre-payment. This will cause the yield to be different in comparison to a security with the same published coupon and maturity. Simply because of pre-payment. The yield calculated, as described in detail previously, will be based upon a conservative level of pre-payment. Further the timing of pre-payment will usually coincide with yields at their peaks; this is a scenario when most mortgages are liable to be redeemed. An OAS analysis is a more systematic analysis of pre-payment. It treats pre-payment as an option like feature, which is accurate, because the bond can be redeemed at par depending upon the level of interest rates. The OAS then is given by

$$\text{OAS} = \text{yield spread} - \text{cost of option (in \% terms)}.$$

Finally one other measure which may confront the reader is the total return measure. This assesses the return generated during the holding period, not necessarily the published maturity because of pre-payment.

The total return is comprised of two sources the interest earned, which is dependent upon the received coupons and the rate at which they are subsequently reinvested, and the value of the bond when it is subsequently sold resulting in a capital gain or loss. This will itself depend upon the holding period. Because most bonds redeem at 100 they tend toward this value as redemption approaches. Obviously a vital ingredient of total return is the subsequent cash flow. Again we can either use the standard PSA methodology or more sophisticated techniques briefly described in the next paragraph.

Other ways of evaluating pre-payment

The PSA methodology, although valuable, cannot be justified as a realistic treatment of pre-payment and given that it is such a vital component in determining the cash flows of a mortgage-backed bond, there must be a subsequent question mark placed on any valuation employing this technique. A more realistic valuation is obtained through simulation techniques.

At its simplest, simulation involves the creation of many, many different interest rate environments. Not just on one particular day but rather over the whole lifetime of the bond. These interest rates are then fed into a pre-payment model. The price of the bond is then the average price over all the different scenarios. It should be borne in mind that the interest rate scenarios are not just totally random selections but are based on today's rates and volatilities.

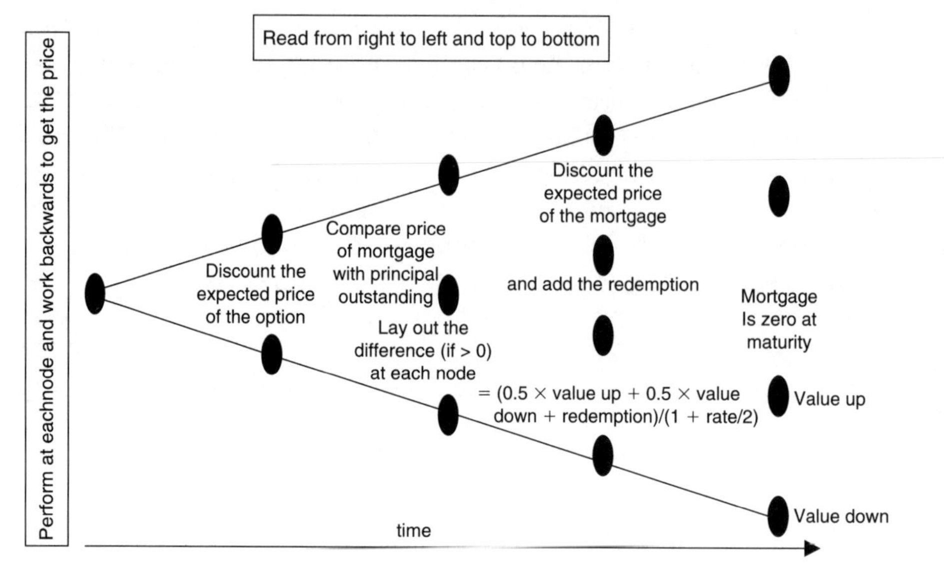

Figure 4.13 The pricing methodology of pre-payment.

One other valuation technique that is common is the binomial tree. This can be thought of as a path in time followed by the interest rate. With reference to the Figure 4.13, time runs along the page from left to right. The possible rate structure at each point in time is displayed as dots arranged vertically. To use this in anger you calculate the bond price at each so-called node. This enables a determination of the option value at each point in time. We can then multiply this value with the probability of reaching this rate. This is pre-specified, because from each point the rate can either go up or down by a known amount. Finally we discount this probability weighted value by the appropriate interest rate at each node. Of course the parameters used on the tree are not totally random, but rather industry standard models, which give a fairly accurate description of interest rate behaviour.

Modelling mortgages

The pricing methodology is shown in Figure 4.13.

4.6 The importance of credit derivatives

The use of a default swap

Prior to examining securitization structures employing credit derivatives, let us first examine why they are used. Typically a bank will be

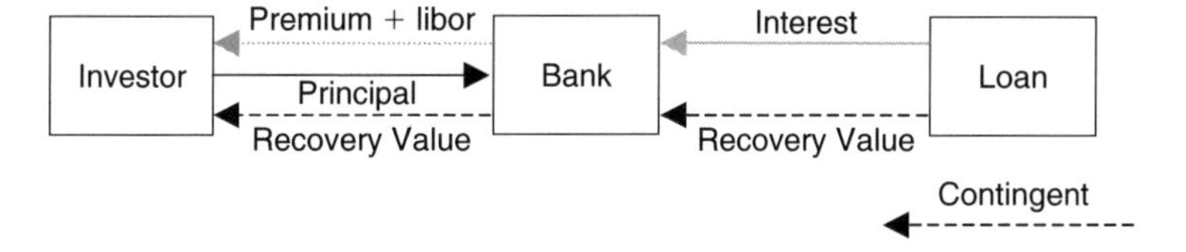

Figure 4.14 A single loan hedge.

motivated to change their exposure to a number of credits, either for regulatory purposes, or the more mundane reason of the action from a portfolio review. If the bank cannot physically transfer the loans, for relationship reasons or because of the absence of any liquid secondary market, then it may transfer the economic risk. The alternative is to foreclose the loan which again could potentially jeopardize future business.

The investor who is the end holder of the credit risk receives a periodic fee as compensation for bearing the risk. This premium is attractive to many third parties as an alternative, usually diversified source of income.

We refer you to Figure 4.14 consisting of one loan 'securitized' by the bank. A somewhat idealized example, but more complicated structures only differ in extent, not principle, as we shall see.

The credit derivative within this structure produces a stream of cash flows which are ultimately transferred to the end investor provided an event does not occur in the loan portfolio. The return received by the investor, appears as a periodic payment on a funded synthetic asset (the investor could also take unfunded exposure). The holder of protection, the bank in Figure 4.14, will be hedged against any adverse performance of the underlying loan portfolio, and the credit risk is assumed by the investor – the principal funding provides the collateral central to its viability.

Having given a simplified conceptual example we now discuss the details. The bank has employed the mechanism of securitization to create a synthetic structure reducing the capital that must be set aside and consequently 'freeing up' this portion of its balance sheet.

We can see in Figure 4.15 that the underlying securitization is identical to the previous example, but there are extra rectangles representing the SPV and the collateral.[4] The credit derivatives are

[4] A standard interest rate derivative is present in most deals to change the profile of the loans from fixed to floating or vice versa depending on the libor profile of the associated notes.

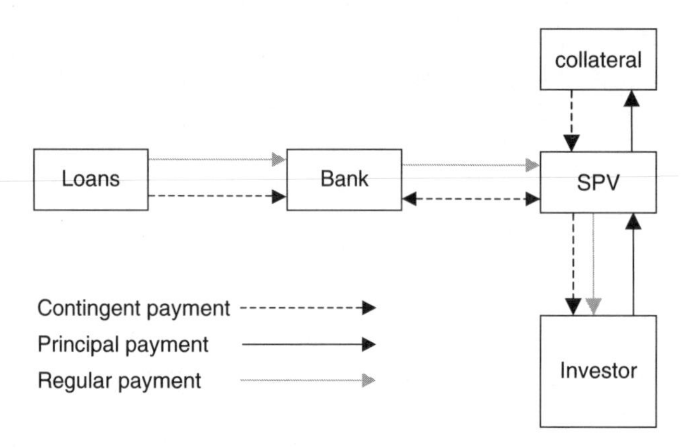

Figure 4.15 The arrangement typical of a securitization employing credit derivatives.

transacted between the vehicle and counterparty, in this case the bank. Thus the investor buys the resulting securities issued from the SPV just like any other public offering, but is unaware the coupon on the notes is being generated through credit derivatives. The derivatives are providing the protection on the banks original loans, consequently the bank has created a synthetic neutral position in the credit. The notional paid upfront by the investor is used as collateral by the SPV (the investor bears the risk of both the loan portfolio and the collateral and receives a higher 'coupon' in comparison to either of the individual exposures).

Glacier

We introduce some applications of credit derivatives. Figures 4.16 and 4.17 depict historically important deals within the industry. These were the first examples of banks actively using credit derivatives to reduce credit risk within their balance sheet. The end investor buys the assets which are structured to take on the appearance of fixed-income securities. Thus from their perspective they have no knowledge of the underlying financial engineering going on between the bank, the vehicle and counterparty.

The deal below was a watershed in 1997 and represented the first occasion on which a bank, in this case Swiss Bank Corporation, securitized a large number of loans without physically transferring them. This was arranged through the foundation of a bankruptcy remote company called 'Glacier' which purchased the economic risk of the loans through a series of credit-linked notes. The SPV subsequently

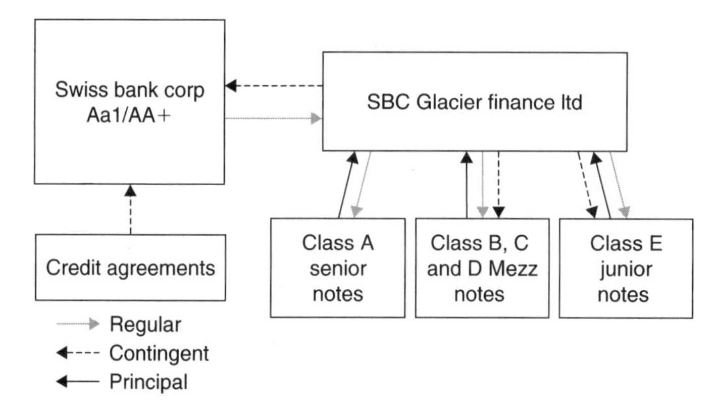

Figure 4.16 An important CDO. *Source:* UBS.

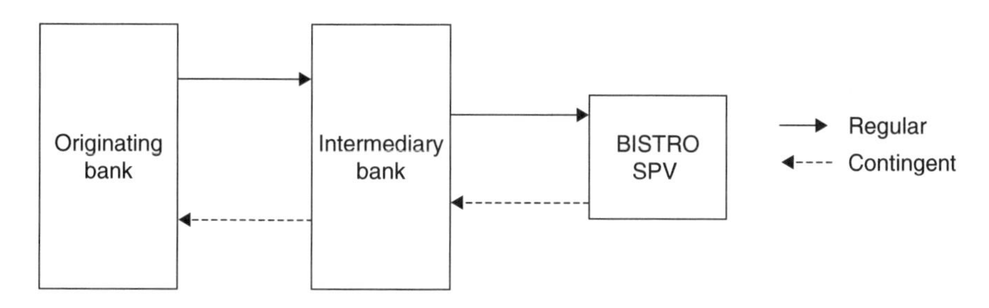

Figure 4.17 Chase/JP Morgan's BISTRO. *Source:* JP Morgan.

issued bonds under the existing MTN programme. These generate the collateral placed against defaults in the underlying loan portfolio.

Broad Index Secured Trust Offering

The generic name conferred by JP Morgan/Chase in 1997 to a securitization for a commercial bank seeking regulatory relief. Within the arrangement the bank physically maintains the loans on its balance sheet, but just transfers the economic risk through the purchase of unfunded credit derivatives. This mimics the rather more traditional securitization from a regulatory perspective. The protection is purchased from JP Morgan/Chase, who in turn purchase from an SPV. The Broad Index Secured Trust Offering (BISTRO) SPV is collateralized with government securities which it purchases through the issuance of notes sold to third party investors. In a departure from previous securitizations the notional issued is substantially less than the underlying loan portfolio. The transactions are set up to ensure that the risk of loss is less than the amount of securities sold.

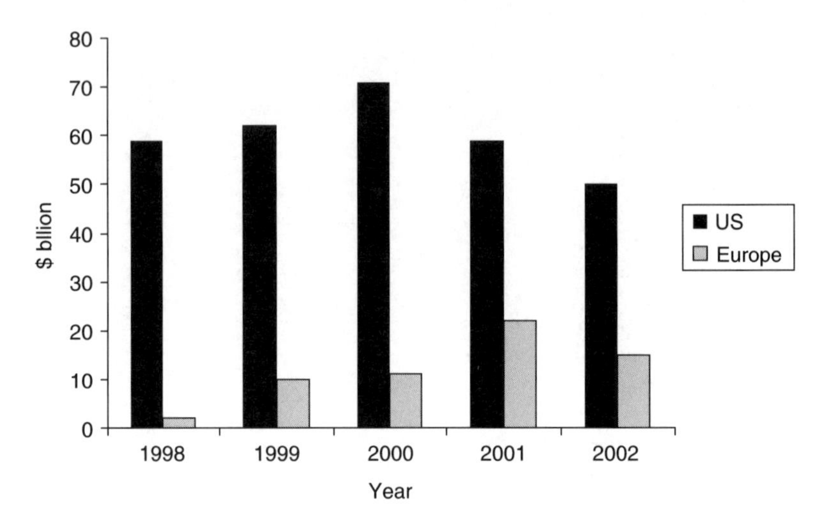

Figure 4.18 Funded CDO issuance 1998–2002.*Source:* Dr. KW.

4.7 Collateralized debt Obligations

Types of CDO

The term CDO is a common definition applied to any securitization backed by a pool of debt. There are two main categories, the balance sheet and the arbitrage. The distinction between these types can be made on the basis of collateral and motivation. These types of structures are an important variety of asset-backed issuance within continental Europe. Figure 4.18 shows the growth of this phenomena.

Complimentary to this diagram is the issuance of CDOs by European countries, displayed in Figure 4.19.

The balance sheet CDO is a mechanism deployed by banks to remove assets from their balance sheet. As such the backing usually consists of loans which are no longer efficient to hold from a regulatory perspective. The arbitrage CDO on the other hand typically consists of a pool of high-yield bonds, or loans, constructed by an investment professional contracted for the purpose. Where the backing on a CDO is mainly composed of loans it is referred to as a CLO, and where the collateral is predominantly bonds it is called a CBO.

Table 4.3 illustrates the main differences.

Arbitrage CDOs

The term arbitrage in the CDO comes from the difference in income generated from the pool and the cost of funding for the overall structure.

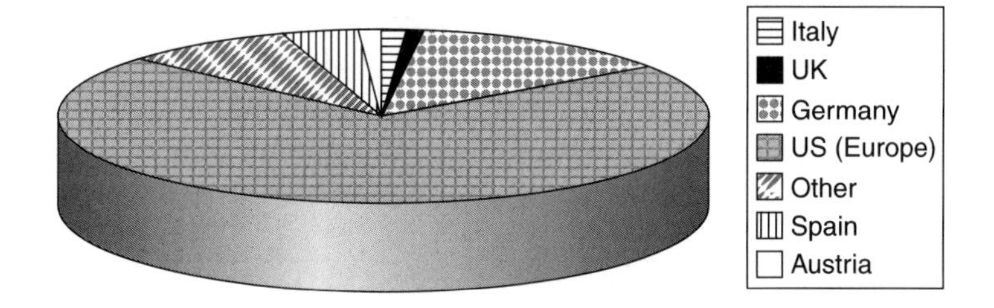

Figure 4.19 CDO issuance by country of origination in 2002. *Source:* Dr. KW.

Table 4.3 The contrasts between the forms of CDO.

Balance sheet CDOs	Arbitrage CDO
Collateral	
High grade, bank originated commercial and corporate loans	High-yield corporate bonds or corporate loans
Motivations	
Reducing balance sheet to improve capital ratios	Arbitrage opportunity between costs and return on assets. Increased marketability
Issuers	
Domestic and international banks	Insurance companies, funds
Investors	
Leveraged funds – hedge funds, trading books (banks)	Institutional clients

This has to be positive for the viability of the vehicle. The arbitrage comes about because of the difference in funding between the major tranche of high-investment grade assets (purchased by the manager) and high-yield investment rates (the underlying collateral).

Figure 4.20 illustrates the type of arrangement common within the arbitrage CDO. The portfolio is selected by the manager to fulfil the obligations of the subsequent securities issued to the investment community on the right hand side.

The portfolio will consist of assets in which the selected manager has experience. Most structures are composed of a combination of high yield, investment grade bonds and loans. There can also be a balance of bonds issued by other CDOs however. Often the deal is driven by the equity investor who will specifically contract a manager who has a track record in the relevant security to which he seeks exposure. The whole deal is usually arranged through an investment bank.

Both arbitrage and balance sheet CDOs have similar structures consisting of the asset backing, the creation of a bankruptcy remote vehicle (SPV) and the structuring of liabilities in order to appeal to the net end investor.

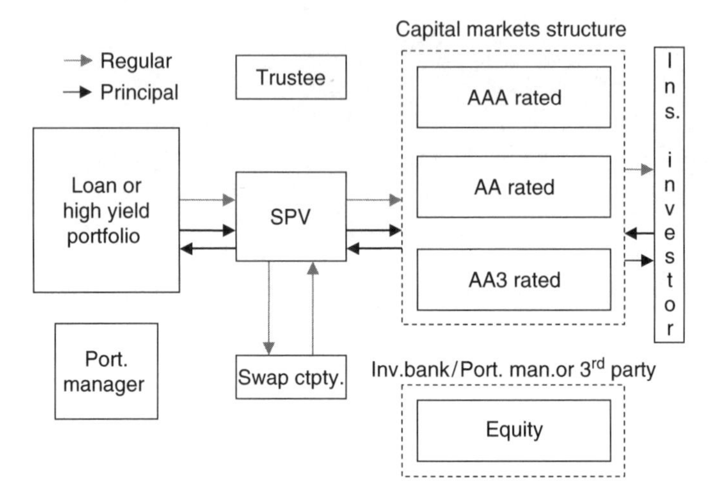

Figure 4.20 The structure of an arbitrage CDO.

Synthetic CLOs

A recent development has been the advent of the synthetic CDO. This consists of the creation of an SPV but just the economic risk of the collateral is transferred through the use of credit derivatives. The benefits to the investor are exactly the same in the synthetic CDO. The SPV arranges this by issuing a note which can either be funded or unfunded.

Within this arrangement the loan portfolio, for example, remains on the bank's balance sheet and the investors bear the credit risk on the underlying collateral. To compensate them for bearing this risk they receive the premium payable by the bank. Ultimately in the form of periodic 'coupons' on the note.

Figure 4.21 shows a common synthetic CDO.

The synthetic CLO has a number of similarities with traditional ABS securitizations. The mechanism of servicing assets and the subsequent issuance of debt by a bankrupt remote vehicle are common. The collateral is different, for ABS this consists of mortgage or credit card receivables, rather than high-yield loans, bonds or high-yield bonds.

CDOs have security tranches, the rating of which is determined by the amount of credit enhancement within the structure, the performance of the collateral and the priority of cash flows. This credit enhancement is the key focus for the agencies, acting on behalf of the investor.

The agency will systematically evaluate the ordering of the principal and interest, the pre-payment conditions and the method of allocation for default and recovery.

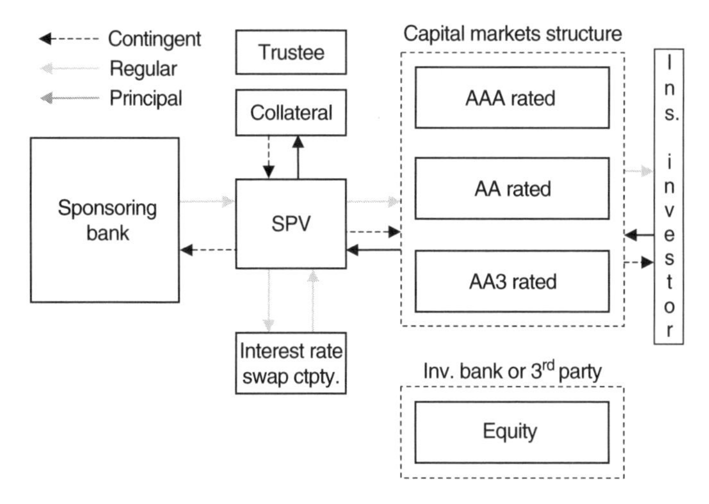

Figure 4.21 The common structure of a synthetic CLO.

4.8 CDO asset types

The arbitrage CDO can be further broken down into two categories, the so-called cash flow and market value (or managed) CDO. Within the former the principal on tranches is repaid using cash generated from repayments on the collateral. In the market value the principal is paid by selling the collateral.

Cash flow CDOs share more similarities to the ABS than their market value counterparts. In particular the collateral is an amortizing pool of loans expected to make both coupon and nominal payments for the duration of the liabilities.

Cash flow CDOs have investment periods longer than the traditional ABS structures – typically 4 years or longer, trading of the underlying collateral pool is restricted usually for reasons of liquidity. In particular loans do not often have a deep secondary market.

For these reasons the valuation accorded to the pool is based on the par value of the underlying assets. The market value variety on the other hand often has quite a liquid secondary market. This allows the portfolio manager to freely trade the backing. This has a number of profound implications. The portfolio will evolve because the manager is trying to maximize the value of the collateral. This is an exercise in default diversification, which is subtlety distinct from traditional mutual fund activities. For example, the manager must anticipate credit events and mitigate the effect by selling positions prior to their deterioration or/and purchasing assets that are expected to diversify. This means she has to pick and choose according to her view the best performing assets – no easy task. Furthermore the investors active in the resulting debt structures have to place as much emphasis on the track record of the manager as they do investigating the backing; in this sense market value CDOs resemble leveraged hedge funds.

Cash flow CDOs are commonly backed by performing loans and high-yield debt, which are current, in the sense that they have not defaulted. The market value CDO has a more heterogenous structure, and the collateral pool may consist of a split between assets which support the liability payments and another category which enhances the equity portion. The balance is towards the investments supporting the resulting investment grade securities. Often the equity portion is invested into distressed debt and other broad categories of capital market instruments such as the preferreds.

The liability side of a CDO structure is relatively generic consisting of investment and non-investment grade classes with an underlying equity tranche that serves as the first loss. They typically have a maturity profile of up to 10 years. You will encounter the term 'ramp up' period appearing in the context of a market value CDO; this means that the investment manager does not fully invest the proceeds from the saleable assets immediately. This is typically because the market is not conducive to a major bidding process. These may only occur during periods of high turnover. Rating agencies scrutinize the situation

Table 4.4 The assets and liabilities of a market value CDO.

CDO balance sheet	
Assets	Liabilities
High-yield bonds	Senior debt
Collateralized loans	Mezzanine debt
Leveraged loans	Subordinated debt
Bilateral loans	
Special situation debt	
Emerging market paper	Equity
Investment grade bonds	

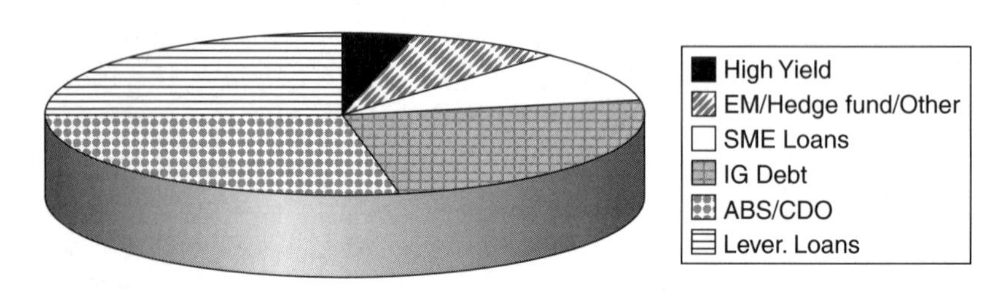

Figure 4.22 Global CDO collateral breakdown 2002. *Source:* Dr. KW.

closely because without some other form of collateral there may be insufficient liquidity in the initial period.

Table 4.4 shows the components of a typical balance sheet for a market value CDO. Note that any actual deal will consist of one or more or any combination of the assets listed, but the liabilities will be all the items noted (Figure 4.22).

4.9 Credit enhancement

We commence with a conceptual overview, which hopefully will establish the ideas. Consider one asset having a certain default frequency of 20 per cent (this asset is assumed to be long dated and pays out an annual interest amount). Holding this asset can be considered to be quite risky. However if we had 200 such assets then it is a reasonable expectation that 160 of them will survive and 40 of them will be lost. If we further give these first 160 payments, rather than the assets themselves to an investor then she will be highly delighted. The question comes down to what do we actually sell, and because we are in the world of sharp finance for how much?

We simply sell fixed-income instruments, the coupon is the payment. Now if we only sell about 80 per cent of the notional receipts then what would the rating agencies have to say about our 'bonds'? They would be impressed to the extent that they would be accorded at least an investment grade. We can take the argument further and consider the remainder of the cash flows, these can be attached to another instrument which has the characteristics of not always offering a sure return but if there is a return it is not limited to a pre-specified amount. We decide to call it equity.

Of course this structure is unrealistic, but the actual applications only differ in terms of complexity not in principle. This type of enhancement is the basic *subordinated* mechanism, prevalent in most of the current structures.

There are other forms of credit enhancement discussed below. The distinction can be based upon either an external mechanism to the SPV, or an internal arrangement.

External credit enhancement

An arrangement where a third-party *guarantees* to cover losses on the issue. The cover usually guarantees a proportion of the issue rather than its entirety. One of the oldest forms of credit enhancement is the *letter of credit*. This represents a guarantee from the bank to meet payments in the event that the trust is unable to maintain its commitment to service the bond issue. The guarantee will pre-specify the amount covered, a fee is payable to the bank providing this cover.

Internal credit enhancement

The senior *subordinated* structure represents the most common type of arrangement encountered for the provision of credit enhancement. The mechanism consists of ranking a bond below the senior securities to subsequently absorb all losses due to default. The consequence is that the senior notes are unaffected by most deleterious effects within the asset pool (which is obviously the aim.) This so-called junior debt will trade at a high yield to compensate the investor for the risks attached.

We can see in Figure 4.23 a typical structure employing this facility. The senior notes are AAA and AA, comprising an annuity together with an amortizing zero. Underpayments caused by stress in the asset pool are absorbed by a junior annuity.

The other common types of common internal credit enhancement are *over collateralization* whereby the SPV has assets of greater value than the subsequent debt issuance. If defaults occur within the backing then the difference is paid to the investor through the surplus accumulated in previous periods.

Under collateral structures, are also possible, provided the cash flow on the underlying assets is large enough to cover the outgoing payments.

Finally you will encounter a form of credit enhancement known as *excess spread*. This is simply the difference between the amount of cash flow coming into the vehicle and the amount of debt servicing.

Construction of financial securities

A typical CLO consists of the senior/subordinated structure. Within this framework the precise details of the asset details depend very much on the characteristics of the asset backing. Unfortunately no two

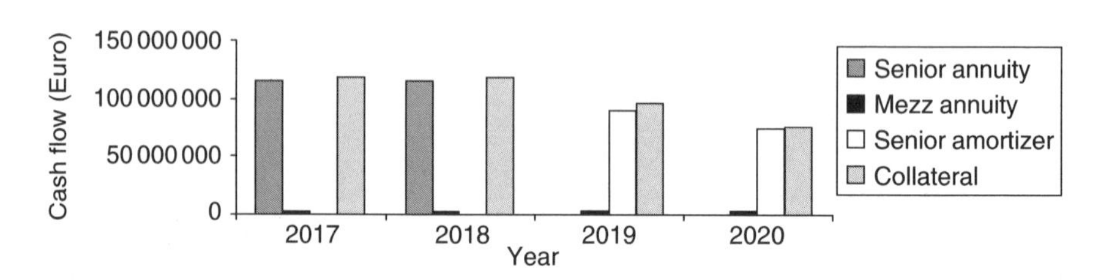

Figure 4.23 Asset backing and resulting securities.

securitizations have exactly the same profile, the methodology used in the formation of these assets and the subsequent evaluation by the rating agencies however is generic. In this section we look at a structure in detail, evaluating the formation of the assets and the subsequent stress testing applied by the agencies to evaluate their performance. Indeed these two steps should be considered to be interrelated since the stress analysis will help shape the profile of the securities.

Thus we divide our labour into two areas; on the one hand we need an understanding of the receivables and on the other how to construct the resulting financial assets given the constraints imposed by the income stream.

The asset portfolio

The securitization we consider consists of a large number of commercial loans warehoused on the bank's balance sheet. The regulatory environment has changed in such a way as to prejudice the collection of low grade assets. Our august bank thus wished to seek regulatory relief by absolving the loans from the balance sheet. Is this possible? We answer this by examining a potential candidate discussed below.

Asset backing

The profile of the loans is displayed in Figure 4.24. The curve is comprised of the payouts consisting of both interest and redemption amounts, as the loans are medium to long dated then initially the bulk of the payments will be comprised of interest and then as we move towards maturity, redemption will become dominant. The majority of the loans were based on a floating[5] coupon structure; this means

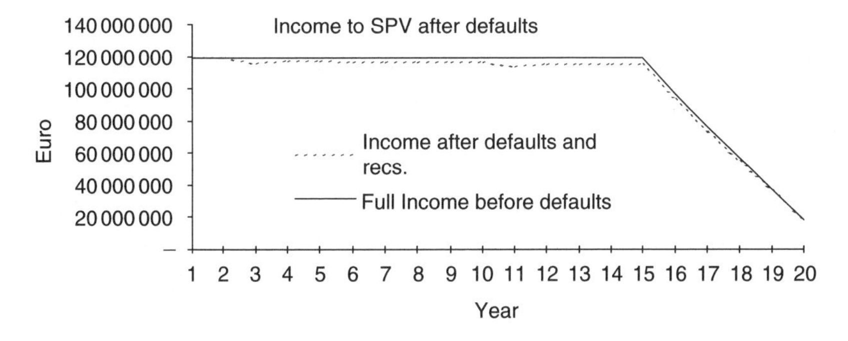

Figure 4.24 The collateral profile of the case study.

[5] We replace the floating payment by the relevant forward rate.

every year the obligor has to pay a variable percentage of the loan value. There securitization consisted of approximately €100 denominated loans each having a nominal of €10 million confined to the financial sector. We will explore in due course the 'lower' profile.

Figure 2.18 in the chapter on the loan portfolio shows the resulting securities. If you look at the profile, even the novice will notice the similarity between the asset redemption and interest schedule and the pay-off profile of the underlying loans. This is not an accident; the job of the structurer is to carefully design the securities such that they match the receivables.

There are many constraints on this task; these include the primary objective of making the structure as efficient as possible. This entails trying to ensure most of the incoming loan proceeds are distributed as fully as possible without the build up of an underlying cash reserve. Otherwise the effect would be a lowering of value for the overall structure.

Of course some reserve is desirable to cover the contingency of inadequate receivables for debt servicing. The difference could be accessed from this 'reserve' in the case of internal enhancement.

We can anticipate the need for some kind of amortization with recourse to the downward sloping loan profile, this requires the payoff of principal to begin in 2015 and end in 2023. This requirement could be fulfilled by long dated zero coupon bonds. They are flexible instruments which are used for interest rate hedging by banks and insurance companies. For example if you hold a conventional bond and worry about an interest rate rise then the value can be protected by selling a zero of similar maturity. Insurance companies can use the appropriate zero to match a liability. Zeros also find a home amongst the private investor; they represent a tax efficient investment because the return is often treated as a capital gain by a number of tax regulations. Strictly though there is no uncertainty attached to the gain, hence the appeal.

Notice that only three structures are actually priced. i.e. will be sold to institutional clients. This is because the rest of the structure is required to support the saleable portion.

We discussed in Section 4.9 the use of the senior/substructure. This is the prevalent method within CDO obligations. The market terminology refers to this as a 'waterfall chart' (Figure 4.25). The idea is that we can think of the income from the the loan portfolio as a stream of water, with the volume per unit of time roughly analogous to the cash flow per month.

Part of this stream of water is diverted into the first waterfall; this appeals to our aesthetic qualities. In order to look attractive the waterfall will have a certain size and thus require a certain quantity of flow.

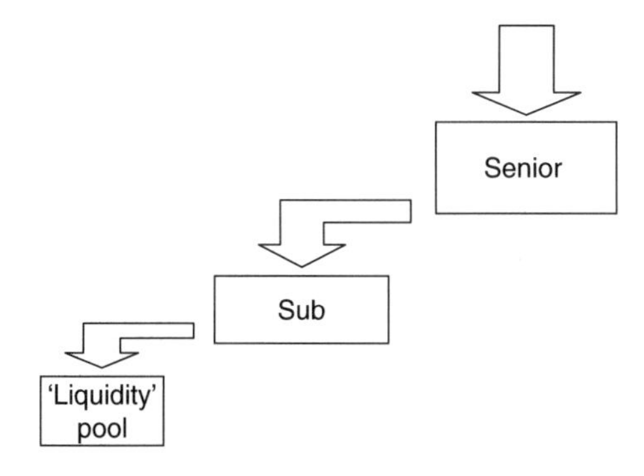

Figure 4.25 The waterfall mechanism deployed in most structures.

If we still have sufficient water left over, then we can divert the difference into another waterfall, perhaps smaller than the former. We think you get the idea. The analogy can be pursued further. We can think of diverting a smaller stream and collecting this into a pool. This would be the over collateralization, and in terms of drought can be used to maintain our elaborate set of waterfalls.

Well enough of analogies, let us examine how the rating agencies actually simulate loan under-performance and the impact on the structure. This process is called 'stressing' the backing in order to assess whether a given structure can handle an anticipated adverse economic environment.

What would be a realistic 'worst case' scenario for the asset securitization? It is unlikely that all loans would simultaneously default, and this situation is not tested for. A much more rigorous test would be to assume each loan has the same probability of default over its lifetime given they are confined to the financial sector.

The further assumption is that there is some correlation between defaults within the portfolio. We might further expect the possibility of default to depend on a variable at large, for example the general state of the economy or perhaps a sector influence.

4.10 Detailed evaluation of asset backing and enhancement

The important insight is that the propensity towards default is a random process; this means we cannot predict it in advance. However we can prescribe an equation which decomposes the driver into what is called an idiosyncratic, or obligor specific term and a systematic term:

$$E = \varepsilon + \beta I.$$

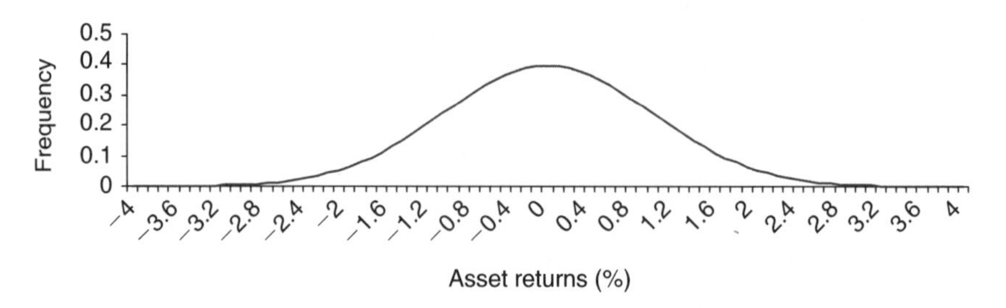

Figure 4.26 The distribution of returns.

(This is referred to as a structural model which assumes the returns on the equity of the company issuing the debt can furnish information on default.)

Here E is the expected return on equity; ε is the company specific term; βI is the systematic component.

Usually we expect the returns to have a normal distribution; this means that the returns have a bell shape about the average loss. The distribution of returns are shown in Figure 4.26.

If we assume the company is isolated from the general economy then we can generate its behaviour through an independent random process. The idea is rather than looking at historical loss distributions we wish to generate samples assuming we know average characteristics. If you wish to use Excel to illustrate this then you can use the random number generator, however this just generates a uniform sequence between 0 and 1, to get a random draw from a normal distribution use

$$\text{Shock} = \text{rand()} + \text{rand()} + \text{rand()} \cdots -6$$

with 12 rand()s.

The rationale for this is the nature of the default process. A historical sample might not be representative considering how rarely some of the events can occur. Also notice that just because we use a normal distribution does not mean that default is a normal process. Rather it depends on the mapping of returns to states. This is covered in detail in Section 2.13.

There is something missing however with this simplistic treatment, this is the driving influence of a common random process. This can be interpreted as the common influence of the market as a whole. The following equation shows how we generate this within Excel:

$$\text{Drawing} = \text{correlation} \times \text{commonshock} + \sqrt{1 - \text{correlation}^2} \times \text{shock},$$

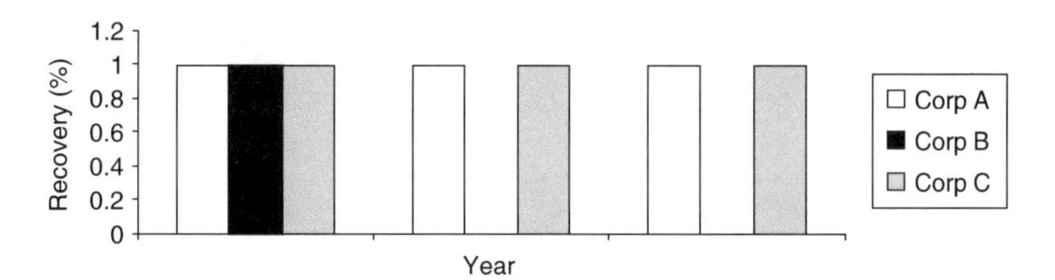

Figure 4.27 Stressing the portfolio.

where commonshock is an independent drawing from our Excel random normal generator. What do we then do with such a random drawing, what is the connection with the loss of income?

You need to evaluate *NORMDIST* (*Drawing*,0,1, *TRUE*) and compare this random drawing with a default threshold, representing 2.5 per cent of the cumulative distribution, for example the precise threshold depends on the nature of the collateral, and treat it as a defaulter if below and survivor if not.

If defaulted we then must address the details of the default process. Usually not all of the loan value is lost. There are usually clauses that allow collection on some of the loan value possibly because there is collateral set against it.

The amount collected on the loan after default is given by

$$\text{Amount} = \text{recovery} \times \text{exposure}.$$

Once the loan has defaulted it stays that way, thus it has either defaulted or is a non-defaulter. Stressing the portfolio is shown in Figure 4.27.

The cumulative default likelihood grows as the exposure time increases, so the loan has to be considered over some pre-specified horizon period. In our example we have taken the maturity of the longest dated loan (Figure 4.28).

We arrive at a profile of the ‘stressed’ cash flows; the question is then how are the resulting cash flows on our structures affected?

These are evaluated by a consideration of the payoffs involved, they are ranked either sequentially or ‘Pari-passu’, whereby they are ranked equal. Figure 4.29 is a flow chart depicting the ordering of cash flows.

Broadly the coupons on each of the bonds are paid according to their seniority class, the remaining money, if any, enters the liquidity pool. This is used to service subsequent payments when the income is insufficient. The structure is designed so that this pool is as small as possible given likely scenarios. Too large a pool detracts from the overall value of the portfolio.

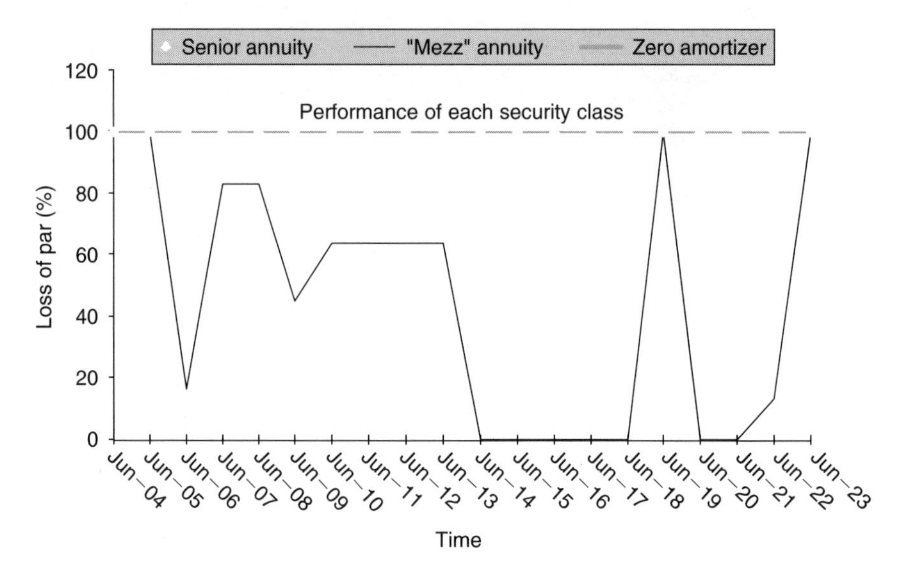

Figure 4.28 Impact of defaults on indenture.

Figure 4.28 shows the impact of default arrivals on the structure; the senior obligations are always satisfied. However the 'mezzanine' debt defaults, on a large number of occasions between 2016 and 2023, the equity component does not accumulate until about 2023. This is quite acceptable behaviour, however, and would constitute strong evidence that the senior rating accorded to the debt is justified.

The initial equity returns are unfortunate, but representative of this type of investment. The holder would anticipate this but expect to postpone gains. Further this is a vital component of any securitization. This typically has the characteristic of paying no income initially but the strong possibility of high returns at a later date. These high returns are furnished from the cash pool which increments as a result of the income being greater than the servicing needs of the rated debt. The equity payoff is designed to be paid at a forward date to allow for this. The equity piece of the deal is often held by the originating bank; usually because no other party is interested, or the bank wants to promote credibility in the deal (there is no better way than becoming a shareholder). Highly leveraged funds can often be equity investors.

We are now equipped with the conceptual framework to answer the question posed at the outset. The extent to which this transaction would gain regulatory relief depends vitally on the size of the first loss or equity tranche. Typically the bank would retain most of the credit risk because it effectively is forced to retain this portion. Indeed an equity tranche larger than 8 per cent results in no capital relief.

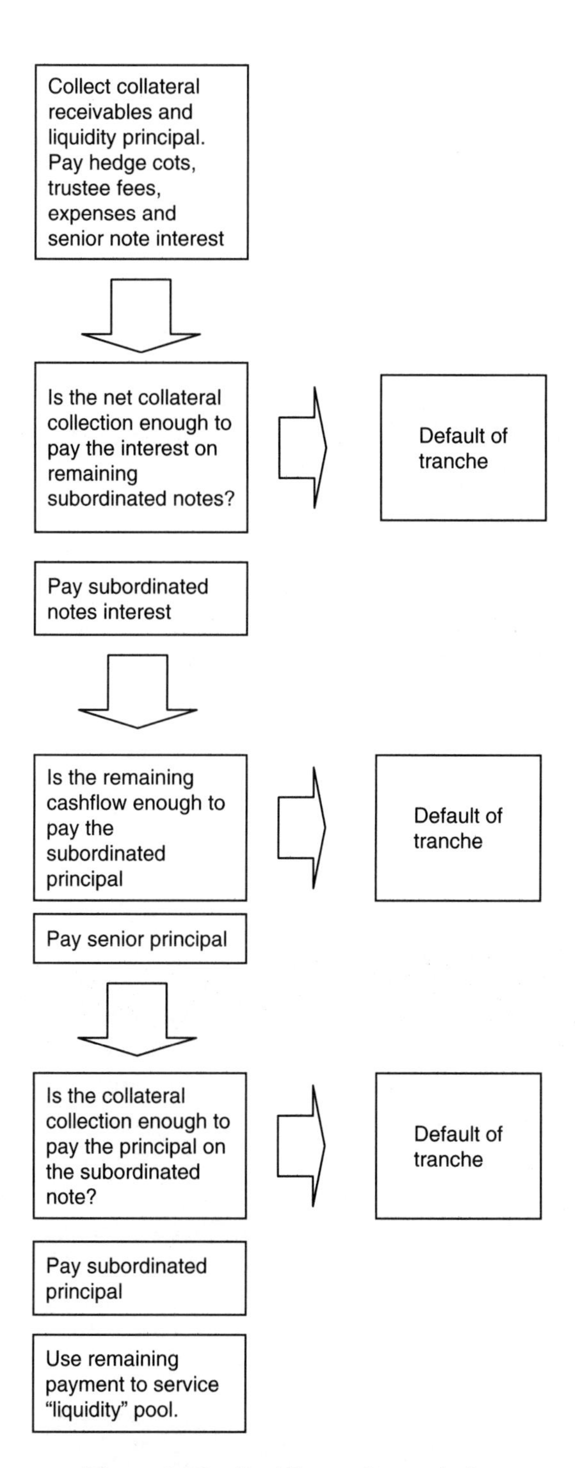

Figure 4.29 Deciding on the seniority.

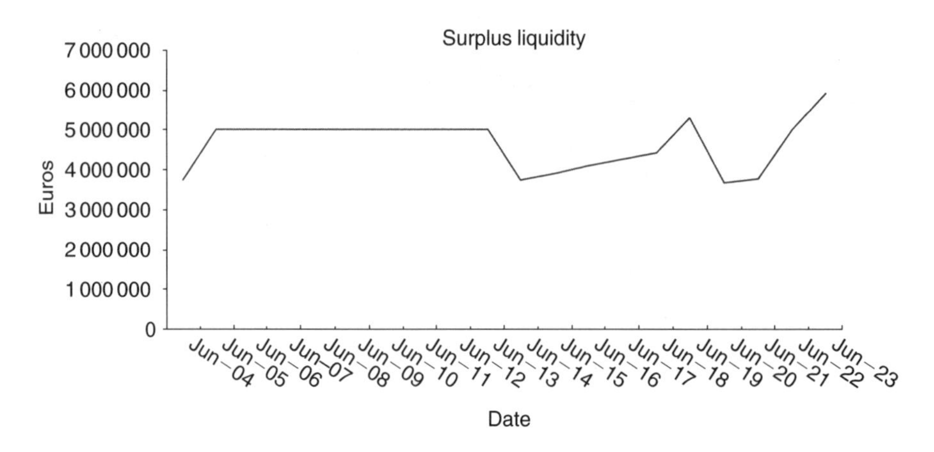

Figure 4.30 The liquidity within the structure.

Smaller retentions result in relief equal to the difference between 8 per cent and the retainer.

There are other considerations, however including the cost of funding such an arrangement. If the bank accessed low cost financing then the difference between the aggregate level achieved through the securitization route is unattractive since even the most senior tranches are typically sold at a premium to libor prevalent in the asset-backed market. The alternative arrangement to participating loans is the synthetic arrangement covered in great detail in Section 4.7.

4.11 Investor analysis

Construction of financial securities

We now drill down into the 'profile' and consider the assets that comprise the offering to the investors. A consideration of this base is vital to originating the instruments and is another integral component of their design. There is little benefit in promoting a particularly efficient structure which purportedly would enjoy a large valuation if the investor demand for the individual components is low. To obviate the chances of this, the structuring team would work closely with the organizations origination and fixed-income sales team to understand the nature of the investor marketplace and which instruments would appeal.[6]

[6] We have described these entities as being an integral component of the bank. For many commercial banks this is not the case and the service would be made available from a partner bank.

The first instrument is a middle dated annuity. This is a class of security which pays out a constant stream of income. Each payment can be thought of as being comprised of both interest and principal; to begin with most of the payment will be interest but as the time to maturity increases then more will be comprised of nominal. There is a formula to calculate its value; this is displayed in the equation below:

$$P = A\left[\frac{(1 + r)^n - 1}{r \times (1 + r)^n}\right],$$

where P is the principal amount and r is the annuity rate lasting for n years.

For example if we consider the first tranche, which has a common annual payment of \$115 000 000 lasting for 15 years, $r = 4\%$:

$$P = \$115\,000\,000\left[\frac{(1 + 0.04)^{15} - 1}{0.04 \times (1 + 0.04)^{15}}\right]$$

giving

$$P = \$1\,278\,614\,560.$$

This value is very approximate, and considerably overvalues, for reason we postpone to a later discussion.

Annuities comprise two tranches of the structure. If we examine the loan profile we can infer why this was the case. The shape can be approximately described by two distinct patterns. The first part comprises payouts up to a maturity of about 2018; this is almost a horizontal line. The second shape starts from 2018 and extends to 2023. This is a downward sloping line and is caused by a heavy loan redemption schedule over this period.

As annuities produce a horizontal profile they are a natural candidate for the securitization of the payments until 2018. The question then arises as to whether there will be sufficient investor appetite for these long dated instruments. The demand for the various tranches comes from different sources of the investment community. Generally the principal aim is to securitize as much as possible as high-investment grade. This would then appeal to the large institutional investors who are usually only allowed through regulatory authorities to deal in such paper. Further appeal would be anticipated from the retail marketplace.

The long dated annuities would be structured as investment grade assets, and would find a natural home within the pension funds that have a large demand for long dated constant payment. This is because policy holders at some point convert their investment into a stream of annuity payments.

The redemption schedule from 2018 until 2023 is trickier, and we need to appeal to the concept of amortization and zero coupon. These are intimidating sound phrases but the underlying ideas are straightforward. A good example is provided by an interest and principal mortgage. Here the monthly payment to the lender consists of both interest on the underlying loan and a contribution to pay off some of the outstanding capital. The underlying loan would be said to be amortized over the lifetime of the mortgage. There is no need however for the loan to be paid according to this schedule however and many different structures exist within the capital markets.

A zero coupon structure is simply a bond that pays out no interest. How can this have any appeal? Well, the interest is embedded so to speak in the terms of the bond. They are always offered at a discount to the nominal. The discount is such that over the lifetime of the zero the difference in value between the cost and the redemption at par gives a return comparable to other bonds having the same maturity.

Back to the structure then. We can anticipate the need for some kind of amortization simply with recourse to the downward sloping loan profile, this requires the payoff of principal to begin in 2018 and end in 2023 or thereabouts. The demand for zeros comes from both banks and insurance companies; they are flexible instruments which can be used for interest rate hedging. The two instruments described so far constitute the investment grade portion of the structure. The bank wishing to free capital from its balance sheet wishes to obtain a high price as possible. How are they valued?

Valuation of the investment grade assets

To properly value any fixed-income instrument you require something called the 'zero coupon curve'. This is none other than the time value of money. If I lent out some money I would expect a higher rate of return the longer the lending period to compensate me for the inability to profit from any changes in the shorter term rate. This plot of interest rate against maturity goes by the rather intimidating name of a 'term structure'. Once I have this plot I can use it to exactly discount cash flows to determine how much they are worth today. It is a marvellous device; it enables a comparison of payments occurring at different times. Figure 4.31 shows a typical plot.

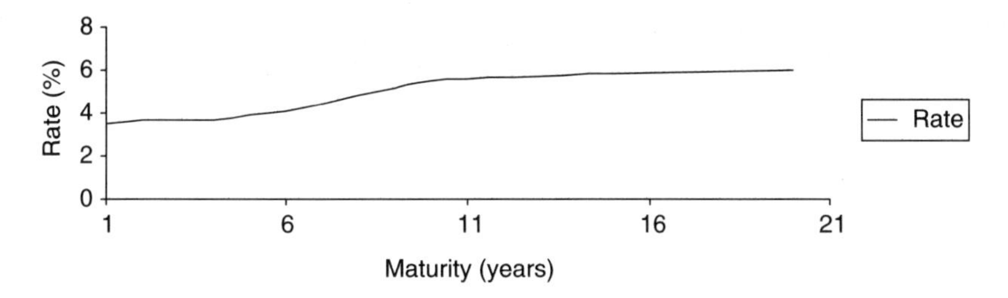

Figure 4.31 A typical term structure.

To value any cash flow stream then we use the equation below:

$$\text{Present value} = \sum_{i=1}^{i=N} \text{cashflow}_i \times \text{discount factor}_i.$$

Here we multiply each cash flow occurring at time t with the discount factor at the corresponding time. These individual components are then summed up. The only further piece of information required is the relevant term structure to obtain the discount factor. This is determined from a combination of the risk free rate and a correction which allows for a possible default on the obligor. This default is assessed by the market and added to the risk free rate in the form of a spread. (The spread can have maturity dependence.) The discount factor thus has the form:

$$\text{Discount factor} = \frac{1}{[1 + \text{risk free rate} + \text{spread}]^t}.$$

The spread accorded to the obligor not surprisingly depends on the credit rating assigned to the borrower. We have three investment grade tranches, this means that spread over the risk free rate will be quite small because of the low likelihood of default. Figure 4.31 shows the pricing curve or term structure used to obtain the value of the senior tranches.

The last investment grade asset is the shorter dated maturity annuity; this has a smaller monthly 'coupon'.

References

Masters *et al.*, The JP Morgan Guide to Credit Derivatives, *Risk Metrics Group.*
O'Kane, Credit Derivatives Explained, *Lehman Brothers.*

5

The credit risk of interest rate products

Counterparty credit risk

5.1 Introduction

In this chapter we discuss standard interest rate products from the perspective of credit rather than libor risk. We use the term 'libor' as a synonym for general interest rate risk. The risk on a fixed income asset generally consists both of a risk free and a spread element. The former is caused by variations in the market rate for risk free borrowing, impacting an obligations present value. A good credit standing will enable borrowing at the risk free rate. Generally this will be restricted to governments in OECD countries and well-capitalized corporates.

For most mere mortals however we have to borrow at the risk free rate plus a spread representing our credit worthiness. From the perspective of the lender, the present value of the loan will depend on both the current market rate and the on going credit standing of the borrower. These risks are distinct. Consequently a fixed income bond will have a price which reflects both the risk free rate and the credit worthiness of the borrower.

We have treated bonds in great detail in Chapter 1. What about interest-rate derivatives, how does credit enter into the discussion? There is a twofold effect on the handling of a derivative product. Firstly the pricing of the derivative must reflect the credit worthiness of the counterparty and secondly an amount of capital must be reserved against a default of the counterparty.

In this section we focus on counterparty credit risk (CCR) for OTC contracts and how banks manage this exposure. This is a distinct aspect of derivative risk. The usual discussions on derivative risk pertain to all risk associated with their use, these types can conservatively be categorized as legal documentary, liquidity, operational, market and hedging.

CCR however is the amount of current and future exposure to a counterpart as a consequence of a derivative transaction, the likelihood that the counterparty will default and the magnitude of the recovery upon default.

The credit risk of a counterparty can be broken down into two distinct components. The risk of loss due to the counterparty defaulting, and then the actual exposure which will be the amount you would lose. This is referred to as the replacement cost of the instrument which is the marked to market value of the derivative contract. The proviso is that this must be positive or zero in the case of a short position. For example if you have sold an 'in the money' contract and the deal was unwound at some later date having increased in value. Then a loss (from your perspective) would have to be realized. If the counterparty defaulted, in the reverse of the above trade this obligation would cease. Hence the replacement cost is always the positive marked to market value of the contract.

The replacement cost will be dependent upon current market factors. For example if you have an interest rate swap on your book, the current value will be dependent upon current swap rates relative to the rate upon deal inception.

There is a further integral aspect of CCR. This is centred around the notion of default in the future. The marked to market analysis arrives at the current exposure of the instrument and implies a loss given a default today. But on an equal footing will be a consideration of the impact of a default in the future. This will be dependent upon a number of unknowns, first will be the possibility of default in the future and secondly the exposure in the event of future default.

5.2 Exposures

Current exposure

This section will analyse in more detail the impact of immediate default and the arrangements within the banking community to mitigate the effect. The current exposure will be the positive, or zero, marked to market value for the derivative.

We can split derivatives into categories. For example swaps are bilateral obligations. When evaluating the exposure and credit risk we have to take this into account. Then more simply we have unilateral obligations such as standard fixed income interest rate options. Here the exposure and credit risk is one sided.

Prior to the above you may have been thinking that the credit risk on a swap is simply the exposure to the counterparty, that is identical to the risk on a bond or loan with the same maturity. However this is not the case; the bilateral nature of the instrument must be addressed. This is because a loan has interest and principal receipts at risk. An interest rate swap transaction has only the interest payments at risk because the principal is usually not exchanged. Furthermore the periodic flows are usually smaller than those of a comparable loan because the flows are based on the difference between the fixed rate deal at inception and the current libor set.

Central to the discussion is a subtle interplay between market and credit risk. To be specific a loss is suffered if two events occur simultaneously. Firstly the counterparty becomes distressed and defaults. However there will only be a loss of value on the contract if the swap is making a profit. This will be purely dependent upon the current market environment.

We have been describing exposure to just one counterpart through an interest rate derivative contract. Most business activities however run multiple positions. What then is their current counterparty credit exposure? It is simply the sum of positive market values on all transactions with a single counterparty, subsequently summed up across all the counterparties.

This is usually managed under a formal netting arrangement. This is both enforceable and acceptable to the relevant regulatory body.

Future exposure

The future exposure to a counterpart represents the risk of a loss arising from a potential default. This is some times referred to as future credit loss, or the future replacement cost of the contract.

The future replacement cost will depend upon the joint likelihood of default and the evolution of market variables such that the contract has a positive value. Without wishing to go into the nitty-gritty of interest rate behaviour, suffice to say that the evolution is stochastic. This is a big word for stating a position of ignorance. Simply, we do not know where future rates will be. However we are not totally ignorant and it is acceptable in the marketplace to apply a distribution of rates. So in essence we have given up trying to talk about one particular outcome but instead talk about a possible set of outcomes with attached probabilities. The credit loss is then simply the product of the probability of default with the average expected exposure.

Although this is a book on credit risk. Counterparty credit exposure is one of those many areas where the overlap between standard market and credit risk must be addressed. Conceptually it helps to think in terms of pigeon holes, although reality is always at the level of the interaction.

Assuming we know the probability of default in the future (after all you have read the chapter on fundamental credit). What is the method of evaluating the potential future exposure on our derivative contract? There are three main techniques which, in no particular priority, are Monte Carlo simulation, historic simulation and analytical approaches.

Monte Carlo simply generates the marketplace many, many times. Each time subtly different but dependent upon the structural characteristics of the financial assets. For example an interest rate will move relative to the current rate and have some degree of correlation with other rates, but other than this its evolution will be random. The future value of our instrument will be the average value implied by the set of rates under all these different scenarios.

Historic simulation can be thought of as obtaining the historic average over a number of sequential trading days and using this to calculate the exposure. Usual rules apply when suggesting history is a proxy for future behaviour.

These methods tend to be slow computationally. Particularly noticeable if you are sat at a trading desk and awaiting an assessment of future exposure. This is the reason for employing an analytic technique. A main stream analytical approach consists of decomposing changes in present value into two distinct ingredients. One is the sensitivity of the instrument to the market environment and the other is the amount that the market will move, included in this will be the likelihood of co-movements. Just such a methodology is employed by the Risk Metrics™ architecture consisting of the so-called 'delta-gamma' approach. This divides labour into assessing the sensitivity of the instrument and the subsequent application of covariance matrices derived from zero coupon bonds (or swap rates) to capture the likelihood and co-movement of the market place.

Example

The example (Figure 5.1) illustrates the potential future exposure of an interest-rate swap. Figure 5.1 is commonly deployed in a number

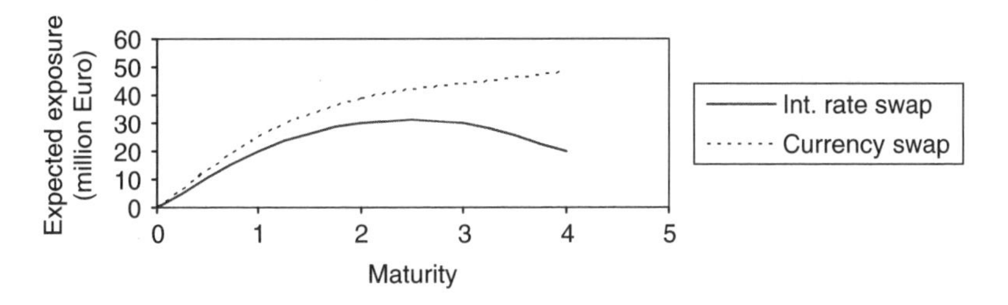

Figure 5.1 Counterparty exposure for various contracts.

of textbooks leading to the perception that the exposure on an interest-rate swap is always synonymous with this figure. We emphasize this is just a special case of a more general situation.

The lifetime of the swap is 5 years and we assume the deal was done on a €500 million notional. At the end of the first year rates have declined by 1 per cent. If the bank is receiving fixed payments the present value will be a stream of cash flows each worth 1 per cent of 500 million which gives a total nominal exposure of €20 million (the present value exposure will be rather less).

At the beginning of the second year, if rates have declined a further 1 per cent then we have an exposure of €10 million for 3 years, which gives a total figure of €30 million. The argument continues in this manner. It is quite unusual for rates to drop by 100 basis points, this is why we drew attention to its somewhat pedagogical nature. We can see from Figure 5.1 that although the interest rate environment is favourable to the bank, the effect of the remaining time to maturity will diminish this benefit as time advances. Consequently the exposure forms a cusp rather than an upward sloping line.

We have spoken at some length about both the current exposure and the potential exposure of an interest rate product within the market portfolio. The credit risk is their sum:

$$\text{Credit risk} = \text{replacement cost} + \text{potential future exposure.}$$

How do banks actually manage these exposures? Through daily marking to market all the positions and then netting exposures on deals with the same counterparty. (Which as previously stated is applicable only under an enforceable netting agreement.) If the position is exchange traded there is negligible credit risk because it is subject to guarantee.

We have described various techniques for estimating the potential exposure of a deal. However if a bank is not party to this type of relatively sophisticated modelling then an alternative is to apply matrices of risk factors which differ by instrument type and maturity. These matrices are supplied by the regulators indeed, financial institutions

Table 5.1 Weightings for maturity.

Contract type	Residual maturity		
Category	<1 year	1 < 5 year	>5 year
Interest rate	0%	0.5%	1.5%
FX	1.0%	5.0%	7.5%
Equities	6.0%	8.0%	10.0%

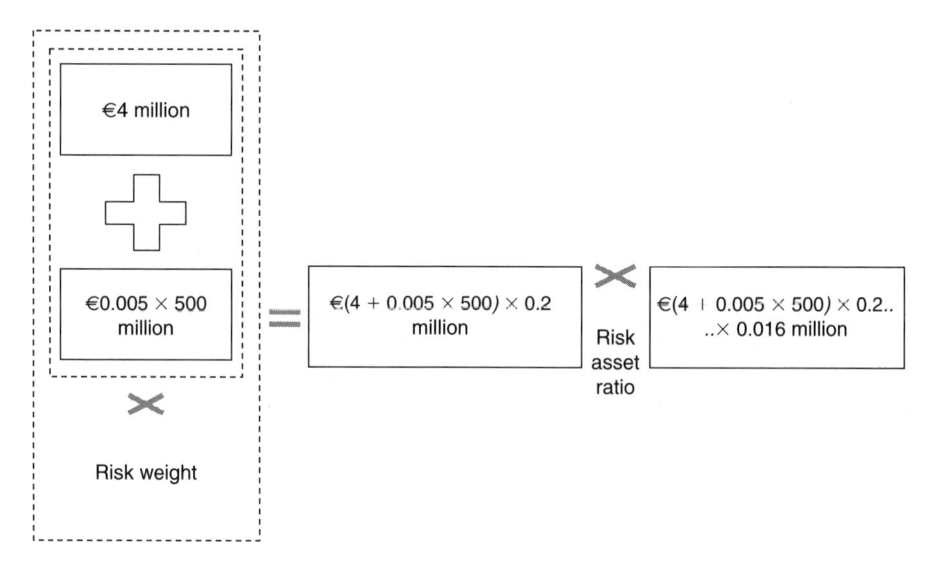

Figure 5.2 Standard exposure method.

have a range of regulations and controls they must uphold. A primary one is the level of capital held to provide a cushion for the activities the bank engages upon. This is enshrined within the Basel Convergence Agreement applicable to G10 locales from 1988. It is a cross-border requirement universally adopted by banks around the world. This agreement was formalized under the Basel Accord of 1992 which lays out, amongst others, the rules for counterparty capital assignment.

There are two relevant aspects; one is the treatment of specific assets within the trading portfolio. Each trade is bucketed according to the categories in Table 5.1. The weights represent adjustments applied to the total exposure of the deal. After the particular deal specific corrections are made, there is a general treatment. Founded on the requirement that all cash and off balance-sheet instruments within the trading portfolio be assigned a weighting based on their perceived credit risk. The weighting determines the level of capital set aside, this is known as BIS1 or the Basel Capital Ratio (Figure 5.2).

It is perhaps useful to show a detailed example on the amount of capital a bank must set-aside to guard against CCR using the matrix

Table 5.2 Basel 1 risk weights.

Categories %	Charge %	Instruments
0	0	Sovereign debt (OECD countries)
20	1.6	Senior debt (OECD banks)
50	8	Undrawn loans (corporate credit)
100	8	Corporate debt and non-OECD sovereign debt

technique. We show above an outline of the methodology, in the example above we analyse a 5 years swap 1 year into the trade which has a current mark to market value of €4 million. On the supposition of not having access to sophisticated modelling techniques we must then apply the Table 5.1 to determine the potential future exposure.

The future exposure will be half a per cent of €500 million. This will be added to the replacement value to determine the total exposure. We then find the position that the bank occupies within the Basel weighting matrix (assuming it is an aa2 European bank). This implies the risk weight will be 20 per cent. Multiply this figure by the total exposure to determine the risk adjusted balance. We are nearly through; we just have to finish off the job – multiplying by the risk asset ratio of 1.6 per cent. This will give us the risk capital representing the monetary amount of the cushion.

This is a stand-alone example. When it comes to a portfolio of deals we apply the standard exposure methodology to each exposure and sum up across all the trades, which amount to a weighted sum. The weightings are given by the appropriate credit standing of the counterparty in Table 5.2.

There are a number of shortcomings with this approach. Of paramount concern is the ignorance of correlation and diversification effects. This will tend to overestimate exposure and raise the capital that must be allocated. A further problem is to assign the default risk to a set of weights which are only loosely connected with the actual possibility of that counterparty defaulting.

The maturity correction applied to the transaction is also inaccurate, because of these difficulties Basel is moving to an approach which embraces credit risk modelling. The reader is referred to Section 2.16 for a more detailed analysis.

5.3 FRN analysis

We consider the example of an FRN, these are very widespread instruments within the credit markets. Similar to a normal bond but instead of the coupon being fixed it varies depending upon the prevailing level of a reference rate at each coupon reset date. The reference rate is typically libor, a margin is added which is dependent upon the credit worthiness of the borrower. (The FRN can also be viewed as comprising one half of an interest rate swap. This picture is particularly important from the risk management perspective.)

The note always pays out the current market rate of interest consequently it has a value which is close to par. This carries the implication that the market risk associated with the note is quite small.

Floating financing is employed by many different types of organization as a way of providing capital. The decision to adopt a floating rate bond as opposed to a fixed issue is determined by the likely investor appeal for the debt. Most corporates do not like floating rates because they introduce accounting risk and consequently prefer the certainty of paying a pre-determined rate. An FRN may still be issued however because of the investor constraint. The issue is subsequently swapped.

Many financial institutions will purchase floating assets, as an alternative to cash deposits, because they are usually very liquid in addition to being very safe investments on a mark to market basis.

A credit-linked note is none other than a synthetic floating rate note. Issued by an SPV to satisfy demand for credit exposure in funded form.

We display the characteristics of the FRN in Figure 5.3. The note pays libor on each coupon date, the usual arrangement is for the payment to be made in arrears (i.e. the payment is based on libor set at the previous coupon).

Time runs from left to right. At the outset the investor pays par for the note, this is represented by the downward arrow. She subsequently receives a stream of income at regular dates in the future. The amount varies, hence the different arrow lengths, these are traditionally depicted as 'wavy lines'. At maturity the principal is returned.

Why is the FRN priced at par? Because the price of borrowing in the future is determined today; the market estimate of future borrowing is the forward rate. In the diagram the future libor rates are replaced by the forward rates purely for valuation purposes. The forward rate obeys the relationship:

$$\text{Rate(from year } n-1 \text{ until } n) \times \text{discount factor}(n) = \text{discount factor}(n-1) - \text{discount factor}(n).$$

Meaning a wavy line can be replaced by an upward fixed arrow 1 year previously and a fixed downward arrow at the coupon payment date.

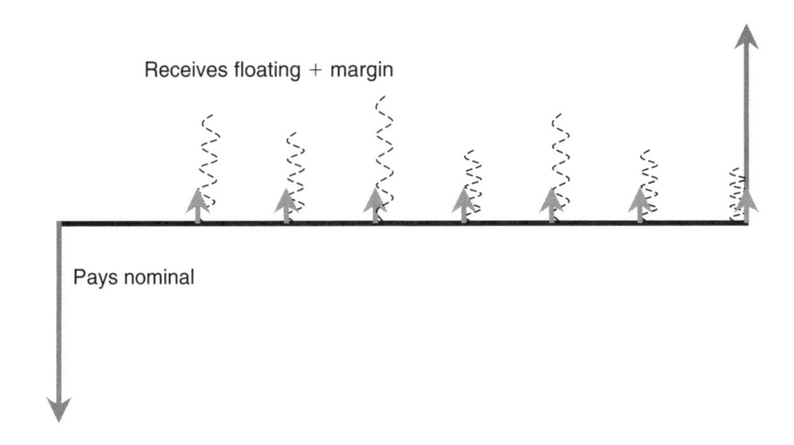

Figure 5.3 The cash flows of a 7 year FRN.

The arrow amounts are the notional. By definition of the forward rate values we net and end up at the notional as we anticipated.

If you are still puzzled, then you may know that the market does not actually price based on expected values of market rates. Rather the pricing mechanism is one of forming a replica portfolio matching the payoff for the instrument at maturity. This means there is no arbitrage opportunity. To apply this to the case of an FRN consider replicating the payoff of a 2 years FRN by depositing money for a year and then redepositing in 1 year and withdrawing it after 2 years. Such an arrangement will only ever be worth 100, because you are just receiving the prevailing market rate of interest. But we know another instrument priced at 100 – the FRN, the conclusion is that the rate of borrowing in the future can be replaced by the forward rate. The upshot is that the rate of borrowing in the future is determined by today's spot borrowing rate.

This is only true for 'libor' rated issuers (deemed risk free). We have to modify this picture because credit has to be addressed. Typically the borrower is not often a highly rated credit hence they are penalized by having to pay libor plus a premium (i.e. the margin). The resulting FRN will still be priced at par, because it is issued at par, it will subsequently trade at par unless the credit worthiness of the company changes.

We are going to look at an FRN issued by an AA credit denominated in euros. First we will look at the cash flows the investor will receive, and subsequently analyse the risk of the FRN from the credit perspective.

Table 5.3 shows the term sheet of the trade.

Once we have examined the term sheet the next step is to construct the cash flows and then value the FRN by discounting these flows using an appropriate rate. We are dealing with an instrument that pays a floating amount on each coupon date, how do we know what these cash

Table 5.3 The term sheet of a AA FRN.

Detail	Term
Issuer	European bank
Value date	27/01/03
Deal date	24/01/03
Maturity date	30/09/06
Notional	€100 M
Currency	Euro
Reference	Euribor
Quoted margin	42 bps
Value convention day	one business
Cash DCT	Act/365f
Coupon frequency	Quarterly

flows are going to be in advance? The simple answer is that you do not, and unfortunately the book cannot reveal a source of crystal balls.

But we can with conviction use the arbitrage argument from the previous page. This enables us to determine the implied libor for each coupon date. We add to this the quoted margin because the cash flow received by the investor is higher than libor because the borrower has a lower rating than the inter-bank libor market. We apply an extra discount to the pricing curve implied from the libor rates, termed the FRN margin. This precisely values the FRN, otherwise we would tend to overvalue the paper because we would be discounting at too low a rate for that borrower (Table 5.4).

We can write down the discount factor as

$$\text{Discount factor}(t) = \frac{\text{discount factor}(t-1)}{1 + (\text{libor}(t-1, t) + m}.$$

We then put this into the column representing discount factors for each period and find the *PV* from the margin determined from the current level of asset swaps.

As mentioned the quoted and FRN margin are only equal at the inception of the deal. The reason for the discrepancy is that the quoted margin is based on the spread which priced the deal to par at origination. It will no longer value the trade if the credit quality of the issuer has changed. The credit spread of the borrower is a very dynamic entity, in the sense that it moves in a random manner on an intra-day basis. For this reason we have to discount by a margin having an explicit time dependence.

Table 5.4 Pricing the FRN.

Date	Cashflow (Libor + margin)	Discount factor
31/03/03	0.920	0.99
30/06/03	0.828	0.99
30/09/03	0.748	0.98
30/12/03	0.651	0.97
30/03/04	0.736	0.96
30/06/04	0.824	0.96
30/09/04	0.843	0.95
30/12/04	0.852	0.94
30/03/05	0.897	0.93
30/06/05	0.963	0.92
30/09/05	0.994	0.91
30/12/05	1.014	0.90
30/03/06	1.045	0.89
30/06/06	1.107	0.88
29/09/06	101.129	0.87

We now have to explore the risk management picture. You may have been thinking up to now that you know all about the market risk of FRNs. However because we have a note issued by an AA borrower there is an extra component of risk, which is purely credit in its nature. Its impact is manifest in the value of the note as a result in either a narrowing or widening of the spread relative to its inception value. How do we quantify its effect? Well, we quite simply move the spread up by one basis point to reveal a new discount factor, reprice the deal and the difference will give us a sensitivity to the credit spread.

We can similarly also determine the libor or market sensitive rate risk to borrowing by shifting the libor curve itself up by one basis point. This is perfectly acceptable and equivalent to a more economical description, which gets to the heart of what an FRN actually represents. We will demonstrate this approach.

A question to ask your colleagues – what is the duration of an FRN? The instrument itself represents a rolling deposit and redemption at the forward libor rate. Since this always will be the fair market rate by definition, the note will always be priced at 100. Consequently the duration is zero. This means from a risk management perspective that we are able to represent the FRN as the principal only on each reset date. However if a coupon reset has already occurred then the note has libor risk and can be perceived as a zero coupon bond with a duration equal to the next coupon date.

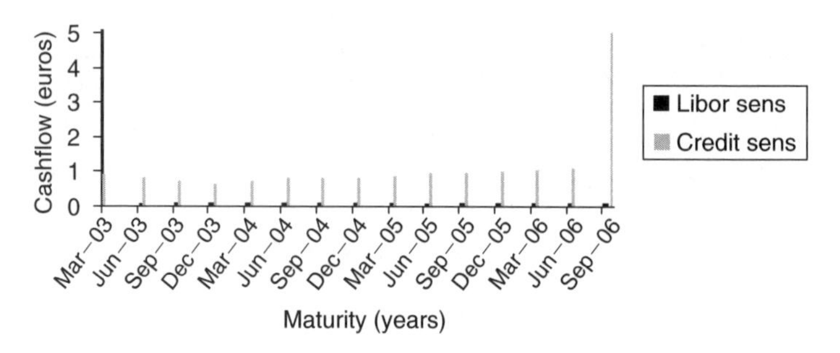

Figure 5.4 Market vs. credit risk of an FRN.

If the issuer has a sub-libor credit standing, they will have to pay a fixed annuity equal to the quoted margin on each of the coupon dates. The picture of risk for our credit FRN is displayed in Figure 5.4. Notice that the libor sensitive flows can be represented by an upfront payment on the next coupon date together with the margin payments. The sensitivity to credit however is represented by the full payments on each coupon date.

5.4 Swap

A rigorous treatment of CCR would involve addressing the correlation between credit and market risk. At this stage we just build on our rather simpler examples. The goal is to identify the aspects of market and credit risks that interact to produce the net exposure.

A credit loss will be sustained if the counterparty undergoes a deleterious credit change and the swap is in the money from the owner's perspective. (This is distinct from the bond world where the owner of the paper is always in the money from a credit standpoint.)

We now describe a way of addressing credit risk involving optionality commonly employed within the dealing community. There are two stages to the procedure; the first is to calculate the risk free value of the cash flows. The second component will represent the losses due to default net of recoveries by the obligor on these remaining cash flows.

To determine the potential future exposure the approach values the swap at a horizon date. If we did not have the bothersome task of having to worry about credit it would be sufficient to take the present value of the remaining cash flows discounted at the forward rates. To address the extra element of credit risk all we do is correct this value by assuming that the counterparty may default over the remaining life of the deal. The probability of this default will vary by rating category and consequently we must incorporate the effects of potential migration on the counterparty.

Optionality enters the picture because we have a credit exposure to the counterparty only if the instrument is in the money. We can write down the above approach mathematically as shown below:

$$\text{Value at horizon} = \text{risk free value} - \text{expected loss from horizon until maturity.}$$

The expected loss will depend upon the credit rating category the counterparty migrates into. Thus we need to do the calculation for each possible end rating and then take a weighted sum to get the total. Each non-default rating produces the equation below:

$$\text{Expected loss} = \text{average exposure} \times \text{default probability (from horizon until maturity)} \times (1 - \text{recovery fraction}).$$

The average exposure represents a weighted probability for many values from the horizon until maturity. (We use the average because we have to allow for the possibility of the counterparty defaulting at any point within this period.) Including a test to determine whether it is in the money.

We require the probability of default for each of the rating categories between the horizon date until the maturity. One problem is that the agencies usually only supply 1 year default rates. To get the cumulative default rate we multiply the 1 year four times. I am sure that the reader is aware of the rather swingeing assumptions in doing this.

There is a slight subtlety what we must address because the deal may have defaulted in the time up to the horizon. Thus calculating the average exposure over the remaining life does not make very much sense. We can write the expected loss in the event of default as

$$\text{Expected loss default} = \text{expected exposure year end} \times (1 - \text{recovery fraction}).$$

Let us apply the above methodology to an example consisting of our 5 year swap. With the horizon date at 1 year, assume the counterparty is AA and the recovery in the event of default is 0.25. We can write for an upgrade to AAA:

$$\text{Future value} = \text{risk free value} - \text{default}_{\text{AAA}} \times \text{average exposure} \times (1 - \text{recovery})$$

Table 5.5 Value of swap at the horizon.

Horizon rating	4 year default probability	Value
AAA	4×0.0000	PV
AA	4×0.0001	$PV - 0.0004 \times AE \times 0.75$
A	4×0.0005	$PV - 0.002 \times AE \times 0.75$
BBB	4×0.0037	$PV - 0.0148 \times AE \times 0.75$
BB	4×0.0138	$PV - 0.0552 \times AE \times 0.75$
B	4×0.0620	$PV - 0.248 \times AE \times 0.75$
CCC	4×0.2787	$PV - 1.148 \times AE \times 0.75$
Default	1	$PV - \text{EE} \times 0.75$

using *AE* to represent the average present value exposure over the remaining lifetime[1]:

$$\text{Future value} = \text{risk free value} - 0.00 \times AE \times (1 - 0.25).$$

We can now easily do the rest of the non-default states since the average exposure is common, thus if the counterparty migrates down to speculative grade:

$$\text{Future value} = \text{risk free value} - 0.0148 \times AE \times (1 - 0.25).$$

As we stated earlier if the counterparty has defaulted in the period up to the horizon date then we need the expected present value of the exposure at the year end, which we denote by *EE*. In the case of default then

$$\text{Future value} = \text{risk free value} - EE \times (1 - 0.25).$$

We summarize the results of our labour in Table 5.5. To find the credit risk, the final column has to be multiplied by the transition probabilities for each of the states.

Reference

Gupton, Finger and Bhatia, 'Credit Metrics™–Technical Document, *Risk Metrics Group.*

[1] Using the global corporate 2002 default probabilities form Standard and Poors.

6

The fundamentals of credit

Methodologies

6.1 The standalone loan

The average loss expected on an individual loan. This is given by:

$$\mathrm{EL} = \text{exposure} \times \mathrm{EDF} \times \text{loss severity},$$

where EL is the yearly expected loss, exposure is the amount of the loan, EDF is the expected default frequency and loss severity is the amount recoverable in the event of a default. The word EDF is quite intimidating but is simply the probability of default in a 1 year period.

This equation is already far too complicated and needs to be broken down further. Let us just consider the case of a loss severity of 100 per cent and an exposure of €1 then we can write the expected loss as

$$\mathrm{EL} = \mathrm{PD}.$$

Now, we only have one abstract variable which is just the probability of default. To understand why this is the case, let us apply the binomial model of default (over a 1 year period) to the case of a single loan of €10 million. It is based on the quite natural assumption that the loan either defaults or it does not. If it defaults we get nothing back and if it does not we have our original exposure of €10 million. This arrangement is displayed in Figure 6.1 for the case where the default probability is 2 per cent.

Then we can determine our expected loss as follows:

$$\text{EL} = 2\% \times 10\,000\,000 + 98\% \times 0 = \quad 200\,000,$$

that is the expected loss is just the default probability scaled.

Now we introduce the notion of the unexpected loss, which is the variation of the expected loss. This is very simple to evaluate because there are only two possible outcomes within a binomial model either a loss or no loss. This will give a volatility,[1] called the unexpected loss UL of

$$\begin{aligned}
\text{UL}^2 &= 2\% \times (10\,000\,000 - 200\,000)^2 + 98\% \times (0 - 200\,000)^2, \\
\text{UL}^2 &= 2\% \times (9\,800\,000)^2 + 98\% \times (200\,000)^2, \\
\text{UL} &= 10\,000\,000 \times \sqrt{98\% \times 2\%}, \\
\text{UL} &= €\,1\,400\,000.
\end{aligned}$$

This will be formalized into a general expression for the expected loss and the volatility of the expected loss. Again assume the losses are binomial and that the default probability is constant. We consider two distinct cases (the basis of the distinction is the amount lost given a default). In the first case we examine a recovery rate of zero.

The probability that the asset defaults within the horizon period under consideration is

$$\begin{aligned}
\text{Expected loss} = {} & \text{default probability} \times \text{exposure} \\
& + (1 - \text{default probability}) \times 0.
\end{aligned}$$

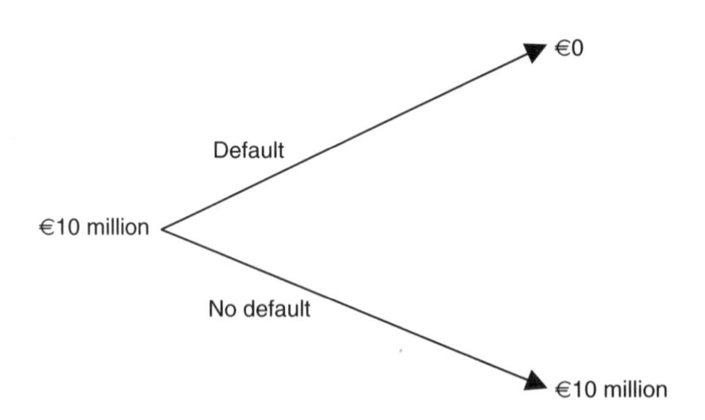

Figure 6.1 The outcomes for the loan.

[1] Notice this is a very special case of a constant default rate. There is a volatility of loss but no volatility in the default rate, more generally the default rate will itself be stochastic.

This simplifies down because one half is zero:

$$\text{Expected loss} = \text{default probability} \times \text{exposure}.$$

The volatility of this expected loss is given by the standard derivation. This is just

$$\text{Volatility} = \sqrt{\sum_{\substack{\text{number of}\\ \text{returns}}} \text{prob. return} \times (\text{asset return} - \text{average return})^2}$$

in the context of asset returns (since this is the application that the majority of readers will be familiar with). For our topic the loss replaces the return, and thus average loss replaces the average return. As we have a binomial process the counter stops at two and so we have:

$$\begin{aligned}(\text{Volatility of loss})^2 &= \text{default probability} \times (\text{exposure} - \text{expected loss})^2 \\ &\quad + (1 - \text{default probability}) \times (0 - \text{expected loss})^2.\end{aligned}$$

This simplifies down into

$$\begin{aligned}(\text{Volatility of loss})^2 &= (\text{exposure})^2 \times \text{default probability} \\ &\quad \times (1 - \text{default probability}).\end{aligned}$$

Now we relax the assumptions on constant recovery and countenance extra volatility because the losses, given a default have a distribution, in this case the volatility of loss is modified according to the formula:

$$\begin{aligned}(\text{Volatility of loss})^2 &= (\text{exposure})^2 \times [\text{default probability} \\ &\quad \times (1 - \text{default probability}) + \text{default probability} \times (\text{volatility})^2].\end{aligned}$$

We depict this situation graphically as shown in Figure 6.2.

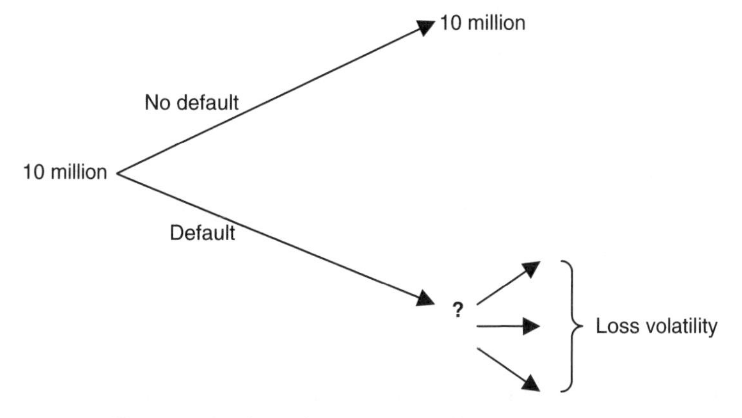

Figure 6.2 Including volatility after default.

6.2 Standard measures

Cumulative default frequency

This is simply in recognition of the fact that the chances of default generally increase over time, we christen the variable

$$q_k,$$

where k is the year. It represents the probability that the issuer will default up to time k.

Marginal default probability

This is the potentially variable default probability for year k, call it p_k.

The marginal default probability in any given year is obtained by taking the differencc between the cumulative default probabilities of successive years. Consequently we have

$$q_k = p_k + q_{k-1}.$$

Conditional default probability

The two notions above are relevant to a given asset. If we wish to know what is the probability of an asset defaulting in a period, given that it has survived up to that period, then we need the conditional default probability

$$\text{Conditional probability}_k = p_k \times (1 - q_{k-1}),$$

where q_k usually has a time dependence.

For example, if the yearly default probability is constant and equal to 2 per cent, the probability of default in the second year will not be equal to 2 per cent, but slightly less and equal to $(1 - 2\%) \times 2\% = 1.96\%$. So the conditional probability is slightly less than 2 per cent. If we consider 3 years the cumulative probability will be $2\% + (1 - 2\%) \times (2\%) + (1 - 2\%) \times (1 - 2\%) \times (2\%)$. Only four outcomes are possible, this is illustrated in Figure 6.3.

Default intensity

The time dependent probability of defaulting, denoted by λ, in a very small period of time.

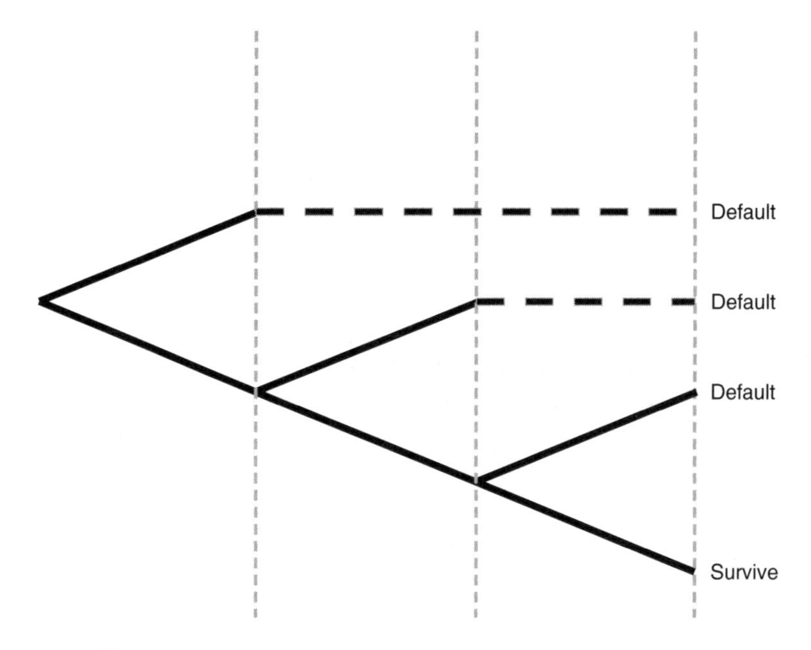

Figure 6.3 The number of outcomes for a default process.

Survival probability

The probability of surviving, denoted by $Q(t)$, up to a horizon period t. This can be related to the default intensity by

$$Q(t) = \exp\left(-\int_{o}^{t} \lambda(u)\,du\right).$$

The survival probability is conditional on surviving previous periods. We gave a derivation of this in Section 1.11. The marginal for any period is the difference of the survival probabilities neighbouring the period.

6.3 A portfolio as a set of standalones

Who really cares about individual loans and their financial characteristics? Business is in the context of a collection of credits. The portfolio, unfortunately from the perspective of default, is a very complicated beast. The industry approaches it in a sequence of stages, each stage adds in another layer of reality. Or we could say complexity. It is rather like the application of a physical science to explain experimental evidence, you are never quite sure how relevant the model actually is, but provided it has some explanatory power there is a danger that the science is substituted for reality when it comes to thinking about the subject. Portfolio modelling is probably at this stage.

As a portfolio manager the biggest risk is one of concentration. This describes the case of too much exposure either to a name, sector or economy. Any model worth its salt should identify concentration risk. However one reservation over default modelling is that it has only recently been able to address such issues in a remotely reasonable manner.

What then is the source of difficulty? Well let us go to the top of the mountain first in order to gain an overall perspective, since we know the nature of what we are trying to describe (which is a big step in itself). The shortcoming is that we do not quite have the tool-set as yet to adequately address the reality in a practical sense. The reality is that a portfolio consists of many loans. Each counterparty has a unique chance of defaulting; this default rate is a variable rate which changes intraday. There will be some correlation between the borrowers. But do not get too comfortable with correlation between two issuers only because there is a high possibility of many joint default events occurring. This is not adequately captured using just a traditional correlation approach. Furthermore the volatility of the portfolio losses cannot be captured using just a mean variance approach. This is because the volatility only really tells you the average thickness of the losses, we introduce Figure 6.4 which perfectly depicts this, where we have two loss distributions which have the same volatility but any portfolio manager would agree the losses are completely different.

Credit is the classic case of the community having a pre-conception and then applying it blindly to another subject matter believing this prescription is the correct one. The majority of institutions still believe the risk in a credit portfolio can be adequacy addressed using an approach based on mean variance volatility. Carrying the implication

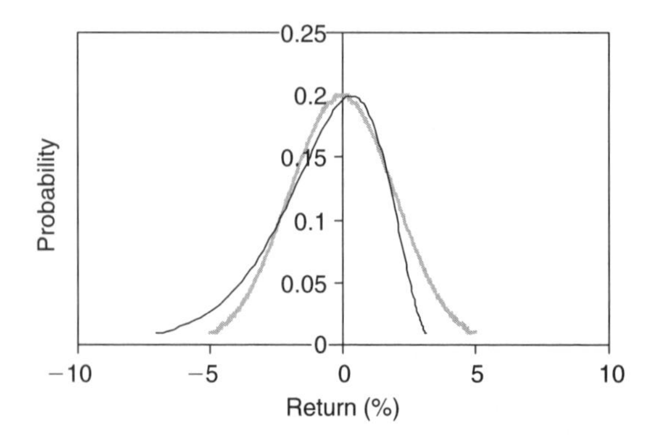

Figure 6.4 Two distributions having the same volatility.

that default correlation can be captured using pairwise tables of default probabilities.

We will systematically go through the models because this is a pedagogical exercise and you will need some of the notions introduced to appreciate the more worthy 'default models'.

The starting point is to treat a portfolio as, you guessed it, a series of what are termed standalone loans. So the picture you have in your mind is a constant default rate, a bunch of loans and the source of volatility within the portfolio will be the random losses due to the constant probability of default. There is furthermore no correlation between defaults. Thus the analysis is straightforward because the portfolio loss distribution is just the famous 'binomial' as discovered by Pascal (Figure 6.5).

This shape comes about because the source of randomness is the chance within a portfolio, for example of 100 loans, that 50 default or 10 default or 3 default. We know from simple statistics how many ways we can pick 3 names out of a hat from 100 names. This is applied to the loan portfolio. In general the way we pick r obligors from a pool of n is given by the coefficient:

$$C_r^n = \frac{n!}{(n-r)!\ r!}.$$

Thus in order to get the probability of 3 defaults out of 10, where the individual obligation default probability is 2 per cent,

$$\text{Probability} = \frac{10!}{7!\ 3!} \times (2\%)^3 \times (1 - 2\%)^7 = 8\,\text{bps}.$$

This can be understood if we think of a portfolio of two assets. Either both could default, both could be unchanged, or either one could default making four in total. You can extend this argument up to many assets.

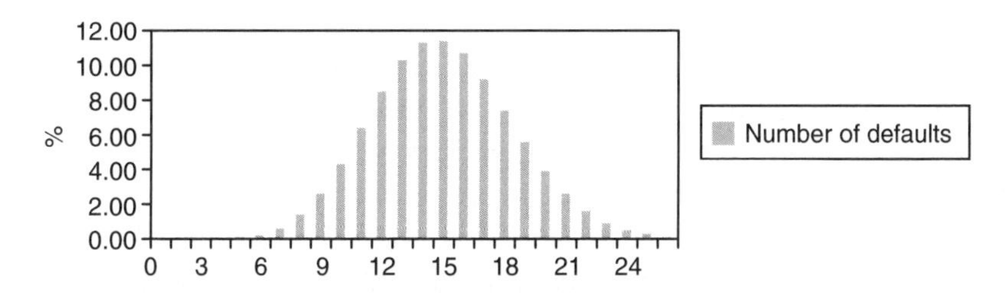

Figure 6.5 The binomial distribution of defaults.

6.4 Introducing correlation

So far so good, but what about if we want to introduce correlation into this framework? There are two main ways we can do this. The so-called joint default probability approach and the technique of inferring the correlation from observations on the number of defaults within a large portfolio. Both of these approaches assume a constant default rate or a number of rates, still constant but applicable to different categories. This will obviously be more realistic. Introducing correlation implies, one company failing might have an impact on the possibility of another defaulting.

The example we consider is the default probability, given two distinct default rates which are constant. This situation arises when we either have two distinct sectors or ratings within our portfolio. To get to the correlation, we begin with the covariance from the standard formula:

$$\text{Covariance}_{\text{1st,2nd}} = \sum_{n=1}^{4} \text{probability}_n \times (\text{loss}_{\text{1st},n} - \text{average}_{\text{1st}}) \times (\text{loss}_{\text{2nd},n} - \text{average}_{\text{2nd}}).$$

The sum is up to four because there are four possible outcomes. Asset one defaults while asset two does not. Vice versa, and then both could default or both could stay unchanged.

We denote the probabilities for each of these contingencies with probability_n.

We can then expand the above equation to give

$$\begin{aligned}\text{Covariance}_{a,b} &= \text{probability}_{\text{both default}} \times (1 - \text{average}_{\text{1st}}) \\ &\times (1 - \text{average}_{\text{2nd}}) + \text{probability}_{\text{2nd defaults only}} \times (0 - \text{average}_{\text{1st}}) \\ &\times (1 - \text{average}_{\text{2nd}}) + \text{probability}_{\text{1st defaults only}} \times (1 - \text{average}_{\text{1st}}) \\ &\times (0 - \text{average}_{\text{2nd}}) + \text{probability}_{\text{neither defaults}} \times (0 - \text{average}_{\text{1st}}) \\ &\times (0 - \text{average}_{\text{2nd}}).\end{aligned}$$

The joint default probability is usually referred to as α. *This is a different animal, one that we have not encountered so far.* What is the meaning of a joint default probability? If the correlation between two borrowers is high, one default is quite likely to be followed by another. The reason for this is that the obligors could be in the same business sector. The problem however remains that the correlation depends on the joint default probability and the individual default levels by themselves are difficult to obtain. The usual way to determine the joint default probability is from the properties of the individual obligors and then to infer the rate. The probability of only one asset, say the second, defaulting is then $\text{average}_{2\text{nd}} - \alpha$. (Using the fact that the individual probability is the average loss for a unit exposure and assuming 100 per cent loss severity.) Thus we can write the above formula as

$$\begin{aligned}\text{Covariance}_{1\text{st},2\text{nd}} &= \alpha \times (1 - \text{average}_{1\text{st}}) \times (1 - \text{average}_{2\text{nd}}) \\ &+ (\text{average}_{2\text{nd}} - \alpha) \times (0 - \text{average}_{1\text{st}}) \times (1 - \text{average}_{2\text{nd}}) \\ &+ (\text{average}_{1\text{st}} - \alpha) \times (1 - \text{average}_{1\text{st}}) \times (0 - \text{average}_{2\text{nd}}) \\ &+ (1 - \text{average}_{1\text{st}} - \text{average}_{2\text{nd}} + \alpha) \times (0 - \text{average}_{1\text{st}}) \\ &\times (0 - \text{average}_{2\text{nd}}).\end{aligned}$$

This simplifies down, if you are feeling adventurous or have a few moments – its just mindless algebra. Alternatively you can take my word that the above formula becomes

$$\text{Covariance}_{a,b} = \alpha - \text{average}_{1\text{st}} \times \text{average}_{2\text{nd}}.$$

Let us connect this groundwork with the correlation, first let us reference the standard formula as

$$\text{Covariance}_{1\text{st},2\text{nd}} = \text{correlation}_{1\text{st},2\text{nd}} \times \text{volatility}_{1\text{st}} \times \text{volatility}_{2\text{nd}}.$$

However we already have an expression involving the covariance above, this means it can be eliminated from the expression:

$$\alpha - \text{average}_{1\text{st}} \times \text{average}_{2\text{nd}} = \text{correlation}_{1\text{st},2\text{nd}} \times \text{volatility}_{1\text{st}} \times \text{volatility}_{2\text{nd}}.$$

We can rejig the above formula to get the correlation in terms of the joint default probability and variables that are dependent on the properties of individual assets only:

$$\text{Correlation}_{1\text{st},2\text{nd}} = \frac{\alpha - \text{average}_{1\text{st}} \times \text{average}_{2\text{nd}}}{\text{volatility}_{1\text{st}} \times \text{volatility}_{2\text{nd}}}.$$

Please do not get too involved in the mathematics to the extent that sight is lost on the underlying finance. The bunch of formulae above are stating that the joint default probability is greater than the independent default probabilities if the covariance is positive (as we would anticipate). If the covariance is negative then the joint default probability is less than the product of the individuals. (For the special case of independence you just multiply the individual probabilities.)

The above equation completes our goal, which is the derivation of the joint correlation. What is the meaning of a joint default probability? If the correlation between two loan borrowers is high, if one defaults then there exists quite a strong likelihood that the other will default. The reason for this is the case that the obligors could be in the same business sector. The usual way of applying the equation is to determine the joint default probability from joint default observations and the default properties of the individual obligor.

The problem however remains that the correlation depends on the joint default probability and the individual default levels which by themselves are difficult to obtain. Due to this we explore another method.

Default correlations from default volatilities

Another widespread method to obtain the default correlation is to infer it from underlying data. The big assumption is that the data is homogenous in the sense that the individual companies that comprise the bulk applies to issuers having the same sector and rating. The assumption is then made that there exists a uniform default rate which is constant over the life time of the observations and this rate applies to all the obligors. This introduces randomness in the portfolio causing a number of loans to default over any given period.

The further assumption is that the spread of losses are caused by a binomial default process and not from other potential sources of randomness, such as recovery. The actual number of defaults will depend also on the correlation between the obligors.

We are going to count the number of defaults at the end of the period and compare this with the original number of loans – this will give us the number of defaults. From this we apply the formula for the expected number of defaults and imply the correlation.

Onto the mathematics then. We consider a company whose assets consist of loans, worrying that any obligor could default. For ease of maths we assume that on default everything is lost. We address the actual number of defaults that occur as opposed to the monetary loss, so this assumption need not be too restrictive. (The converse is that if an obligor does not default the loan is valued at par.)

Let R be a random variable that is either 1 if a company defaults or 0 if it does not. You do not actually have to make the connection with monetary loss, we can just think of R as a variable dependent on default. However for those of you who like something less abstract you can think in money terms. In which case we have a portfolio of €1 loans.

Thus $R_{\text{firm}} = 1$ if the firm defaults and $R_{\text{firm}} = 0$ if it does not. Thus we could consider an average uniform default rate:

$$\text{Average} = \frac{1}{N} \times \sum_{\text{firm1}}^{\text{firms}} R_{\text{firm}}.$$

Then the volatility of an individual firm due to default is

$$\text{Volatility} = \sqrt{\text{average} \times (1 - \text{average})}.$$

This expression was derived at the beginning of the chapter.

This is the same for all firms. Now do not fall into the trap of any high school statistics student. Just because a variable has values 0 and 1 does not mean that the average value is 0.5, it depends on the actual result of a lot of outcomes. We can consider observing a lot of similar firms over the course of 10 years. If 1000 started out trading, then perhaps only 10 will disappear, meaning that the average is 0.01 despite the variable having value 1 and 0.

We require an expression for the volatility of the number of defaults. Well, if we use the standard expression and denote that the volatility is a function of the default rate:

$$\sigma^2(\text{total default}) = \sum_{\text{firm}\,i}^{\text{firms}} \sum_{\text{firm}\,j}^{\text{firms}} \text{correlation}(i, j) \times \sigma(R_i) \times \sigma(R_j).$$

Now the volatility of all the firms is a constant and given by the above expression. Thus

$$\sigma^2(\text{total default}) = \sum_{\text{firm}\,i}^{\text{firms}} \sum_{\text{firm}\,j}^{\text{firms}} \text{correlation}(i, j) \times \text{volatility}^2$$

and substituting the symbols we get an expression in terms of the required and measurable properties, which is the average default rate:

$$\sigma^2(\text{total default}) = \sum_{\text{firm}\,i}^{\text{firms}} \sum_{\text{firm}\,j}^{\text{firms}} \text{correlation}(i, j) \times (\text{average} \times (1 - \text{average})).$$

We can further state that the correlation of an obligor with itself is one. This leads to

$$\sigma^2(\text{total default}) = (\text{average} - \text{average}^2) \times \left[N + \sum_{\text{firm}\,i}^{\text{firms}} \sum_{\text{firm}\,j,\, j \neq i}^{\text{firms}} \text{correlation}(i, j) \right].$$

Remember that rather than pairwise correlation we are interested in an average correlation and define this as follows:

$$\overline{\text{Correlation}} = \frac{\left[\sum_{\text{firm } i}^{\text{firms}} \sum_{\text{firm } j, j \neq i}^{\text{firms}} \text{correlation}(i, j)\right]}{(\text{assets}^2 - \text{assets})}.$$

As there are only 'cross' elements. We can now substitute this to get

$$\sigma^2 = (\text{average} - \text{average}^2) \times (\text{assets} + (\text{assets}^2 - \text{assets}) \times \overline{\text{correlation}}).$$

Now, finally, the average loss is observable, together with the loss volatility. Consequently we can imply the default correlation.

6.5 Other approaches to default

A major approach to portfolio default modelling is not unsurprisingly a type of mean variance approach under which the default rate is assumed to have some mean and randomness in the same sense that a stock has a random nature. The basic requirement is that the data on defaults is available as a time series, that is, an average and volatility can be calculated. Once this not inconsiderable foundation is in place all we need is to link the volatility of default to the volatility of loss at the portfolio level.

We start off with the assumption that once again there is a homogeneous default rate, but this time it can be volatile. We want to find out the expected loss and the unexpected loss for this portfolio.

The expected loss for an individual counterpart is simply the exposure multiplied by the expected probability of default. The portfolio expected loss is just the sum over the counterparties:

$$E(L) = \sum_{\text{assets}} E(\text{asset } i)$$

because the default probability is the same, the expected loss is just the total exposure times the default probability. In equation form

$$E(L) = E \times E(d).$$

Consequently, the expected loss does not depend on the properties of the individual loans. For example, if we have 100 loans within the portfolio with an exposure of €1 million each and a default probability of 1 per cent then the expected loss is €1 million. If we had a portfolio of two loans with an exposure of €50 million with the same default probability of 1 per cent and one of the counterparties defaults the loss will be €500 000. However the expected loss for the other is the same so the total expected loss is still €1 million despite the different structure of the portfolio.

The loss volatility is the sum of the individual loss volatilities for the very special case that the portfolio is equally weighted and the obligors have no correlation.

The fact that all the issuers depend on the same default rate enables some simplification because the volatility of the loss for an individual is just the exposure times the volatility of the default rate. This is very different from the binomial approach where the default rate is constant and the loss just has two outcomes. Thus substituting in the constant volatility:

$$\text{Volatility}^2(\text{loss}) = \left[\sum_{\text{asset } i}^{\text{assets}} \text{exposure}^2 \text{ (asset } i)\right] \times \sigma^2(d)$$

and

$$\text{Volatility(loss)} = \text{assets} \times \text{exposure} \times \sigma(d).$$

For the example above if the default probability volatility was 3 per cent then the unexpected loss would be €3 million.

Volatility with different rates which vary and are correlated

The next level of complexity is to assume a variable default rate but further to assume there is some correlation between obligors. The natural assumption is to break the portfolio down into sub-portfolios which have a common default rate. So in essence we have a small number of classes of known default rates. But within each class the rate is random. Let us first consider the case where our portfolio can be divided into two sub-portfolios.

In this situation the default probability for sector one is d_1 and for two is d_2. The expected loss for this portfolio is

$$E(L) = E_1 \times E(d_1) + E_2 \times E(d_2)$$

and the unexpected loss on the portfolio is

$$\text{Volatility}^2(\text{loss}) = E_1^2 \times \sigma(d_1) + E_2^2 + \sigma(d_2) + E_1 \times E_2 \times \sigma(d_1) \times \sigma(d_2) \times \text{correlation}(1, 2).$$

This can be generalized up to a number of sectors which have a common volatile default rate. The expected loss on this portfolio is

$$E(L) = \sum_{\text{sector}_i}^{\text{sectors}} \text{exposure}(\text{sector}_i) \times \text{expected}(d_{\text{sector}_i})$$

and the volatility of this portfolio is

$$\text{Volatility}^2(\text{loss}) = \sum_{\text{sector}_j}^{\text{sectors}} \sum_{\text{sector}_i}^{\text{sectors}} E_{\text{sector}_i} \times E_{\text{sector}_j} \times \sigma(d_i) \times \sigma(d_j) \times \text{correlation}(i, j).$$

Higher order defaults

This is the probability of more than two loans defaulting simultaneously and as such will be an important contributor to the 'higher moments', that is the kurtosis of the distribution. The copula approach is probably the most fruitful, given that non-normals on marginals can be accommodated. The difficulty surrounds actually calibrating these distributions to market data. The recent paper in the Journal of Risk Metrics using Cornish Fischer expansion techniques highlights one avenue.

6.6 Copulas

A rather esoteric phrase which is unfortunate because the underlying idea is straightforward even if some of the applications can get a little abstract. This is an introductory book so we are going to concentrate on the concept and spare you some of the elaboration.

We are going to use a synonym, this is 'sewing'. You may have encountered an eiderdown, sewn together from individual patches. The link is that the eiderdown represents the portfolio loss distribution, the patches represent the asset loss distribution and the sewing is the copula.

Enough of analogies. The reason for this fertile area of credit is because it serves as the natural framework for enlarging the notion of 'latent' variables. These have been discussed under the banner of the KMV and the Risk Metrics™ approach which simply posits the driver of default is an underlying stochastic process, that is there is a mapping:

$$(0,1) \Rightarrow X \leq D.$$

If the share price falls below a certain level the entity defaults. This can be generalized to N stocks. In which case we have N distributions – these are known as the marginals.

The next step is combining the marginals into the portfolio called the joint distribution function, or dependence, or copula. You have actually done this before. A common application for two stochastic processes is the general economy and a stock whose return is dependent on this level of activity. To find the conditional default probability you calculate the threshold level of return α driven by

$$\sqrt{\rho} \times \text{economy process} + \text{stock process} \times \sqrt{1-\rho},$$

where ρ is the correlation such that the stock has defaulted. This enables us to eliminate the stock component. Then we need the probability of default given the state of the economy. Thus the probability is given by $\Phi\left((\alpha - \text{economy}\sqrt{\rho})\,/\sqrt{1-\rho}\right)$ where we must 'condition' on the state of the economy. We can write this in even more abstract form $\Phi[\Phi^{-1}(Z)]$. This looks like a copula.

Now there is no reason we stop at one asset. Indeed you have met the case of two assets, in the case of the simple loan portfolio, we needed the multivariate distribution, given the normal marginals were below their default thresholds. Thus:

$$\Phi\left[\Phi^{-1}(\text{asset one defaults}),\ \Phi^{-1}(\text{asset two defaults})\right].$$

We can extend this to N variables, but importantly to other distributions. The joint distribution will also depend on the level of correlation and higher order processes.

6.7 Moody's Diversity Score

Generally our portfolio of credits will consist of assets where default behaviour is to some extent correlated. Typically we observe periods when larger numbers of stresses occur. The task of the portfolio manager is to try and construct a very well diversified set of holdings. This objective can be quantified. The measure is used widely within the industry and goes by the rather apt appellation 'Moody's Diversity Score'. The formula is straightforward and we reproduce it as follows:

$$C^{\text{many}}_{\text{some}}\,\text{default probability}^{\text{some}} \times (1 - \text{probability})^{\text{many}-\text{some}}.$$

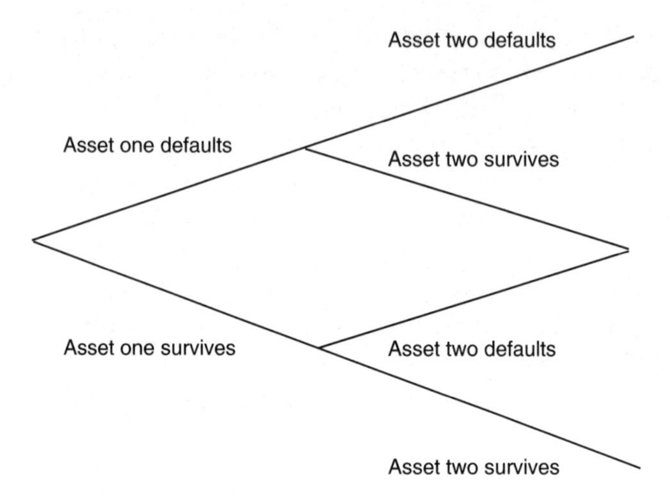

Figure 6.6 Potential outcomes with two assets.

The derivation of this appeared earlier in this section. It can be understood in the context of independent defaults. Each asset's behaviour is uncorrelated and has the same default probability. So for example, if we have two assets in our portfolio, the tree diagram in Figure 6.6 shows the outcomes.

If we wants to know the chance of two defaults then we count the number of routes with two up branches and multiply by the probability.

6.8 KMV's risk calc

So far the emphasis has been on the professional manager of credits with access to systematic quantitative modelling. What about the rather more traditional business of providing loans to smaller business: Is there anything in the quantitative cupboard? Indeed, the logic based approach. This takes as input a wide variety of observable characteristics relevant to the credit worthiness of a small business. As output, it predicts the likelihood of default.

Moody's RiskCalc™ is a good representative of this type of approach. Which is to *a priori* identify a set of independent, observable factors and then test how well they explain defaults. The considerations going into the model consist of the following:

- Low data requirements for the user.
- Small number of factors which should be intuitive.
- Good explanatory power.

Table 6.1 The relevant factors for the UK experience.

Category	Definition
Leverage	Liabilities/assets (current liabilities – cash) /assets
Profitability	Net P&L/assets
Debt coverage	Ordinary P&L/liabilities (ordinary P&L + depreciation and amortization)/interest charges
Liquidity	cash /assets
Activity	Trade creditors/turnover
Growth	(Turnover(*t*) − turnover(*t* − 1))/turnover(*t* − 1)

Source: Moody.

The mathematics of these approaches are straightforward in the following equation, the probability of default is given by

$$\text{Default probability} = \frac{\exp(\alpha_0 + \alpha_1 \times \text{factor}_1 + \alpha_2 \times \text{factor}_2 + \cdots)}{1 + \exp(\alpha_0 + \alpha_1 \times \text{factor}_1 \times \alpha_2 \times \text{factor}_2 + \cdots)}.$$

This functional form is chosen so that the probability is well behaved ('S shaped' in Moody's parlance) on the underlying. The argument is that the sensitivity of default to an underlying factor is not large when above or below a certain critical level.

The actual factors for the UK experience are listed in Table 6.1.

References

Gupton, Finger and Bhatia, Credit Metrics™ – Technical Document, *Risk Metrics Group.*

Kocagil, Escott, Glormann, Malzkorn and Scott, Moody's RiskCalc™ for Private Companies: UK, *Moody's Investors Service*, February 2002.

Jarrow and Turnbull, Pricing Derivatives on Financial Securities Subject to Credit Risk, *Journal of Finance*, Vol. 50, 1995.

Jaschke, The Cornish-Fischer Expansion in the Context of Delta-Gamma Normal Approximations, *Journal of Risk*, Vol. 4, No. 4, Summer 2002.

Index

Page numbers in italics refer to figures and tables.